WHY KIDS KILL PARENTS

CHILD ABUSE AND ADOLESCENT HOMICIDE

Kathleen M. Heide

SAGE PUBLICATIONS

International Educational and Professional Publisher
Thousand Oaks   London   New Delhi

First paperback printing 1995 by Sage Publications, Inc.
Hardcover edition originally published 1992 by Ohio State
University Press, Columbus.

For information address:

 SAGE Publications, Inc.
2455 Teller Road
Thousand Oaks, CA 91360
E-mail: order@sagepub.com

SAGE Publications Ltd.
6 Bonhill Street
London EC2A 4PU
United Kingdom

SAGE Publications India Pvt. Ltd.
M-32 Market
Greater Kailash I
New Delhi 110 048 India

Printed in the United States of America

Library of Congress Cataloging-in-Publication Data

Heide, Kathleen M., 1954–
    Why kids kill parents : child abuse and adolescent homicide / by Kathleen
    M. Heide: foreword by Hans Toch.
        p. cm.
    Includes bibliographical references and index.
    ISBN 0–8039–7060–9 (pbk.)
    1. Parricide—United States. 2. Problem families—United States.
    3. Family violence—United States. 4. Adolescent psychotherapy—
    United States.   I. Title.
    HV6542.H45   1995
    364.1'523'0835—dc20   94–30935

    97 98 99 00 01 10 9 8 7 6 5 4 3

Text and jacket design by Bruce Gore.

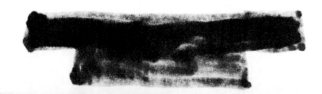

■ WHY KIDS KILL PARENTS

This book is dedicated to my family:
Especially to
my parents, Eleanor and Victor Heide,
who gave me life, love, opportunity, and
the encouragement to strive for excellence;
to my brother, Thomas,
whose outlook on life and accomplishments
and whose pride in me
empowered me to take a stand and be counted;
to my Aunt Therese and Uncle Vinny
and "the boys,"
whose love and willingness to lend a hand
were always apparent.

And to my mentors at Vassar College
and the School of Criminal Justice,
State University of New York at Albany:
Jane Ranzoni and Marguerite Q. Warren,
whose ways of thinking about issues
and living life
changed my worldview.

■ CONTENTS

■ FOREWORD

Hans Toch
Distinguished Professor,
State University of New York,
University at Albany

THIS BOOK is a humane, intelligent, and caring book about families that breed violence. The author, Kathleen Heide, has the rare ability to research a problem while feeling for those who are enmeshed in the situation and have no one to speak for them. The book shows what can happen when good science and advocacy go hand in hand.

Kathleen Heide tells the story of a group of youngsters who do not customarily evoke empathy. Her subject is adolescent parricide offenders, mainly children who have violated a universal and basic taboo (vested in two biblical commandments) by killing their mother or father. Heide summarizes what we know about such young murderers and about the parents they kill. She caps her summary with beautifully written case studies, which sound stranger than fiction but are representative of horrifying realities.

Such is the core of this book, but the content transcends its subject by discussing problems of good and bad parenting, dysfunctional families, child abuse, and social reform. Clinical practitioners will prize a section on therapy, which highlights the process of reparenting. Clinicians will also find the book useful as a primer of differential diagnosis, especially of murderers.

Unlike other reformers, Kathleen Heide does not buttress her case by inflating victimization statistics. She relies instead on the interconnectedness of social problems, which makes parricide the tip of a very ugly iceberg. Parricide is a very rare event which occurs in families whose members feel threatened, cornered, engulfed, desperate, and lost. Escalating conflict, bickering, and cruelty (including unspeakably sadistic cruelty), punctuated by the child's unsuccessful efforts to escape, are only part of the picture. Alcoholism is endemic in such families, as are other forms of substance abuse. Psychopathology or pathology is routine, and family members feed off pathology with mutually destructive results. In parricide constellations one factor is especially horrifying: the omnipresence and availability of firearms with which the murders are committed. Ironically, most of the families are among those law-abiding citizens whose right to bear arms is proclaimed by gun lobbyists.

Violent acts committed by members of dysfunctional families pose a dilemma to courts and a challenge to society. Knowledge of events preceding the act often invites compassion for the offender. But violence is not a solution to problems society can tolerate. Do-it-yourself justice is unacceptable in civilized communities because institutions have been created that temper and sublimate revenge. Resources should in theory be available to victims to make it unnecessary for them to help themselves by destroying their victimizers.

But what if societal resources fail? What if victims are reluctant (or afraid) to draw on them? What if problems fall between the cracks of the system or are lost in red tape? The rules obviously hold, no matter what: Thou shalt not kill a tormentor. Call the cops. Or run if you have to—then call the cops.

There are exceptions to these rules: If your life is in jeopardy and you cannot escape, the system recognizes it by exonerating you. But what if you feel you are in danger and others disagree? And if you could escape but feel you cannot do so? And if the danger is less tangible than loss of limb? These are the sorts of questions legal dilemmas are made of.

Other questions have to do with states of mind and incapacities. To be responsible you have to know what you do when you do it, and you must be able to refrain from doing it. But reconstructing an offender's state of mind is difficult. Those who do such reconstructing disagree in their conclusions. Worse, they may disagree depending on who retains their services.

Controversy may also surround the facts. Take a casual parricide by a teenager whose driving privilege has been curtailed. Faced with disproportionate penalties, the teenager recalls a history of brutal incest. The father's ex-spouse testifies that the teenager's story is consonant with her view of the man. Would one doubt the testimony or believe it? Is it sufficiently corroborative? Juries must decide such questions, and judges must face them in arriving at verdicts and sentences.

A special highlight of the book is the outcome of each of the stories. One of the three case studies has a happy ending. The boy pleads to second-degree murder, receives and serves prison time, and uses this time constructively. His comportment has been exemplary. He lives with his mother, and (aside from difficulties in coping with school) has made an adequate adjustment.

The other stories have ended less well. One parricide offender is acquitted by reason of insanity. After three months, he has committed four armed robberies because (he says) he "needed the money to give to his mother." One of the reasons for the mother's financial problems is that her son—who has no driver's license—has had a serious traffic accident. The judge who presided over the original trial adjudicates the boy's new "self-help" offense and finds mitigating circumstances. The boy serves time, is left adrift, and absconds. A warrant is outstanding for his arrest.

The third case is that of a girl who receives a long sentence in prison. At first she thrives in confinement, participating in programs and social life. After some time, however, she becomes bitter and self-isolating, sulking, neglecting her appearance, and living the life of a hermit. In this state of mind she faces ten more years as a self-styled Victim of Injustice.

Is there room for happier endings to such stories? Heide makes a convincing case for the proposition that happier endings require attention to offenders' problems. It is irrelevant in this connection whether the problems are products of victimization or not. It does matter whether the problems make the offenders dangerous or simply unhappy, disturbed, and self-destructive. The point is that if we do nothing, or not enough, we can expect more unhappy endings, including more dysfunctional families and violence.

We would like to see imprisonment more sparingly used, but in the short run there is little chance that this will happen. An alternative is to improve the experience of confinement, to make it more regenerative. If society cannot afford years of residential treatment (Kathleen Heide's prescription), we must try to approximate this ideal in custodial settings. We could do a great deal for inmates if persons willing to assist the offender in the community would work in the prison instead. In the long run, imprisonment will decrease in proportion as self-help solutions result in acquittals, convictions on reduced charges, or mitigation of sentences. Such a trend is most likely to eventuate if victim advocates can produce testimony that is accepted and attended to by courts. This book contains examples of such testimony.

The book also discusses programs in the schools and in the community that are designed to sensitize citizens and service providers to the problems of dysfunctional families. Need is most critical, according to Heide, where alcohol and drug use by parents breeds not only violence but habitual child abuse or neglect. With wholesale implementation of programs, unsuitable parents can expect to see more children removed from their homes for purposes of protection. They will see more allegations of abuse investigated and more services mandated.

The trend is beneficent, but carries some risks. At extremes, a modern witch hunt can be sparked if vengeful adolescents (as in Salem) raise fashionable charges. But Salems are less of a danger where science and due process prevail, moderating gullibility and zealotry.

Advocacy is also a competitive game in a society like ours. When we respond to one group at the expense of another, humane observers call us to task. Experts contend because they have different values, sensitivities and perceptions. Balanced accounts (such as this one exemplifies) will, one hopes, prevail.

The resolution of such questions as "What is a just response to a parricide by an abused child?" is a societal one. Our society permits divergent ideas (and data) to surface and to compete for adoption. In such a system a scientist and clinician such as Kathleen Heide can play a precious role. The work summarized in *Why Kids Kill Parents* is a testament to this role. It is also a credit to its author, who cares about ameliorating suffering and reducing despair.

■ PREFACE

TERRY ADAMS and his two older sisters had long been physically and emotionally abused by their parents, both alcoholics. When Terry's sisters reached 18, they left home. Once they were gone, Terry became the sole target of the abuse. At the age of 16, he decided there was no alternative but to leave as well and make it on his own.

Terry had to go through his parents' bedroom to get out of the house. While he was attempting to escape this way during the early morning hours, Mr. Adams woke up and confronted his son. Terry told his dad that he was tired of the way he was living, that he was old enough to make it on his own, and that he knew what he was doing. Terry asserted that he could quit school legally. Maybe he could not leave home legally, Terry told his dad, but he didn't care: he was leaving anyway. Mr. Adams slugged his son, knocking him down. When the youth got back up, his father pushed him over, and he fell into a closet where several guns were kept—including a .22 caliber rifle. Terry grabbed the rifle and fired at his father. He remembered his father screaming, "Oh, my God!"

Terry's mother, who was in bed when her husband was shot, woke up when the gun went off. Terry could not remember actually shooting his parents, particularly his mother. All he could remember was her face "when she sat up in bed . . . the agony within the terror. . . . The rest of it is more or less, sort of hazed out for me. I remember waking up completely. Standing there looking at two dead bodies. Two people. What have I done now, you know. Like it was a dream."

Both killings were the reactions of a terrified youth. Overwhelmed by stress at the moment he fired the shots that killed his parents, Terry may not have been aware of what he was doing and, hence, not have been culpable.

Court records showed that four petitions alleging neglect, abuse, and physical abuse in the Adams home had been filed and investigated by the state social services agency. Three of the petitions named Terry as the victim and had been filed in the two years preceding the homicides. The latest referral was made when Terry was 15. At that time the state agency received a report that Terry was being physically and emotionally abused by both parents. The report followed Terry's admission to the hospital for stomach problems. Hospital authorities could find no physical reason for the problems and decided that they were caused by emotional problems related to the home situation. Terry was first placed in a foster-care home, then with his oldest sister and her husband, with whom he remained for three months. After that the boy returned to his parents under protective services supervision, which officially lasted nine months. Ten months after the state agency terminated supervision, Mr. and Mrs. Adams were dead. Terry Adams was charged with two counts of first-degree murder.

The youth was advised by his public defender to plead guilty to two counts of second-degree murder and was sentenced to life imprisonment. The judge who sentenced Terry to life was the same judge who had presided over the dependency proceedings alleging abuse. Upon being sentenced, Terry wrote the following "Request for Freedom":

> I cry out at night, "I'm so sorry! I just couldn't take the fear and pain anymore, I won't hurt anyone again!" It doesn't matter what the degree of pain and fear was on me, all that matters is what I've done. I try to tell them I [am] so very young and have a lot to do with my life, but it doesn't matter. The public just says, "You shouldn't of done it, you shouldn't of done it!" I hear them lock the bars around me and I say to myself, "I can't stay in prison all my life, I've lived in a world of bounage [bondage] before and now once again." The world has no pity for me. They just don't understand. I couldn't take it any more, I [am] human and make mistakes, I just made a big mistake and now I'm paying for it by doing life.

As part of an in-depth study of adolescents convicted of homicide I interviewed Terry about two years after he killed his parents, and we corresponded for several years more. Four years after the homicide Terry wrote:

> A big change has taken place in my life. It happen[ed] about eight (8) months ago while going through the photo album. A couple of the pictures from my home town took me back to what happen[ed] in the truest since [sense]. For three years I lived in a make-believe world on what really happen[ed]. Then I realized I loved Mom and Dad. Down deep inside I loved them. That hurt when I realized it. I couldn't believe

it. I began letting out all the awful things that happened and what really took place that morning.

I couldn't believe it was happen[ing] all over again and I didn't have control . . .

Almost seven years after the double homicide, Terry was released on parole. He felt emotionally stable. Two months later, on the seventh anniversary of the murders, he called me, saying that he feared for his future if he did not resolve issues stemming from his past.

It took Terry seven years to begin the process of recovery. He made arrangements with the paroling authorities to relocate to a halfway house for men in Tampa. Within a few weeks he began therapy with a treatment team headed by Don McCann, a therapist whose expertise includes working with severely abused clients.

Terry Adams represents the abused child who kills from desperation, the *typical adolescent parricide offender* (APO), who is the major focus of this book. Part 1 focuses on the relationship of child abuse, neglect, and the dysfunctional family in order to understand the motivational dynamics behind these parricides. Part 2 details clinical case studies of three adolescent parricide offenders. The case studies address pivotal issues in adolescent parricide cases, including the sanity of the accused, the relevance of the youth's perceptions and personality development, and the relationship of post–traumatic stress disorder to the homicide. The final part of the book explores treatment strategies. Because of the crucial role of abuse in these homicides, the book concludes by focusing on a number of strategies that can be developed and implemented in an effort to reduce the incidence of child maltreatment.

■ ACKNOWLEDGMENTS

I WISH TO express my deep appreciation to colleagues, professional associates, and friends who contributed to this book. Special thanks are due to my editor, Alex Holzman, of Ohio State University Press, and my literary agent, Frances Goldin, who were among the first to see the importance of adolescent parricide and whose editorial suggestions and support helped bring this project to completion. I am very grateful to my good friend and editorial consultant, Frances Knowles, who read every chapter of this book at least twice with enthusiasm and excitement and provided astute comments. Nancy R. Woodington deserves special mention for doing an outstanding job of copyediting and also for making excellent editorial suggestions.

I want to thank my colleagues at the University of South Florida who helped and supported me as I launched and developed this project: Travis J. Northcutt, Jr., Ph.D., Dean Emeritus, Department of Social Work; Susan M. Stoudinger-Northcutt, Ph.D., Department of International Studies; Edward M. Silbert, Ph.D., Associate Dean, College of Arts and Sciences; Julia M. Davis, Ph.D., Associate Provost; Judith Ochshorn, Ph.D., Department of Women's Studies; William G. Emener, Jr., Ph.D., Department of Rehabilitation Counseling; and William R. Blount, Ph.D., Ira J. Silverman, Ph.D., Mitchell Silverman, Ph.D., Leonard Territo, Ed.D., Harold J. Vetter, Ph.D., and Magdalene C. Deutsch, Administrative Secretary, Department of Criminology. I also thank my graduate and undergraduate students for their interest and enthusiastic participation in discussions of adolescent homicide in lecture classes, seminars, and directed research. Their contributions to and excitement at my work and its application have been very inspiring to me. I especially thank Joseph Kuhns III, M.A., G.S.E. (Graduate Student Extraordinaire), Cindy Boyles, M.A.,

G.S.E., and Debbie Haggag, B.A., U.S.E. (Undergraduate Student Extraordinaire) for their help, good cheer, and laughter. Special thanks are also due to Media Relations and Publications staff, particularly graphic designer Richard Scott for his ideas and input, which were instrumental in designing the book cover.

I also want to thank Don McCann, M.A., licensed mental health counselor, and Roy Persons, Ph.D., licensed psychologist, for helping me to understand treatment issues especially pertinent to abuse victims and for teaching me effective intervention strategies.

I am grateful for the efforts of Robert Kriegner of the Florida Department of Corrections, Bureau of Planning, Research and Statistics, and his staff in Tallahassee, Florida, in identifying the population of adolescents committed for homicide in Florida and in helping me to obtain data about them. I thank the Department of Justice, Federal Bureau of Investigation, Uniform Crime Report staff for providing the Supplementary Homicide Report data on which the national analyses of parricide contained in this book are based. Special thanks are due to Ronald D. Hickman, Southern Illinois University, Computing Center Services; Richard Dembo, Ph.D., University of South Florida, Department of Criminology; and Suzanne Shealy, Ph.D., for help in preparing the FBI data for analysis.

A number of people devoted their time and talents to reviewing one or more chapters of this book to ensure its accuracy and relevance for professionals in the law, social services, and education. I am grateful to the following individuals for sharing their experience and expertise with me.

- Eldra P. Solomon, Ph.D., licensed psychologist, Tampa, Florida
- Marguerite Q. Warren, Ph.D., Professor (retired), State University of New York at Albany, School of Criminal Justice
- Anne H. Cohen-Donnelly, D.P.H., Executive Director, National Committee for the Prevention of Child Abuse
- B. Wesley Pardue, J.D., HRS District Legal Counsel, State of Florida Department of Health and Rehabilitative Services, District 6 Legal Office
- Craig Alldredge, J.D., Assistant Public Defender, Office of the Public Defender, Thirteenth Judicial Circuit (Florida); Chairman of the Mental Health Committee, Florida Public Defenders' Association
- The Hon. Barbara Fleischer, Circuit Court Judge, Thirteenth Judicial Circuit (Florida)
- Lee William Atkinson, J.D., Executive Assistant to the State Attorney, Office of the State Attorney, Thirteenth Judicial Circuit (Florida)
- Lorette McNeill-Enochs, J.D., Office of the Chief Counsel, U.S. Department of Energy

- Gerald S. Myers, former executive director of the National Association for Children of Alcoholics
- Nancy Wilson, M.S.W., social worker, De Jarnette Treatment Center, Adolescent Unit, Staunton, Virginia
- Lerea Goldthwaite, former director of the Sexual Abuse Treatment Center, Hillsborough County Crisis Center, Tampa, Florida
- Kris Marsh, M.A., Visiting Assistant Professor, University of South Florida and Florida Mental Health Institute, Professional Development Center, Department of Law and Mental Health
- Phyllis Weislo, Trainee Specialist, University of South Florida and Florida Mental Health Institute, Professional Development Center, Department of Law and Mental Health
- Mady Flemal-Sidwell, former circuit director, Guardian ad Litem Program, Thirteenth Judicial Circuit (Florida)
- Richard Dembo, Ph.D., Professor, University of South Florida, Department of Criminology
- James B. Halsted, J.D., Ph.D., Associate Professor, University of South Florida, Department of Criminology
- Lisa Day, computer education instructor, Tampa Palms Elementary School, Tampa, Florida
- Jane "Happy" Silverman, M.A., kindergarten instructor, Temple Terrace Elementary School, Tampa, Florida
- Gina Boland, R.N., addiction specialist, Tampa, Florida
- Elinor Le Boss, past president of the Board of Directors, Hillsborough County Sexual Abuse Treatment Center, Tampa, Florida
- Debbie Haggag, former undergraduate directed research studies student

I wish to thank my good friends, especially Eldra Solomon, Elinor LeBoss, Jack and Gina Boland, Frances Knowles, Lerea Goldthwaite, Marsha Vanderford, Diane Bernardi, William Stockinger, Michael Zmistowski, Lisa Day, Frank Ranzoni, Mark Totta, Craig Darlak, and Lorette McNeill-Enochs, who believed in me and in this book, and brought enormous joy, laughter, peace, and purpose into my life.

Last but not least by any means, I thank "Terry Adams," "Peter Jones," "Scott Anders," and "Patty Smith"—my pseudonymous adolescent parricide offenders—for trusting me with the most intimate details of their lives and giving me permission to tell their stories. I join with these young adults in hoping that this book's message will be received by those empowered to make changes in our social service, educational, and legal systems so that other adolescents in situations similar to theirs can receive the help that was denied to them.

■ INTRODUCTION

SINCE THE initial publication of *Why Kids Kill Parents*, adolescent parricide offenders have continued to make front-page news. In my roles as a criminologist and psychotherapist, I have continued to conduct clinical assessments of some of these adolescents who recently have stood accused of murdering their parents. As a researcher who has systematically studied adolescent homicide and family violence for more than 10 years, I have examined these cases closely to look for patterns, to test hypotheses, and to verify previous findings.

As a clinician frequently appointed by the Court or retained by defense counsel, my interest in parricide cases, as in other types of murder cases, has been to unravel the motivational dynamics that propel defendants to kill others. At this level of analysis, the individual is my primary focus of inquiry. Corroboration of facts is critical in determining the credibility of the defendant's statements. Accordingly, in addition to clinical interviews with the youth, I routinely conduct clinical interviews with family members, study pertinent materials, including existing school, medical, social services, and psychological records, and examine law enforcement reports, autopsies, and depositions of key witnesses.

My task as a clinician is to understand the defendant and his or her role in the killing. When subpoened to testify at trial, my responsibility becomes one of helping judges and jurors to comprehend how the defendant makes sense of the world and to identify what events led this individual to kill. At the sentencing hearing, I am typically asked questions regarding the defendant's risk to the community, what treatment would benefit the defendant, and what is the prognosis, that is, the likelihood that this individual can, at some point in time, be returned to the community.

My role as a scientist who has conducted clinical assessments of more than 100 adolescent homicide offenders is broader than my role as a psychotherapist. Every adolescent parricide case since the publication of *Why Kids Kill Parents* has allowed me, in varying degrees depending upon the nature of my involvement, to assess to what extent findings presented and conclusions drawn appear valid in other cases.

This situation has been particularly gratifying. The 12 characteristics, synthesized from my review of the literature and my own cases, delineated in Chapter 3 have typically been readily apparent in cases that I have personally examined or that have been reported in the media. The five factors discussed in Chapter 4 as targeting youths at higher risk of killing an abusive parent have also been identified in subsequent cases. In addition, the devastating effects of being a victim and a witness to violence, as described in Chapters 2 and 6 and illustrated in the three detailed case studies, have been reported in cases that I and other mental health professionals have examined since the book's publication.

Several adolescent parricide offenders whom I evaluated since the publication of *Why Kids Kill Parents* have been textbook cases. Such cases are encouraging because they provide additional evidence that the findings previously reported are genuine.

Publication of a book such as this one presents certain risks. A defendant on trial for killing a parent might read it and adjust his or her statements and testimony to correspond with the life experiences of severely abused children in an effort to escape responsibility for premeditated murder. Accordingly, I explore in the clinical interview what materials these youths have read about kids who kill parents. Prior to finalizing my conclusions, I verify that they had not had access to my book.

Why Kids Kill Parents is to be distinguished from books and articles that have recently appeared in the popular press on adolescent parricide offenders. This book, unlike others, does not start with the premise that adolescents who kill parents have killed because they have been abused and saw no other way out of an intolerable situation. Although these dynamics seem to be the most typically encountered among adolescent parricide offenders, this determination is a scientific one. It can be made only after careful examination by a mental health professional who has extensive experience and expertise in evaluating child abuse, family violence, homicide, and adolescent homicide.

This book presents a typology of parricide offenders in Chapter 1. The three types of individuals who kill parents include **the severely abused child, the severely mentally ill child,** and **the dangerously**

antisocial child. When adolescents kill their mothers and fathers, severe mental illness is typically ruled out. The question frequently becomes "Was the adolescent a severely abused child, or was he or she 'a psychopath'?"

This question was the one that appeared to polarize the nation, including the two juries, in the recent trial of Lyle and Eric Menendez, who at the ages of 21 and 18, respectively, allegedly killed their parents, Jose and Kitty Menendez. The defense argued that "the boys" were abused by both parents. Defense attorneys contended that the brothers killed their mother and father because they feared that their parents were going to kill them for threatening to reveal the sexual abuse within the family. The prosecution argued that the abuse was a fiction. The State maintained that the "young men" plotted to kill to inherit their parents' $14 million estate because they feared that they were going to be disinherited.

I did not evaluate Lyle or Eric Menendez. Accordingly, I have no direct knowledge of this case and cannot evaluate the veracity of Eric and Lyle's statements about the nature and extent of the alleged child maltreatment. However, my opinion on the case has been repeatedly sought by mental health professionals, lawyers, the media, students, and the general public. The question was almost always framed like this: "Do you think those guys were really abused, or do you think that they did it for the money?"

Evidence was presented at the Menendez trial that, *if true,* would indicate that Lyle and Eric Menendez were victims of several different types of abuse and neglect defined in Chapter 2 of *Why Kids Kill Parents.* Trial testimony suggested that Eric and Lyle Menendez were overtly sexually abused and raped by their father and covertly and overtly sexually abused by their mother. Reported accounts suggested that they had, in addition, been physically, verbally, and psychologically abused by both parents. Statements made at trial further suggested that the Menendez boys had been emotionally neglected by both parents. Testimony further suggested that they had been physically neglected by their mother, who allegedly failed to protect them from their father's alleged sexual abuse and rape.

However, even if these statements were in fact true, the verification of child maltreatment does not necessarily uncover the underlying motivation for the double homicides. The Menendez brothers could have been both "battered children" and "sociopathic." The two categories are not, as the opposing lawyers in the Menendez case seemed to argue, mutually exclusive. Some children raised in abusive homes become "conduct disordered." In fact, the development of "antisocial personality disorder" is typically rooted in early and pervasive childhood maltreatment. Put another way, the Menendez brothers could have been abused AND still have killed their parents for the money.

The critical question in the Menendez case is, as in any parricide, what propelled the homicides? Individuals who are severely abused often have mixed feelings about their abusive parents. These feelings may include fear, anger, hatred, hurt, and a desire for revenge, as well as love. If Lyle and Eric Menendez killed Jose and Kitty Menendez out of hatred and rage stemming from years of severe abuse, that motivation is clinically significant, but it is not self-defense.

It is interesting to note that the behavior of Lyle and Eric after the homicides was markedly different from the behavior typically shown by severely abused adolescents who kill their parents. The Menendez brothers concocted an elaborate alibi and maintained their innocence for several years. They acknowledged their involvement in the homicides only after it was determined that statements that they had made to their psychologist about their role in the killings would be admissible. Shortly before the trial it was publicly disclosed that the Menendez brothers had been abused—information that neither had at any time ever disclosed to their therapist. The psychologist testified that, when Lyle and Eric were discussing the killings with him, they did not indicate that they had been abused and feared for their lives. In contrast, adolescents who kill their parents typically are apprehended immediately after the killing and state that they killed the parent to end the abuse.

Severely abused children who kill their parents have a number of characteristics that the Menendez brothers do not appear to share. For example, prior to the killing, these youths have typically attempted to get help from others and have tried to escape the family situation. Severely abused children who kill their parents do not report seeing psychotherapists on a regular basis, from whom they withhold information about the abuse that they have endured for years. Severely abused youths who report feeling trapped and perceive no other way out of the family situation do not have in their histories, as Lyle Menendez did in his, that they had attended a major university 3,000 miles away from their parents' home.

These discrepancies and others that appear in the case do not rule out that Lyle and Eric Menendez were severely abused children who killed because they believed they were about to be killed by their parents. However, they raise questions that need to be asked to understand the motivation that propelled the killings of Jose and Kitty

Menendez. More important, these questions need to be addressed to advance scientific knowledge of the phenomenon of parricide.

I have been surprised by the number of my therapy clients, university students, and others familiar with my work in parricide who have told me that, as adolescents, they had seriously entertained killing their abusive parents but did not. In a study of women who had been severely abused, my colleague, Eldra P. Solomon, Ph.D., and I found that 50 percent reported that prior to the age of 18 they had seriously considered killing their abusive parents. Parricide appears to be the tip of a very ugly iceberg. In addition to asking why some adolescents kill their parents, we need to be asking why more youths do not. It is my hope that our nation will seriously consider the recommendations made in the final chapter of *Why Kids Kill Parents*. These recommendations are designed to reduce the conditions that propel some youths to kill their parents and countless more to consider such action.

PARRICIDE: FACTS AND ISSUES

1 | The Phenomenon of Parricide

A FATHER is gunned down . . . a mother is bludgeoned to death . . . a family of four—mother, father, and two small children—is butchered alive . . . by a son . . . a daughter . . . a son and a daughter acting together.

The term *parricide*, while technically referring to the killing of a close relative, has over the last decade increasingly become identified in the public mind with the murder of an individual's father (patricide) or mother (matricide). This book focuses on one group of parricides, parents slain by their adolescent children. Between 1977 and 1986, the killing of a parent was almost a daily event in the United States. More than 300 parents were killed each year.[1] An in-depth analysis of the FBI Supplementary Homicide Report (SHR) data for this period[2] revealed that parents and stepparents murdered were typically white and non-Hispanic. Stepparents killed tended to be younger than biological parents who were slain and male parents younger than their female counterparts. The mean (average) age of stepfathers killed was 46; stepmothers, 50; fathers, 54; and mothers, 58.[3]

In the great majority of cases, the child who killed a parent or stepparent was a white, non-Hispanic male. More than 70 percent of those killing fathers, stepfathers, or stepmothers were under 30 years of age, while almost 70 percent of those killing mothers were between 20 and 50.[4]

Fifteen percent of mothers, 25 percent of fathers, 30 percent of stepmothers, and 34 percent of stepfathers were killed by sons and daughters under 18.[5] Juvenile involvement in the killings of parents and stepparents may seem relatively low compared to the attention that it has attracted. Juvenile involvement in parricide is actually quite high, however, in relation to the proportion of juveniles arrested for

3

homicide. Over the period 1977–86,[6] less than 10 percent of those arrested for homicide were under 18.[7]

Identifying the exact number of parents and stepparents slain by juveniles is not possible because of limitations in the SHR data set. These data and publicly available FBI data, however, make it possible to state that in every year of the ten-year period as many as 65 natural parents—45 fathers and 20 mothers—may have been killed by youths under 18.[8]

ADOLESCENT PARRICIDE OFFENDERS

Adolescence is a turbulent period characterized by growth spurts, development of primary and secondary sexual characteristics, enhancement of motor skills and intellectual abilities, and psychological changes. While one cannot precisely define when adolescence begins and ends, child development experts set its beginning at puberty, perhaps as early as age 11, and extend it to age 19 or 20.[9]

Adolescence seems a more amorphous term than *juvenile status,* which is defined by law in U.S. federal and state justice systems. Lack of uniformity in juvenile court status across jurisdictions suggests, however, that the difference between the two terms is more apparent than real. The federal system and 38 states designate individuals under 18 as juveniles. Of the remaining 12 states, eight have restricted the age of juvenile court jurisdiction to youths under 17, and three have restricted it to youths under 16. One state has extended juvenile court status to youths under 19.[10] In recognition, perhaps, of developmental differences, several states have provisions for extending juvenile court jurisdiction to age 21. Others allow youths who are tried as adults and young adults convicted before age 21 to be sentenced as "youthful offenders."[11]

Bender and Curran (1940) recognized the importance of distinguishing between preadolescents (children under 11) and adolescents who kill in understanding the motivational dynamics behind the crime and in prescribing treatment. Children under 11 typically do not understand the concept of death[12] and have tremendous difficulty accepting that their actions have led to an irreversible result.[13] In addition, preadolescents who kill are much more likely to be severely mentally ill than adolescents.[14] Adolescents are more likely to kill because of the life-style that they have adopted or in response to situational demands or environmental constraints that they perceive to have been placed upon them.[15]

Adolescents who kill parents also differ from adults who kill parents. Adolescent parricide offenders (APOs) under 18 may shoot the same gun or wield the same knife as their adult counterparts, but weapons usage does not make the two types of slayers equivalent. Yet the law may, and increasingly does, hold youths under 18 who kill their parents accountable to the same degree as adults who commit the same crime.[16] In June 1989, the Supreme Court held that 16- and 17-year-olds convicted of murder may be sentenced to death.[17]

Adolescents, unlike adults, are at a higher risk of becoming parricide offenders when conditions in the home are unfavorable because of their limited alternatives. Unlike adults, adolescents cannot simply leave. The law has made it a crime for young people to run away. Although running away is technically considered a status offense applying only to children, it still subjects the youth to juvenile court intervention. In some states, for example, Florida, if a juvenile runs away several times, he can be found in contempt of court and held in a detention facility.[18]

Juveniles who commit parricide usually consider running away, but many do not know any place where they can seek refuge. Those who do run away are generally either picked up and returned home or go back voluntarily. Surviving on their own is hardly a realistic alternative for youths with meager financial resources, limited job skills, and incomplete education. State regulations invariably mandate their attendance at school, most commonly until age 16, and federal law imposes strict limitations on when and how much juveniles, particularly those under 16, can work.[19]

Adolescent parricide offenders also, on the whole, have far less experience than adults and cannot be expected to cope as well with deplorable environmental conditions. Adolescents are not as likely to see alternative courses of actions and weigh different strategies; their cognitive development, judgment, and character are not equivalent to adults'.[20]

Because adults have more choices and resources and are more mature than juveniles, an adult's killing of a parent would be expected to be an unusual occurrence. Logically, an adult who found contact with his or her parents intolerable would just leave the familial situation. One would expect to find more psychopathology, or severe mental illness, in adult offenders who kill their parents than in adolescents who commit the same act. Empirical studies and clinical case reports confirm this hypotheses.[21]

Given these differences, discussing all parricide offenders as though they were the same is ill advised. This book focuses on adolescent parricide offenders because the adolescent population is the most receptive to effective intervention and prevention strategies. Even after killing a parent, some young people may become contributing members of society.

A TYPOLOGY OF PARRICIDE OFFENDERS

The professional literature suggests that parricide is committed by three types of individuals: (1) the severely abused child who is pushed beyond his or her limits, (2) the severely mentally ill child, and (3) the dangerously antisocial child. The following typology provides a conceptual framework for understanding parricide offenders.[22] Although psychological assessment of the offender and thorough knowledge of the case are necessary before one can draw firm conclusions about where the offender falls in the typology, media accounts can provide useful illustrations of each type of parricide offender. In some cases, adolescents who kill their parents may not represent a "pure type."

The Severely Abused Child

The severely abused child is the most frequently encountered type of adolescent parricide offender[23] and is the focus of this book. According to Paul Mones, a Los Angeles attorney who specializes in defending adolescent parricide offenders, over 90 percent of youths who kill their parents have been abused by them.[24] In-depth portraits of such youths have frequently shown that they killed because they could no longer tolerate conditions at home.[25] These children, typically adolescents, were psychologically abused by one or both parents and often witnessed or suffered physical, sexual, and verbal abuse as well. They did not typically have histories of severe mental illness or of serious and extensive delinquent behavior. For them, the killings represented an act of desperation—the only way out of a familial situation that they could no longer endure.

One of these cases, the Jahnke case, captured the interest and compassion of a nation.[26] One evening in November 1982, a 16-year-old brother and a 17-year-old sister, Richie and Deborah Jahnke, got several guns from their father's arsenal of weapons. After methodically placing these weapons throughout their home, the two teenagers lay in wait for their father, a 38-year-old IRS investigator, to return home from a dinner with his wife celebrating their twentieth anniversary. As

Richard Jahnke walked toward the garage, Richie discharged a shot-gun into his father's body, ending the elder Jahnke's years of verbal abuse of the whole family, physical abuse of his wife and son, and sexual abuse of his daughter.

The Severely Mentally Ill Child

On occasion, adolescents who kill parents are recognized as gravely mentally disturbed or psychotic.[27] Psychotic individuals have lost contact with reality. Their personalities are typically severely disorganized, their perceptions distorted, and their communications often disjointed. Their behavior may be inappropriate to the setting and characterized by repetitive, purposeless actions. Although they may show excessive levels of motor activity, they also may be lethargic. They may experience hallucinations (seeing or hearing things that are not actually occurring) and bizarre delusions (beliefs that have no basis in reality and that would appear totally implausible to other people in their environment, for example, a belief that one's thoughts are being broadcast through transmitters implanted in one's teeth).[28] Individuals with psychotic disorders often do not understand that they are mentally ill and frequently require hospitalization, at least until their mental disorder has been stabilized.

In some parricide cases involving psychotic individuals, the illness is so visible and well established that criminal prosecution is not completed or is halted for a period of time.[29] Michael Miller, age 20, was charged with first-degree murder and rape after confessing to killing his mother, who was the wife of President Reagan's personal attorney. Mrs. Miller's nude and battered body was found sprawled in the master bedroom of their opulent home in March 1983. Available reports suggested that the Millers were a close-knit, religious family, but that both of the Miller sons had suffered from mental illness. The older son, Jeff, had suffered a "nervous breakdown" while a student at Dartmouth College. He committed suicide in 1981 while in a clinic that specialized in the treatment of schizophrenia. Michael was very upset by his brother's suicide, moved back to his parents' home, and sought psychiatric treatment.[30] Court documents revealed that the psychiatrist who had been treating Michael for eight months prior to the matricide was "of the opinion that Miller has been and is presently suffering from severe mental disorders evidenced by manifestation of acute psychotic behavior and suicidal tendencies . . . and is in need of immediate and intensive psychiatric treatment and observation."[31] After hearing testimony from four mental health experts, the presiding judge found Michael incompetent to stand trial and committed him to a state mental health facility, suspending all criminal proceedings against him until he was restored to competency.[32]

In other cases, mental illness presents no bar to prosecution, as in the case of 19-year-old Jonathan Cantero, a psychotic matricide offender convicted of murder in the first degree in 1989. According to media accounts, the adolescent, following a detailed plan he had drafted, stabbed his mother 40 times in the chest, stomach, and back, and slit her throat.[33] He told police that he tried to cut off his mother's left hand to demonstrate his allegiance to Satan, but was too scared to collect his mother's blood in a vial as he had planned. After the killing, Cantero etched a pentagram (a five-pointed star with Satanic associations) on his palm and used a Polaroid camera to photograph it. He said he had recited the following words over his mother's dead body: "Lord Satan thou I had stricken this woman from the earth, I have slain the womb from which I was born. I have ended her reign of desecration of my mind, she is no longer of me, yet only a simple serpent on a lower plane."[34]

After the murder Cantero partially burned and buried his notes, the photograph, the incantation, and the clothes that he was wearing. When he was arrested two weeks later, he led police to the site where the charred evidence was buried. His notes included two lists that he had drafted describing 11 steps in his plan to kill his mother and eight materials that he would need.

Defense counsel planned for months to argue that Cantero was legally insane at the time of the crime. Two mental health experts who examined him observed that he was extremely delusional and diagnosed him as paranoid schizophrenic. They concluded that he apparently heard voices commanding him to kill his mother at the time of the homicidal incident and was legally insane. Shortly before trial, however, defense counsel entered a plea to murder in the first degree in accordance with his client's wishes. Cantero, although clearly psychotic, had been found competent to stand trial (he knew the nature of the proceedings and was able to assist counsel in his own defense) and was therefore empowered to make his own decisions about legal strategies and pleas. According to the public defender who represented him, Cantero did not want to put his family through the ordeal of a trial, preferring to plead guilty to first-degree murder in exchange for a life sentence. Neither the state of Florida nor the Cantero family was interested in seeking the death penalty, and the adolescent's plea was accepted.[35]

In some accounts of parricide, an established psychiatric history is not mentioned, but a review of the details of the crime suggests that the offender may have been severely mentally disturbed, at least at the time of the crime. The possibility of serious psychological disturbance is particularly likely to be considered where multiple family members are killed and extreme violence is used. When corpses are bizarrely dismembered, the possibility that the offender suffers from mental illness is often considered seriously by both mental health professionals and attorneys who frequently deal with homicide offenders.[36]

The Dangerously Antisocial Child

The term *dangerously antisocial child* here refers to individuals whom professionals in the late nineteenth and early twentieth centuries called psychopathic or sociopathic personalities.[37] The two terms, which have become synonymous in the public mind, have been replaced in the professional literature with two more precise terms— *conduct disorder* and *antisocial personality disorder*—depending on the age of the individual and the presence of specific criteria.[38] Individuals who are diagnosed as having conduct disorders or antisocial personalities, unlike those who are psychotic, are oriented in time and space and free of delusions and hallucinations.

A youth under 18 may be classified clinically as having a conduct disorder when a pattern of disregarding the rights of others has been present for six months or more. The youth must engage in at least three types of disruptive behavior.[39] Severity of the conduct disorder (mild, moderate, severe) is determined by the number of conduct problems and how much harm they cause. Of the 13 criteria listed, nine involve physical violence against persons or property (examples are physical cruelty to people or animals, rape, arson) or thefts involving confrontation with a victim. The remaining behaviors, considered nonaggressive, include episodes of stealing without confrontation, running away from home, truancy, and often lying under conditions other than to avoid physical or sexual abuse. Three types of conduct disorders are currently recognized by the American Psychiatric Association: the group type, the solitary aggressive type, and the undifferentiated type, which cannot be assigned to either of the other two types.[40]

When the individual is at least 18 years old, a diagnosis of antisocial personality disorder may be made if evidence of a conduct disorder existed before age 15 and the individual continued to engage in behavior disregarding the rights of others. To support a diagnosis of antisocial personality disorder, the individual must have a minimum of four of ten characteristics listed: employment instability, failure to conform to social norms, tendency to be irritable and to behave aggressively, repeated failure to honor financial obligations, failure to plan ahead, lack of regard for the truth, reckless disregard for the safety of oneself or others, inability to function as a responsible parent, failure to sustain a monogamous relationship for more than one year, and absence of remorse.[41]

Those having antisocial personality disorders often appear to behave in an irrational manner, consistently demonstrating poor judgment and failing to learn from experience. They typically come across as poised, even charming, largely because they are free of anxiety and guilt about their violation of norms and the rights of others. They are capable of only the shallowest of human emotions.[42]

Media accounts of the two cases below suggested that the APOs involved were dangerously antisocial individuals, killing their parents to serve some instrumental, selfish end. Michelle Ann White, a 14-year-old girl, and her 17-year-old brother, John, were arrested for arranging to have their 41-year-old father killed by a neighborhood youth in Cleveland, Ohio, in February 1979.[43] John White had obtained custody of the children following his divorce ten years earlier. The victim was considered to be a quiet and religious individual. He had a reputation as a hard worker, a meticulous housekeeper, and a strict disciplinarian.

When John White returned home from work one evening, he was allegedly greeted by the neighborhood youth and his daughter, then gunned down by the 19-year-old assassin as Michelle Ann watched. Within minutes Michelle Ann's brother arrived home. Police reported that the two children paid the hit man with three twenty-dollar bills from their father's wallet.

The victim's children used his car, paycheck, and three credit cards to purchase at least $1000 worth of merchandise during the next week. They bought bicycles, video games, a television set, and a toolbox. According to one of the police investigators, the White children made no provisions for disposal of their father's body. For more than a week they cooked meals in the kitchen a few feet away from their father's decaying corpse.

Neighbors of the victim noted that the children often had loud parties when Mr. White was away from home. One neighbor described the White children as angels when their father was home and devils when he was away. The adolescents had little to say about the motive for the killing other than that their father had not permitted them to do whatever they wanted.

In the second case, Paul T. Rogers, an award-winning author, was gravely ill with cancer when he was beaten to death in his Queens, New York, apartment by his adopted and disabled 19-year-old son and the son's 27-year-old drifter friend. The building superintendent found Rogers' body about ten days later. The two confessed to beating the victim with a plank and to withdrawing some $4500 from the author's bank account to purchase "cocaine and other drugs."[44] The possible linking of a number of recent matricides committed by juveniles to the effects of crack[45] also raises the question whether the APOs were dangerously antisocial.

The Need for Psychological Assessment

The categories just described look clear-cut. In reality, cases sometimes contain facts that span categories and make rapid-fire classification prone to error. Assessment of the child by a mental health expert whose area of specialty includes children who commit violent acts is critical to determine whether a juvenile is really dangerously antisocial. The case of Patty Smith (chapter 9) illustrates this point. Patty was initially portrayed by the media as a youth who cold-bloodedly murdered her father because he took away the keys to her car. My in-depth examination of her, a detailed interview with her mother, and an extensive review of case-related materials led me to conclude that she was not dangerously antisocial. Rather, she was a severely abused child who enlisted the help of her friends to kill her father because she could find no other way out.

Children who have been abused and neglected may adopt an antisocial way of responding to life as a means of psychic, if not physical, survival. Antisocial behavior can focus their attention away from problems at home that are too difficult to handle. When faced with an APO with any history of acting out, the question whether the adolescent is truly sociopathic (that is, lacks a conscience), or whether he or she has adopted a pattern of acting out to maintain his or her fragile mental health is one best reserved for the mental health professional. The case of Debra "Muffin" Mattingly illustrates the significance of unraveling the history and meaning of antisocial behavior.

Muffin was 14 years old in 1970 when she and two of her codefendants were arrested and charged with murdering her father. During the year prior to the homicide, she had reportedly been associating with the Vipers, a bike gang known for its apparent fascination with violence and the motorcycle group Hell's Angels. Her codefendants, both societal dropouts, were a 19-year-old male from California who styled himself after Hell's Angels and a 21-year-old AWOL marine who seemed impressed by the 19-year-old's violent fantasies. Others living at the Vipers' residence said that the 19-year-old (known as "Big Spirit") and Muffin (referred to as "Little Spirit") slept with switchblades in their hands and modeled themselves after Bonnie and Clyde. One described Muffin "as tough as nails, the kind of chick who eats nails." [46] Police reported that Muffin, the two young men, and a 15-year-old female who later became a material witness went to the Mattingly house to get some of Muffin's belongings. There they got into an argument with Muffin's father, Richard Mattingly, and bludgeoned and choked him to death.

Muffin had been born to a poverty-stricken couple who divorced shortly after her birth. At that time she went to live with Richard and Ethyl Mattingly, who later adopted her. Mr. Mattingly was an abusive alcoholic whose wife separated from him five times in a 16-year period, typically mentioning his "drunken brutality" as the reason for her departure. In 1962, when Mrs. Mattingly left for the sixth time, she took six-year-old Muffin with her and did not go back.

In 1966 or 1967, Mrs. Mattingly died and Muffin was returned to live with Mr. Mattingly. At her adopted mother's funeral, Muffin saw her biological mother, who was then remarried, for the first time since infancy. Muffin was shaken by seeing her natural mother at the wake and her foster mother laid out in the coffin, and seemed to become obsessed with the idea of seeing her real mother again. After about a year of Muffin's imploring her adoptive father to take her to see her natural mother again, Mr. Mattingly did so. The visit did not accomplish much. Muffin's schoolwork, which had once been excellent, continued to deteriorate. The girl ran away from home several times, once to her biological mother's home, and was placed in a series of detention homes, parochial schools, and summer camps. A few months before the homicide, Muffin told friends that she needed psychiatric help and that she had asked a judge to commit her to a mental hospital. When he refused, she ran away again. Eventually she wound up hanging out in an area of Washington, D.C., known as a gathering place for motorcycle gang members and societal dropouts. There she met the two young men with whom she killed her father.[47]

The Making of the Dangerously Antisocial Child

We live in a society that tends to categorize complex issues in black-and-white terms. When youths kill their parents, severe mental illness is typically eliminated as an explanation almost immediately. The question frequently becomes: Was the juvenile really a battered child or was she or he simply a "psychopath"? The two categories are not mutually exclusive. Some children raised in abusive homes do have conduct disorders and, if adults, would be classified as having anti-social personality disorders. In the Mattingly case, there was evidence that the girl had been raised in an abusive environment. Whether her antisocial behavior was her way of coping or whether the behavior was indicative of her personality structure cannot be determined without more information.

The case of Marc Schreuder is a powerful study of the making of a sociopathic youth. Marc was arrested in 1982 for killing his multi-millionaire grandfather, Franklin Bradshaw, in 1978. Prosecutors alleged that Marc murdered his grandfather to placate his mother, who was seeking access to her father's fortune.[48] Marc was convicted of second-degree murder; his mother was later convicted of first-degree murder largely on her son's testimony. Two books[49] documented the intergenerational cycle of abuse and neglect that led to mental illness in both the Bradshaw and Schreuder families, and eventually to murder.

Coleman's 1985 book is a brilliant study of family psychopathology. He depicted Frances Schreuder as a sociopathic woman who abused and neglected her two sons, Marc and Larry. Frances instructed her sons to steal from her father and to act abusively toward her mother. The author concluded that in attempting to cope with Mrs. Schreuder's treatment of and demands on them, both sons had become mentally ill. Larry was diagnosed as a paranoid schizophrenic; Marc appeared to fit Louise Kaplan's role of the impostor, a character disorder that in many ways mirrors the antisocial personality disorder.

Although Larry's psychosis had resulted in violent outbursts, his involvement in the murder was never established. The psychiatrist who examined Marc opined that Larry was not so easily controlled by his mother as Marc, and hence may not have been sufficiently oriented or motivated to effect a complex assassination plot. In contrast, Marc's character structure enabled him to gun down his grandfather when his mother's wishes became explicit and persistent—his grandfather had to be killed if Marc wanted to maintain his relationship with his mother.

SOCIETAL REACTION

Society has reacted to the killing of one's parents with horror as far back as antiquity. The attention given such figures as Oedipus, Orestes, Alcmaeon, and King Arthur shows that the slaying of mothers and fathers has been a source of morbid fascination for thousands of years.[50]

In a psychoanalytic review of myths and legends, Bunder (1944) noted the significance of parricidal themes in literature and cited an important difference between the murders of mothers and fathers. "The vanquishing of the father, in whichever of its manifold guises it may be represented, is one of the major themes—indeed, it could almost be termed *the* major theme of myth and legend."[51] The analysis of matricides, although not so common in Greek mythology as patricides, suggests that in literature, "incest with the mother becomes converted into what appears to be its very opposite, her murder."[52]

The killing of mothers and fathers by their offspring has captured the public's attention because societal dictates have always commanded children to love and obey their parents.[53] If offspring are unable to express positive sentiments toward their parents and to follow their rules for whatever reason, they have been expected at least not to kill those who gave them life. After all, if parents must fear violent death at the hands of their children, how can they feel safe anywhere with anyone?

Traditional taboos notwithstanding, the more recent response of individuals in the United States to youths and young adults who kill their parents has been mixed, depending on the circumstances.[54] In many cases people have reacted to the parricide more with compassion than disbelief. *Time* magazine, for example, headlined the Jahnke case by quoting a family friend: "It Made Terrible Sense."[55] The conclusions reached in the article were sympathetic to the offenders rather than to the deceased. Although the patricide appeared premeditated, the Cheyenne community increasingly rallied behind the two alleged killers as information about the Jahnke household surfaced.[56]

Two weeks after Richard Jahnke was convicted of voluntary manslaughter, a letter-writing campaign was initiated to influence the trial judge in sentencing. In less than three weeks, the Committee to Help Richard John Jahnke recorded more than 4,000 letters urging leniency for Richard, and only one letter opposed. The committee collected 10,000 signatures on petitions distributed locally and delivered scores of additional petitions from around the United States to the judge. While letters were pouring in to the committee on Richard's behalf, his sister, Deborah, was convicted of aiding and abetting voluntary manslaughter. Following both convictions, defense attorneys were besieged with letters and phone calls urging leniency in sentencing.[57]

The letters did not have their desired effect, however. On March 18, 1983, Richard was sentenced to 5 to 15 years in prison; on April 27,

1983, his sister was sentenced to three to eight years. While appeals were pending and the youths were on bond, a crew from "60 Minutes" arrived in Cheyenne to investigate the story. On January 22, 1984, fourteen months after the parricide, the Jahnke case was the lead story on "60 Minutes." An estimated 46 million viewers watched as the details of Richard's and Deborah's convictions were discussed. Correspondent Ed Bradley described the abuse that the adolescents had endured, the inability of Mrs. Jahnke to protect her children, and the failure of the state social services agency to investigate the child abuse report filed six months before the homicide. Of the more than one thousand letters written to the studio after the broadcast, only ten objected to the sympathetic treatment.[58]

When the Jahnkes' convictions and sentences were upheld by the Wyoming Supreme Court in separate appeals later that year, Governor Ed Herschler commuted both sentences. Richard was ordered to be sent to a hospital for a few months for psychiatric evaluation and then placed in a juvenile facility until age 21. His sentence totaled three years and 13 days. Deborah's sentence was commuted to one year of probation to be preceded by one month's intensive psychiatric intervention. Thirty days later, she enrolled as a freshman at the University of Wyoming.[59]

In three cases that attracted national attention in 1986 and 1987, three female offspring ranging in age from 16 to 30 took action to kill their fathers and succeeded. Although two of these "children" were legally adults, their cases are included here because they were living at home at the time of the killings and did not appear to have separated themselves from their childhood families. All three claimed that they had been abused by their fathers since childhood and that they had killed the victims to end years of physical and sexual abuse. The judicial system dealt with each very differently.

The state of Florida failed in its attempt to have 22-year-old Janet Reese indicted for murder in the first degree. Janet, who claimed that her father had been sexually abusing her since the first grade, shot her 42-year-old father in April 1986, after he came home for lunch one afternoon and forced her to have sex. When grand jurors heard the circumstances, they reduced the charge to manslaughter. The state eventually dropped the charges.[60]

Thirty-year-old Lisa Keller was found not guilty of murdering her father. The defense persuaded jurors that Lisa acted in self-defense when she beat her 70-year-old father to death with a wooden 2" × 4". Family members testified that the victim had beaten his wife and children for many years. Lisa's sister testified further that when Mrs. Keller left the home, the defendant became the primary target of abuse. Psychiatric testimony indicated that Lisa's father had started making sexual advances to her when she was 13 years old.[61]

In a third case, 18-year-old Cheryl Pierson pleaded guilty to manslaughter for making arrangements when she was 16 to have her 42-year-old father killed. The adolescent admitted to offering a classmate, also 16 at the time of the crime, $1,000 to kill her father. Cheryl testified at the presentencing hearing that her father began sexually abusing her when she was 11 years old. After her mother died in February 1985, the sexual abuse continued and Cheryl feared her father would eventually abuse her younger sister. At the presentencing hearing Cheryl's stepbrother and many neighbors and friends testified that they had suspected James Pierson of sexually abusing his daughter, but had done nothing to help her.[62] Cheryl was sentenced to six months in jail and five years' probation.[63] She was released after serving three and a half months.[64] The boy she hired was sentenced to 24 years in prison. Cheryl's boyfriend, also charged in the murder for having given the hit man $400 at Cheryl's request, pleaded guilty to criminal solicitation and was sentenced to probation.

Trends in Judicial Processing of Parricide Cases

Recent judicial processing and disposition of parricide cases involving adolescents with histories of abuse need to be studied and compared as much as possible with earlier periods before trends can be reported with certainty. Some evidence suggests that the reaction of the judicial system to the abused youth who kills the victimizing parent is becoming more compassionate.[65] Cornell, Staresina, and Benedek (1989) briefly described a case in which Fred—a 17-year-old who killed his father—was acquitted by reason of insanity. The authors concluded that "the jury's sympathetic reaction" to the youth who shot his father, "an alcoholic who was extremely brutal and tyrannical,"[66] as he was beating up the defendant's sister apparently influenced their verdict. The authors made the following observations in evaluating the jury's verdict.

> Fred did not suffer from schizophrenia or any similar mental disorder; he did not even profess amnesia for the offense or give any indication that he acted in a dissociated state. Moreover, Fred did not deny the intentional nature of his behavior or his awareness that his actions were wrong. However justifiable the offense might appear from some larger moral perspective, it is far from clear that the insanity statute represented the appropriate legal resolution.[67]

As public awareness of child abuse has increased, arguments by defense attorneys that these children act in self-defense are also winning more favor among jurors. According to Paul Mones, who has assisted in the defense of many adolescent parricide offenders, "Courts are finally waking up to the problem. Kids just don't take these actions unless something is very, very wrong."[68]

In October 1986, a Los Angeles jury acquitted a 19-year-old male of the attempted murder of his father under an unusual set of circumstances. According to court testimony, Johnny Junatanov made arrangements three times to have his father killed. The victim survived the first two attempts on his life. When Johnny was in the process of making arrangements for the third time, he was arrested by the undercover policeman he was seeking to hire as a hit man.

Johnny testified that he was desperate to kill his father. He explained to the jury that his father had beaten him, kept him in handcuffs, chained him since he was a child, and raped him three years earlier. A photograph and testimony by the boy's mother and grandmother and by the victim's employees corroborated the abuse.

The Junatanov case may have been the first in which an adolescent was found not guilty of attempting to kill a brutal parent on the grounds of self-defense when it did not appear that he was in imminent fear of death or severe bodily harm. Self-defense appears to be becoming a more viable argument. Increasingly, defense lawyers are attempting to persuade juries that battered children, like battered wives, reach a point where they believe they are in danger of being killed at any time and kill in self-defense. Juries recently have tended to convict of manslaughter rather than murder and to recommend leniency to the court in sentencing.[69]

In addition to jury verdicts, indications of a change in attitude and practice are noticeable in sentencing and even sometimes in actions taken by grand juries and judges. In the sentencing decision, judges have on occasion clearly taken into account the effects of a history of abuse. In Jacksonville, Florida, a trial judge in 1983 sentenced to 15 years' probation a 17-year-old boy who pleaded guilty to the second-degree murder of his father. In imposing this sentence, the judge followed the recommendations of both the prosecutor and the state agency counselor who wrote the presentencing report. The boy, George Burns, Jr., had shot his father six times in the chest and back immediately following a long evening of arguments—and after years of documented abuse. Authorities had known for several years that the father had physically and psychologically abused his wife and children.[70] The judge was careful to state explicitly that society in no way condoned the boy's behavior. In imposing sentence, however, he remarked: "I believe that the chain of violence and abuse that led to this end were brought about by your father's actions rather than by yours."[71]

In a 1984 case, a 17-year-old Boston youth, Robert Ludwig, killed his father with a hatchet. The judge imposed a suspended sentence of nine to 15 years after a court psychiatrist testified that Robert's was the worst case of abuse he had ever encountered. Friends and neighbors also rallied behind the adolescent.[72]

In June 1989, a circuit court judge presiding over juvenile matters in Pensacola, Florida, found 15-year-old Diana Goodykoontz not guilty of second-degree murder in the shooting death of her father. During the four-day, nonjury trial held in juvenile court, the court had heard testimony that the father had a history of drinking heavily and physically abusing his wife and three children, on one occasion threatening to kill the entire family. Diana testified that her father had made sexual advances to her and that she feared he might rape her. On the day of the homicide her father was drunk and ordered the family into the living room. Believing another violent confrontation was about to occur, Diana refused and retreated into her parents' bedroom, where her father's .357 magnum revolver was kept. She quickly dismissed the idea of escaping through the bedroom window as unfeasible, advancing instead from the bedroom into the hall and firing one shot into her father's chest.

In handing down the court's decision, the judge agreed with the testimony of expert witnesses for the defense that the adolescent was a battered child and suffered from post–traumatic stress disorder. He held that this syndrome caused Diana to have a reasonable belief, based on past interactions with her father, that she was "in imminent danger of great bodily harm" when she shot him. The judge found that Diana "further reasonably believed that the use of deadly force was necessary to prevent that harm from occurring."[73] According to cocounsel Paul Mones, the Goodykoontz case was the first one in which the battered-child defense was accepted by a juvenile court in a nonjury trial in the United States.[74]

Child Maltreatment and Parricide

UNDERSTANDING THE phenomenon of child maltreatment is critical in analyzing the dynamics leading to the killing of a parent. In conceptualizing child maltreatment, the law distinguishes between crimes of commission and omission. Acts committed upon a child that are harmful are considered to constitute abuse; failure to act that results in harm to the child constitutes neglect. Adolescent parricide offenders are typically victims of both.

One type of child maltreatment can lead to the other. A child who is physically or sexually abused by a parent becomes a victim of neglect if the parents fail to seek medical attention for resulting injuries or sexually transmitted diseases. It is useful to distinguish four types of abuse: physical, sexual, verbal, and psychological. Neglect can be categorized into three areas: physical, medical, and emotional. *Emotional incest,* a term initially introduced by Ackerman (1986) and referred to by Bradshaw (1988b, 1990) as *emotional sexual abuse,* frequently accompanies emotional neglect.

PHYSICAL ABUSE

Physical abuse includes inflicted physical injury or the attempt to inflict physical injury or pain that is indicative of the unresolved needs of the aggressor. This definition captures the dynamics of physical abuse by directing attention to both the victim and the offender.[1] It includes both cause and effect and can define physical violence perpetrated on the spouse as well as the child.[2]

The definition can be appropriately utilized when physical violence or force is used in obvious ways like those first described by Straus

(1979) in the Conflict Tactics Scales (for example, threw something, pushed, grabbed, or shoved, slapped or spanked, kicked, bit, or hit with fist, hit or tried to hit with something, beat up, burned or scalded, threatened with gun or knife, used gun or knife).[3] Straus' technique has been modified and used extensively in numerous studies of family violence. Physical abuse can also be more subtle. Parents (almost always mothers) who simulate illness in their children or who intentionally make them physically ill so that their children may receive excessive medical attention while they themselves play the role of concerned parents are also physically abusing their children. This disorder, known as Munchausen Syndrome by Proxy, is frequently fatal for infants whose mothers are not correctly diagnosed and treated.[4]

Physical abuse by a parent may or may not be a reaction to the child's behavior. If the parent's behavior is not appropriate or proportional to anything the child has actually done, it is physically abusive. In some cases the offending parent attacks the child for no reason at all. The child may be simply watching television, walking through a room, or coming into the house when the abusive parent strikes out. In other cases, the parent is clearly reacting to something the child has done. A parent may excessively beat a seven-year-old for taking another child's toy, a 12-year-old for getting an unsatisfactory grade at school, a 15-year-old for being disrespectful to his mother. In such cases the child often can identify the action that provoked the parental attack and may even mistakenly interpret the physical assault as deserved.

If the parent's conduct does not actually cause injury or pain but could reasonably have been expected to have done so, the behavior is still physically abusive. Again, the criterion is that the parent's response to the child is inappropriate and out of proportion.

A case that recently captured national attention illustrates excessive and unsuitable tactics used by one mother in an attempt to discipline her seven-year-old son.[5] Over a two-week period, the boy apparently had stolen $25 worth of baseball cards, six dollars in cash, an earring, a belt buckle, and another child's toy. The mother decided that she needed to teach her son a lesson because he lied to her after each theft. She dressed the boy like a pig by putting blue finger paint on his face and taping a cardboard snout to his head. She tied his wrists behind his back and made him sit on a bench in front of his home with a sign on his chest for about half an hour. Before police arrived to find the boy crying on the porch, 15 neighbors had gathered to read the sign, which said:

I'm a dumb pig. Ugly is what you will become every time you lie and steal. Look at me squeal. My hands are tied because I cannot be trusted. This is a lesson to be learned. Look. Laugh. Thief. Stealing. Bad boy.

The woman told police when they arrested her that her mother had used this technique on her, as well as putting her hands on hot stove burners for punishment. The mother stated that she wanted the boy to understand "for if only 30 minutes that lying and stealing make you ugly like Pinocchio." The woman, acknowledging her conduct might have been wrong, stated, "Mom said it worked on us kids."

Physical Abuse in Adolescent Parricide Cases

Physical abuse was a factor in each of the three parricide cases presented in part 2 and typically appeared to have been the result of the father's anger and dissatisfaction with his life and marital circumstances. Two of the fathers beat their adolescent children more frequently once their common-law wives had walked out on them, claiming that the breakup was the children's fault. By blaming their children for their problems and seeking redress from them, these parents, like others who abuse their children, were denying their responsibility for life events.

Although none of the three adolescents whose stories are told in part 2 was ever hospitalized as a result of physical abuse, all received injuries. Patty Smith sustained a dislocated back after being severely kicked by her father, while Peter Jones had bruises and welts on his back, legs, and arms from beatings inflicted upon him by his father. He was kicked, punched in the head, nose, mouth, and stomach, and led around by his hair. His father also threw things at him—once cutting him—and bent his son's thumb so far that the youth believed his thumb would break. Scott Anders' father hit him "everywhere . . . stomach, face, and head." The beating was so severe that Scott's father would not allow him to go to school because he had "knots" on his head.

In addition to injuries and obvious attempts to hurt, the three cases illustrate the pervasiveness of the threat of serious injury and even death. The fathers of Patty Smith, Peter Jones, and Scott Anders each threatened to kill their children. Patty Smith's father aimed a gun at her; Scott Anders' father propped a shotgun beside him on the night of the homicide after threatening to kill himself and his son. Terry Adams' father attempted to stab his son once, and another time pulled a gun on him.

In cases in which adolescents have killed parents, particularly fathers, severe spouse abuse frequently also exists, often antedating child physical abuse.[6] These adolescents' histories include the horror of witnessing extreme forms of violence as well as the terror of being a victim. The simultaneous experiencing of horror and terror may set the stage for parricide.

Individuals experience horror when they are witnesses to events that are so shocking that their minds cannot fully comprehend them. Though there is no physical threat, the events are traumatizing to them and may stay lodged in their minds for years. Although fear may be an element of horror, the predominant feelings associated with horror are shock and dread, not fear. Individuals react with terror or experience intense fear when their physical survival is threatened. With terror, both body and mind are affected. Terror immobilizes the body just as horror stuns the mind. Events that are terrifying, unlike those that are horrifying, have a beginning and an end: one wins or loses, one escapes or is captured, one is assaulted or spared, one lives or dies.[7]

SEXUAL ABUSE

I differentiate two types of parents' sexual abuse of children, overt and covert,[8] as well as forcible rape. Groth makes a similar distinction between overt sexual abuse and rape by noting that sexual offenses against children can consist of acts of molestation or rape depending on the characteristics of the approach and the dynamics of the offender.[9] Table 2.1 illustrates the differences between the two types of sexual abuse.

Overt Sexual Abuse

Overt sexual abuse is the more readily identifiable of the two. It involves a physical form of offending. A parent who sexually fondles a child or who engages in vaginal intercourse, anal sex, or oral sex with a child has overtly sexually abused that child.

It is estimated that one in four girls and one in seven to eight boys are overtly sexually abused before age 18.[10] Most of the offenders are known to the children; many of them are the children's parents or stepparents. Overt sexual abuse by a parent is a form of incest. When incest occurs between a parent and a child, the parent, regardless of

TABLE 2.1
Overt and Covert Sexual Abuse

Overt sexual abuse	Covert sexual abuse
Physical form of offending	Exposing a child to sexual issues that are age-inappropriate
"Hands-on" violation, direct contact	Raising the child in an environment that is sexually-saturated and/or provocative
Parent fondles child	Parent masturbates in front of child
Parent engages in vaginal intercourse with child	Parent allows, encourages, forces child to watch parent engage in sex with other parent or mate
Parent engages in anal sex with child	Parent shares pornography with child
Parent engages in oral sex with child	Parent routinely sleeps with adolescent child of opposite sex
	Parent forces or encourages child to commit prostitution or to engage in sexual performances or erotic dancing
	Other seductive behavior by parent towards child (e.g., a parent conversing in bathroom with opposite sex adolescent child as child showers, or a parent, while in state of undress, visiting with child **may be** covertly sexually abusing the child)

the circumstances, is always unequivocally responsible. It does not matter whether the child appeared to be a "willing" participant. A child's consent to be sexually expressive with a parent is meaningless because of differences in development and power between adult and child. A child who appears to consent to sexual behavior with a parent may be simply acceding to the parent's sexual demands in an unconscious effort to get his or her own needs for attention, affection, love, safety, and a sense of belonging met.

Covert Sexual Abuse

Covert sexual abuse involves exposing a child to sexual issues that are age-inappropriate or raising the child in a sexually saturated or provocative environment.[11] Although direct sexual contact between parent and child does not occur, parental activities are sexually explicit. A father who masturbates in front of his daughter or a mother who shares pornography with her son is abusing the child covertly.

Covert sexual abuse is typically very stressful for the child. It causes shame and confusion and may delay emotional development. The child generally knows that this activity is viewed as wrong, often within the family itself, and she or he knows, almost always, that it is condemned by the larger society.[12] The parent who covertly sexually abuses a child frequently conveys the implicit message that this activity is a secret between them because the other parent "simply won't understand."[13]

A parent who sleeps in the same bed with an adolescent child of the opposite sex has typically covertly sexually abused that child.[14] It does not matter that no physical contact occurs between the parent and child. Similarly, a parent who sits in the bathroom conversing with an opposite-sex adolescent as the youth showers or who, purposely in a state of undress, visits with the child, is also risking engaging in covert sexual abuse. The proximity of the opposite-sex parent in sexually provocative situations is sufficient to cause discomfort to a child who is going through puberty; it may cause gender confusion.[15] Adolescents know that it is unacceptable from the standpoint of society for them to fantasize about sexual involvement between them and their parents. Yet they are likely to feel very vulnerable because the closeness of the situations described suggests the possibility of increased sexual interaction, typically bringing fear and anxiety.

A parent who forces or encourages a daughter or son to commit prostitution or to engage in sexual performances or erotic dancing also abuses his or her offspring. It does not matter whether the child was willing—or even desired—to be in that setting. This parent has put or allowed the child to be put in a sexually explicit and exploitative atmosphere. In a recent case in Florida, Theresa Jackson was charged with child abuse after her teenage daughter, who worked as an erotic dancer, committed suicide. The prosecution succeeded in proving that Jackson was guilty of child abuse by introducing a psychological autopsy of the victim at trial. This evidence helped convince a jury that the girl took her own life because her mother forced her to engage in erotic dancing to support the family, and the mother was held responsible for her death.

Covert sexual abuse is potentially damaging to a child because of its frequently masked nature and the confusion its behaviors create.[16] It is often difficult for a child to realize that he or she has been victimized. Victims of covert sexual abuse tend to believe that the discomfort that they feel is somehow an indication of their "warped mind," that "there must be something wrong with them." Covert sexual abuse can result in lowered self-worth or self-esteem and can create confusion for the child about identity and personal boundaries.

Children's Reluctance to Report Sexual Abuse

Boys and girls who are overtly or covertly sexually abused frequently do not talk about it to others, even close friends, let alone school counselors, because of their shame and embarrassment.[17] Although they may feel that sexual behavior with a parent is wrong, they are often forced to choose between believing themselves or believing others who are important to them. These children may find it necessary to surrender their perceptions and to give up control of themselves for psychological, and sometimes physical, survival.[18] In learning to accede to others' definitions of reality and to abdicate whatever power they might have had, these children often adopt an external locus of control; that is, they come to believe and accept that events in their lives are controlled by outside forces.[19]

In spite of the increased concern about sexual abuse in the United States, the problem is not clearly recognized. Children are commonly reluctant to talk about their victimization because they know that those who report sexual abuse court disbelief. Our society is uncomfortable with acknowledging the reality of sexual abuse. Some children remain silent because they believe it is their responsibility to take care of the offender or save the family unit from the dissolution that they have been told would result from disclosure.[20] Even more sadly, some children, typically adolescents, resign themselves to the situation and make trade-offs with the abusing parent. In return for not reporting the parent to the authorities, these children accept privileges and material goods.[21]

Forcible Rape

Overt sexual abuse is conceptually distinct from forcible rape. The characteristics of the two types of acts appear in table 2.2. I use the term *overt sexual abuse* to describe sexual activities engaged in by the parent with the child that are often characterized by physical and emotional gentleness on the part of the parent. As noted by Groth in describing the dynamics involved in acts of molestation by pedophiles,[22] the parent relates to the child sexually because of his or her inability to relate sexually and emotionally to a spouse or other age-

TABLE 2.2
Overt Sexual Abuse Distinguished from Forcible Rape

Overt Sexual Abuse	Forcible Rape
Often characterized by physical gentleness on the part of the parent	Characterized by brute force
Reflects parent's inadequacy	Reflects parent's rage
Parent looks to child to fulfill needs for nurturance, love, intimacy	Parent selects child to vent anger and demonstrate power
Parent does not intend or desire to hurt child physically or psychologically	Parent intends and desires to hurt and control child
Child may not be fearful	Child is likely to be terrified

appropriate mate. The parent may be unable to relate to suitable sexual partners because his or her primary orientation is to children (the fixated pedophile) or because the individual is under a great deal of stress, loses control, or evinces poor judgment (the regressed pedophile). The parent's dysfunctional thinking leads him or her to look to the child rather than to an appropriate age mate to fulfill needs for physical closeness and sexual expression.

The parent who engages in overt sexual abuse generally does not want to hurt the child physically or psychologically. Before attempting to have sexual intercourse with his child, a father may spend months, even years, engaging in a series of other sexual behaviors. Such behaviors as undressing one another, being naked in the presence of one another, kissing, fondling, and having oral sex are often presented to the child as though they were a game. The father may take considerable time to stretch the opening of his young daughter's vagina so that it is able to accommodate his fully erect penis without causing her significant pain or injury. Although children generally experience tremendous guilt and shame when they realize that society condemns such intimacy between parents and children, the abusive parent typically did not intend to cause any trauma and frequently fails to appreciate that the action was so terribly wrong.[23]

I reserve the term *forcible rape* for sexual encounters between parents and children in which the parent uses brute force to achieve ends far different from those generally sought by an incest offender. The father who sexually assaults his daughter or son because he is enraged or wants to demonstrate who is boss is no different from an "angry rapist" or "power rapist."[24] The sexual encounter serves to vent anger, demonstrate power, and humiliate the victim. Elements are present in a forcible rape that are often absent in a typical incest encounter: The child feels powerless to resist the attack and is momentarily terrified that she or he may not survive it. The parent-assailant does not select his daughter or son simply because of inadequacy in relationships with other adults. Rather, as graphically illustrated in the case of Patty Smith, he attacks to hurt and control.[25]

VERBAL ABUSE

Verbal abuse consists of words spoken to a child, or remarks made in the child's presence about the child, that either are designed to damage the child's concept of self or would reasonably be expected to undermine a child's sense of competence and self-esteem. Swearing at a child can have a devastating effect on the child's sense of self. A father or a mother who calls a daughter "slut" or "whore" is certainly risking undermining the girl's self-esteem. Telling a child that he or she is "ugly," "stupid," "no good," or "good for nothing" is also obvious verbal abuse. The parent who remarks to another person in the presence of the child that "my daughter will never amount to anything" or "my son will die in the electric chair someday, wait and see" is attacking the child's self-concept.

Belittling remarks (for example, telling a three-year-old child "you're nothing but a baby," or an eight-year-old boy "I thought you were man enough to do it, my mistake") can undermine a child's sense of competence. Statements that tear at the child's ego ("you wimp you," "you'd forget your head if it weren't attached to you") can also damage the child's self-esteem. Parents who blame a child for their problems ("you're ruining my marriage," "if it weren't for you, we would be a lot better off financially," "it's your fault I didn't have a career, I had to stay home and raise you") are also likely to diminish the child's self-concept. Unfortunately, such comments are utilized by some parents to transfer their shame to the child[26] and to manipulate the child by making him or her feel badly.

The case presented earlier of the woman who dressed her son as a pig certainly had elements of verbal as well as physical abuse. The words on the sign—"I'm a dumb pig. . . . Look at me squeal. My hands are tied because I cannot be trusted. . . . Look. Laugh. Thief. Stealing. Bad boy"—would reasonably be expected to damage a child's self-concept. The words remain abusive despite the mother's avowed intentions.

PSYCHOLOGICAL OR
EMOTIONAL ABUSE

The terms *psychological abuse* and *verbal abuse,* although sometimes used interchangeably both by professionals and the public, are conceptually distinct. Psychological abuse is a far broader term than verbal abuse, encompassing words and behaviors that undermine or would reasonably be expected to undermine a child's sense of self, competence, and safety in the world. Verbal abuse is just one type of psychological abuse.

Physical and sexual abuse are also forms of psychological abuse when they are inflicted by a parent or guardian because these acts represent a violation of trust. They destroy the child's sense of security in his or her home and impede the development of competence in interpersonal relationships.[27] If the child tells the nonoffending parent that he or she is being sexually abused by the other parent and is met with disbelief, the child has been psychologically abused by both parents.

Psychologically abusive communications can be extraordinarily complex. These messages are particularly insidious because they often communicate to children that they are not valued for themselves or that they are unable to measure up to their parents' expectations regardless of what they do. Parents who constantly compare one child with a sibling to illustrate where the one falls short and does not measure up rather than accepting and valuing the differences in their children are undermining the child's self-esteem. Parents who express dissatisfaction with a child's accomplishments regardless of the actual performance level, always demanding more, are also psychologically abusing the child. Take the case of a child who works extraordinarily hard to get a B− on a test and is greatly relieved, even pleased, by his performance. When he tells his mother, she says, "Why didn't you get a B?" The next test he works even harder and manages to get the B. He runs home with excitement to tell his mother that he got the B. She says, "Why didn't you get an A?" Eventually he gets the coveted A. Mom remarks at that point, "Was that the highest grade in the class?" "No," he tells her, "one of the 40 kids in the class got an A+." She replies, "Why didn't you get the A+?"

Myriad behaviors can undermine a child's sense of self-esteem, competence, and security. Some acts parents commit are unquestionably cruel (one father strangled his child's pet as the boy watched; one mother called her son a "son of a bitch" and spat in his face in front of his girlfriend). Other acts appear designed to humiliate the child into complying with parental expectations that the child may be unable to meet. One woman whose son had a bedwetting problem decided that she would dissuade her son from wetting the bed at night by hanging out his urine-soaked sheets in the front yard to dry while the neighbors looked on.

Less dramatic psychologically abusive behaviors can also be very damaging to the child's sense of self. A parent who frequently wakes a child up in the middle of the night to accommodate the parent's needs (for example, father wants child to clean garage or mother decides that she must vacuum child's room at 3 A.M.) is communicating that the child's needs are not important.

Early in my study of adolescent murderers I grappled with the scope of psychological abuse when I encountered a case involving parental rejection. Edwin, who was one of 12 children fathered by several men, left his mother's domicile in New York at the age of 15 to live with his father and stepmother in the South. His father and stepmother made him live in the garage and charged him money to watch television. Their behavior made it clear that the boy was not wanted, and eventually he left this house to take up residence with two male strangers who befriended him. When one of these men's friends approached Edwin in a threatening way, the youth shot him.

PHYSICAL AND MEDICAL NEGLECT

Physical and medical neglect are relatively straightforward concepts. Parents are required by law to provide food, clothing, and a safe home environment for their children. In addition, they are expected to supervise their children adequately. Parents who are unable or unwilling to perform these duties, although financially able to do so or offered other means that would allow them to do so, have clearly neglected their children's physical needs. Parents who cannot meet their children's physical needs due to hardship are still considered to have physically neglected their offspring when they fail to make other provisions to ensure that their children's needs are met.

Physical neglect need not be intentional. In adolescent parricide cases in which one parent, usually the father, is physically abusive, the nonabusive parent, usually the mother, must by law assume the responsibility of providing a safe environment. Her failure to provide a safe home for her children is rarely intended. Her neglect is typically an unfortunate by-product of her inability to take care of herself and her offspring in a healthy and effective way.

Parents are also required by law to provide health care for their children. Parents who ignore their children's needs for medical care and treatment when they have the financial means or other resources to meet them are guilty of neglect. Parents whose religious beliefs preclude certain types of medical treatment may not be considered to be neglectful of their children in some states when they choose not to seek medical attention. The state may, however, have provisions in its code allowing investigation and ordering of medical services when the health of a child so requires.

EMOTIONAL NEGLECT

Children have emotional needs as well as physical and medical needs. Research has established that meeting an infant's physical needs is not sufficient to ensure healthy physical development. Babies whose emotional needs are not met frequently do not gain weight and in some cases may actually die from the effects of "maternal deprivation."[28] This condition, known as nonorganic failure to thrive, is typically associated with two factors: inadequate feeding and a lack of bonding between the parents and the infant.[29]

Children need to be nurtured and loved, supported and encouraged to develop a sense of themselves as valuable individuals and to trust others. When emotional needs are met, children are much better prepared to master their school and neighborhood environments. They are also more likely to be able to engage in healthy and mutually satisfying relationships.

Parents who do not give their children clear messages that they are loved, whether by words or appropriate displays of affection, such as being held, cuddled, hugged, kissed, having hands shaken, and being patted on the back, are not meeting their sons' and daughters' emotional needs. Similarly, parents who make no time genuinely to listen to their children and to console and help them with difficulties are emotionally neglecting their offspring. They are communicating to their children, intentionally or not, that the children's needs, and hence the children themselves, are not important.

Emotional neglect was a primary reason that one 12-year-old boy killed his mother and his nine-year-old brother. The boy, whom I will call Timmy Jackson, had initially intended to kill himself. Timmy decided, however, that before he took his own life, he would do "something nice" for his father and nine-year-old brother by killing his mother, whom he perceived as responsible for the unhappiness in the family.

Events did not follow the boy's expectations. Timmy's brother,

Martin, arrived home before his mother. Martin's presence frustrated and panicked Timmy. He tried to persuade Martin to leave the house, but Martin would not go. Timmy eventually shot his brother in the head because he did not want Martin to see him shoot his mother and himself. When his mother arrived home, Timmy shot her in the head. "Scared" by the sight of the blood spattering and gushing from the wounds, the youth was unable to kill himself and called his father.

Mrs. Jackson's way of relating to Timmy and to her husband had hurt the boy very much. Timmy perceived his mother as not wanting him, her older son, as hurting his father by her behavior, and as rarely being home. He interpreted being sent to day care, survival camp, and military school as indications that she did not want him around, which made him feel "angry," "hurt," and "unwanted."

Timmy's reflections on his mother were without exception negative. Mrs. Jackson emerged as overbearing, self-centered, materialistic, insensitive, nervous, lacking in willpower, demanding, unnecessarily restrictive of the boy's activities, and unaffectionate. Timmy stated that he could not talk to his mother because she did not like the things that he liked, such as clothes, pets, and leisure activities. Timmy thought, but was not sure, that the last time his mother had hugged him was on his twelfth birthday. The boy could not remember the last time she had said that she loved him.

EMOTIONAL INCEST

Emotional incest occurs when a parent aligns with a child and relates to that child as though the child were the spouse.[30] Such a child nurtures the parent, acts as the parent's confidant (e.g., discusses adult problems such as sexuality and relationships), and on occasion serves as the parent's protector against the other parent.

Although on the surface the behavior of these children often appears exemplary, it is not healthy. A parent's excessive dependence on a child is inappropriate because it typically creates enormous stress for the child and interrupts the natural developmental process. Children are ill equipped to act as husbands or wives, or, as so frequently occurs in dysfunctional families, to assume the role of parent and take care of their siblings and mother or father. Children may embrace this role because it seems to be the only way to receive parental attention, approval, acceptance, and love.

Emotional incest was one factor in the pathological family dynamics that led Peter Jones to kill his father. Peter functioned in many ways as a surrogate spouse and parent. Both his parents were receiving Social Security disability payments, had been diagnosed as having severe psychiatric illness, and were chemically dependent. Peter's father was an alcoholic who had been taking tranquilizers for about a year prior to the homicide. Mrs. Jones, who had a long history of psychophysiological ailments, had been taking painkillers and tranquilizers for years.

The medication that Mrs. Jones took would at times make her very drowsy and unable to discharge her parental responsibilities. Over the years, Peter increasingly cooked, cleaned, got himself and his younger brother off to school, and took care of his mother. He was a nurturing figure to his mother and felt a responsibility to protect her from his father. In many ways he acted more like a husband than a son. He had long been his mother's confidant and protector. Eventually, he became in essence her hero—killing the man who had abused her for years.

3 | Which Youths Kill

FREDERIC WERTHAM (1941) was the first mental health professional to take an in-depth look at adolescent parricide. When he first met 15-year-old Gino in the hospital ward, the boy was being treated for a nasty hand cut. As he observed Gino, Wertham noted that "there was something immediately likeable about the boy, something direct and simple and honest." When Wertham asked how he had cut himself, Gino replied "without fear or bravado—or regret" that the knife had slipped while he was killing his mother.

As a psychiatrist, Wertham wanted to know why Gino had stabbed his mother 32 times. Realizing that his knowledge of matricide was confined to the story of Orestes, Wertham reported that he turned to the libraries for more information only to discover "there was none to collect. No systematic study of the subject exists, either criminological or psychiatric."[1]

Wertham found few clues to unraveling the dynamics behind this homicide—only the murder itself, the manner of the murder, and Gino's behavior after it—"his first impulse had been to pacify and soothe the frightened children [his younger siblings]; and he had then gone voluntarily to the police with a confession."[2] Shortly after the homicide, 31 neighbors who knew Gino in his daily life—"bakers, pastry-cooks, grocers, undertakers, florists, manual laborers" —signed the following petition:

> We, the undersigned, affirm and declare that we know Gino very well, having had continuous contact with him, and therefore we can with full conscience state that he was a hard worker, scrupulously honest, of good and high moral feelings, of clean habits, and never associated with people of dubious character.[3]

In his extensive analysis of why Gino killed his mother, Wertham used a primarily psychoanalytic approach.[4] After careful consideration, the psychiatrist rejected the possibility that Gino suffered from psychosis or was an antisocial personality. Although he did not explicitly identify Gino as a severely abused youth, the case analysis is replete with data indicative of various types of abuse (physical, covert sexual, and emotional) and neglect (physical and emotional neglect, emotional incest). Wertham's explanation that the matricide was the product of catathymic crisis is consistent with the portrait of a youth pushed beyond his or her limits.

> Catathymic crisis is a circumscribed mental disorder, psychologically determined, non-hereditary, without physical manifestations, and not necessarily occurring in a psychopathic constitution. Its central manifestation consists in the development of the idea that a violent act—against another person or against oneself—is the only solution to a profound emotional conflict whose real nature remains below the threshold of the consciousness of the patient.[5]

Fewer than a dozen case studies specifically addressing the phenomenon of adolescent parricide have appeared since Wertham's 1941 case study. Eight clinical studies in particular are cited repeatedly as authoritative: Sargent 1962; Scherl and Mack 1966; Duncan and Duncan 1971; Sadoff 1971; Tanay 1973, 1976b (one study); McCully 1978; Post 1982; Russell 1984. These case reports can be considered classics; the views they have advanced have largely gone unchallenged.

Although Donald Russell noted as early as 1965 the importance of differentiating between intrafamilial and extrafamilial murders in his study of juvenile murderers, only one empirical study analyzing adolescent murderers this way currently exists.[6] A number of authors who have investigated adolescent homicide have tabulated the relationship between victims and offenders[7] or noted it in the presentation of the case study without making the parricidal nature of the relationship the primary focus of the investigation, analysis, and discussion of the study results.[8] Because of the small sample sizes in these studies, the authors combined all cases in the analysis and discussion sections of the article or the book, leaving it unclear whether juveniles who killed family members represent a distinct type of adolescent murderer.

Perusal of the classic clinical studies of adolescents who have committed parricide reveals that almost all reported cases involved sons. Of the three types of parricide offenders identified in chapter 1, one clearly predominates: the severely abused child. In drawing on cases reported in the literature as well as their own, Cormier et al. (1978) noted that the home environments in which matricides and patricides occurred were both typically abusive, though some differences were observable. Mothers killed were psychologically abusive and covertly or overtly sexually abusive of their sons. Husbands of the matricide victims were passive men who placated their wives and who were physically or emotionally absent and nonsupportive of their children. Fathers killed were cruel men who often beat their wives while their sons watched. Their wives were weak, helpless, and passive women who often depended on their sons for protection. In the few cases where daughters killed or attempted to kill a parent, the parent was also usually abusive.[9]

A history of severe mental illness was absent in all of the classic studies except McCully's (1978).[10] Psychotic features, if present, tended to appear at the time of the homicide or even some months later, and to be transitory.[11] Only one of four adolescent matricide offenders evaluated and treated by Mack, Scherl, and Macht (1973) developed a long-standing psychosis after the homicide.

The literature identified four APOs who were apparently psychotic before the homicides. Analysis of existing records of a parricide case occurring in 1835 revealed that 20-year-old Pierre Rivière had been psychotic for years before he killed his mother, sister, and brother.[12] More recently, McCully (1978) diagnosed a 19-year-old boy who killed his mother, stepfather, and half-brother as having "borderline schizophrenia with sociopathic understructure."[13] Although the psychotic symptoms did not appear until after the homicide, McCully suggested that the teenager's autistic thinking (excessive preoccupation with personal fantasies without consideration to reality)[14] may have been present long before. Close study revealed that this youth had been sexually abused and emotionally neglected. In the third case, two adolescent girls who conspired to kill the mother of one of them were diagnosed as having "paranoia of the exalted type" (grandiose delusions). This "folie à deux" (shared personality disorder),[15] when combined with a completely reversed set of moral values, transformed murder into acceptable behavior for them.[16] In a fourth case, a 15-year-old boy who stabbed his abusive mother to death after hearing messages on his phonograph suggesting that he kill her was diagnosed as psychotic. When evaluated, the youth seemed unaware of the seriousness of the murder charges and believed Satan would save him. The boy's mental deterioration was apparent at least two months prior to the homicide.[17]

The dangerously antisocial child was also rarely encountered in clinical case reports of adolescent parricide offenders. With one exception, noted in the classic literature, APOs tended to have minimal or no delinquent histories.[18] When youths were identified as having been in trouble with the law,[19] legal difficulties tended not to be serious.

One criticism frequently made about clinical studies is their small sample size. While one should be cautious in generalizing from these studies, close examination of parricide cases reported by several authors and my own cases suggests that patterns can be detected.

SAMPLE OF ADOLESCENT PARRICIDE OFFENDERS

I have conducted assessment interviews with approximately 75 adolescents charged with murder or attempted murder. Seven involved youths who killed parents. Two were among 59 subjects in a study of adolescent murderers.[20] Of the remaining five, four were referred by defense counsel for pretrial evaluation. The remaining case was referred by a state prosecutor strictly for research purposes.

These seven youths, six of whom were male, were all white. They ranged in age from 12 to 17. Two had killed both parents. As a group, they killed six fathers, three mothers, and one brother. The murder weapon in all cases was a gun, which was readily available.

Six of the youths fit the profile of the severely abused child. The youth referred by the state prosecutor was one of the two who had killed both of his parents. He fit the profile of the severely mentally ill child. This youth had been diagnosed as having a paranoid disorder.

Although seven may appear to be a small number of cases from which to draw conclusions, it is valuable to describe the characteristics of these individuals, particularly in relation to the literature on APOs. The similarities between my cases and others increase the likelihood that the findings are not peculiar to any state or region.[21] In addition, one can use observations based on these clinical data to generate hypotheses for testing with a larger number of cases. The discussion that follows focuses on the six APOs who fit the profile of the severely abused child.

Analysis revealed that these six adolescents had approached life fairly passively until the homicide. Five tended to perceive themselves as strong and in control of events.[22] Beneath the surface, however, they were being stressed continuously near or beyond their limits and had been for years.

Child maltreatment, particularly verbal and psychological abuse, was readily apparent in these six cases; severe physical abuse was indicated in five. The one female APO, in addition to being physically, verbally, and psychologically abused, was also covertly sexually abused and forcibly raped by her father. All six youths had been emotionally and physically neglected by their parents (two had virtually no supervision because their parents were alcoholics, and none of the six had been protected from harm by their parents). At least one of the youths had been medically neglected; three were victims of emotional incest.

In all six cases there was confirmed alcoholism or heavy drinking in the home. There was strong evidence that each of the five fathers slain was alcoholic; three also used drugs (one smoked marijuana excessively and the other two used tranquilizers). One of the mothers murdered was also alcoholic. Among surviving spouses or ex-spouses, chemical addiction was common. Only one of them had reportedly never been a chemical abuser. The stepmother who had left her common-law husband shortly before the homicide was also an alcoholic and illegal drug user. Two of the other mothers had been addicted to Valium for years as a way of coping with their abusive husbands. The husband of the non–chemically addicted matricide victim drank excessively on occasion.

These families tended to be relatively isolated because of problems in the home. The six adolescents had fewer outlets than other youths because they were expected to assume responsibilities typically performed by parents (e.g., cooking, cleaning). Over the course of the years, the youths' attempts to get help were either ignored or unsuccessful. The juveniles' goals increasingly centered on escaping the family situation through flight or suicide. Over time they felt increasingly overwhelmed by the home environment, which continued to deteriorate. Their inability to cope eventually led them to lose control or to contemplate murder.

Life became increasingly intolerable prior to the murder. In the four cases in which only the abusive father was killed, the mothers were not living in the home at the time. One month before one of the homicides the common-law stepmother did the same thing the boy's mother had done several years before: She walked out. In a second case, the mother was chronically ill and had been hospitalized for several weeks at the time of the homicide. In the other two cases, the mothers had divorced their husbands for physical and psychological abuse, and then allowed their children to live with their fathers more than a thousand miles away. The boy in one of these cases killed his father within a year of being left alone with him; the girl in the other case killed her father within 16 months of his common-law wife's departure.

The APOs' reports in five of the six cases clearly suggested that they were in a dissociative state.[23] The youths had gaps in memory, "blackouts," and a sense that events were somehow unreal or dream-like during the homicide or immediately afterward. In one case, the youth did not remember the homicide; in another, dissociation left only part of the memory of the shooting intact.

These six APOs typically associated with law-abiding peers and were relatively uninvolved in criminal behavior prior to the homicides. The youth killed the parent or parents in response to a perception of being trapped rather than as a result of a violent life-style. In two of the five cases in which there was severe physical abuse, youths were reacting to a perceived threat of imminent death or serious physical injury when they killed their parents. In the three others, they were experiencing terror and horror when they killed even though death or serious physical injury was not imminent. In these cases, the victims were defenseless: Two were shot as they lay asleep in bed; the third, as he sat with his back to his son watching television.

During the assessment interview, the APOs typically expressed some remorse, which may have resulted partly from the passage of time—from one to 27 months since the homicide. The youths seemed uncomfortable with having killed and knew that their behavior was wrong, but experienced conflict over the end result. They felt some relief because the victim could no longer hurt them or others. Their conflict seemed to result largely from a sense of their own victimiza-tion and an awareness of how desperate their situation was when they killed their parents. The extent to which these youths experienced remorse was related to their level of personality development.[24]

The Severely Abused Child as Adolescent Homicide Offender

Preliminary analysis of my original data set of 59 adolescent homi-cide offenders suggested that seven different types could be clinically identified and reliably rated.[25] This typology is in the process of being empirically validated using more than 1200 test items.[26] For now, the clinical types should be considered as preliminary, albeit reliable, sketches of types of youths who kill.

In my typology of adolescent homicide offenders, the severely abused child typically fit the profile of a type called the *situationally trapped kid* because the homicide appeared to be an act of desperation. Close examination revealed that these APOs were markedly different from adolescents involved in extrafamilial homicides. The severely abused APO contrasts with five of the six types of adolescents who killed nonfamily members with relative ease.[27] These types of adolescents—the *player*, the *helpless child*, the *alienated young man*, the *escapist*, and the *criminally identified youth*—tend to perceive the world as a violent place, life forces as overwhelming them, the world as a jungle where only the fit survive, life as a constant struggle to survive, or life as essentially unfair. With the exception of the helpless child, they tend to take an active approach to life. These five types tend to associate with delinquent friends, drink and do drugs often to excess, and engage in such criminal activities as robbery, burglary, theft, and so on. With the possible exception of the alienated young man, they usually do not intend to kill anyone at the onset of the incident, but they are prepared to use violence if they think the situation warrants it. For these types, homicide is a random event occasioned by something that the victim did or did not do, or the youths' perceptions of the victim's behavior.

Although four of these five types do not endorse a criminal value system (the exception appearing to be the criminally identified youth), these types tend to remain a danger to society because of their perceptions of life, their life-styles, and the people with whom they associate. In contrast to that for the severely abused child, the prognosis for a successful reintegration of these types of adolescent murderers into society is poor unless their perceptions and behavioral responses are changed.

The remaining type, the *nihilistic killer* (see chapter 5), seems to derive a sense of satisfaction from acts of destruction that can culminate in murder. Although available data indicate that most APOs are unlikely to be nihilistic killers, the possibility that a particular youth may fit this profile must be explored.

CHARACTERISTICS OF ADOLESCENTS WHO KILL PARENTS

A review of the eight classic clinical studies, Corder et al.'s (1976) empirical comparison, and my own research indicates that the 12 characteristics listed below are associated with adolescents who kill family members, particularly fathers. In table 3.1 these ten

TABLE 3.1
Characteristics Associated with Adolescent Parricide Offenders

Studies Involving Adolescents

	Sargent (1962)	Scherl & Mack (1966)	Duncan & Duncan (1971)	Sadoff (1971)	Tanay (1973)	Corder et al. (1976)	McCully (1978)	Post (1982)	Russell (1984)	Heide (1984–89)
Total # cases	5	3	5	2[a]	8	30	1	4	60	75
Total # parricide cases	2	3	5	2	8	10	1	4	8	7
(F = Father)	(F=2)	(F=0)	(F=4)	(F=1)	(F=2–7)	(F=8)	(F=1)	(F=3)	(F=4)	(F=5)

Characteristics

1. Patterns of family violence (parental brutality and cruelty toward child and/ or toward one another)	X	X	X	X	X	X	X	X	X	X
2. Adolescent's attempts to get help from others fail	not addressed	X	X	X	X	no data	not addressed	X	X	X
3. Adolescent's efforts to escape family situation fail (e.g., running away; thoughts of suicide, suicide attempts)	not addressed	X	X	X	X	no data	X	X	X	X
4. Adolescent is isolated from others/fewer outlets	not addressed	X	not addressed	X	not addressed	X	no	X	X	X
5. Family situation becomes increasingly intolerable	X	X	X	X	X	no data	not addressed	X	X	X

6. Adolescent feels increasingly helpless, trapped	suggested	X	X	suggested	suggested	no data	not addressed	X	X	X
7. Adolescent's inability to cope leads to loss of control	X	X	X	X	X	no data	not addressed	X	X	X
8. Prior criminal behavior minimal or nonexistent	X	X	not addressed	not addressed	suggested	X	no; delinquent history	X	X	X
9. Availability of gun	X	X	X	X	X	no data	X	X	X	X
10. Homicide victim as alcoholic	X	some evidence	in some cases	not addressed	not addressed	X	not addressed	not addressed	X	X
11. Evidence to suggest dissociative state in some cases	some evidence	some evidence	not addressed	X	no	X	no	not addressed	X	X
12. Victim's death perceived as relief to offender/family; initial absence of remorse	X	X	X	X	X	implied	X	X	X	X

[a] One adolescent (17-year-old) and one adult (22-year-old)

studies are compared with respect to these characteristics. The number of cases that the authors examined and the number of cases that involved adolescents killing family victims are noted in the table.

1. *A pattern of family violence* was identified in all ten studies. In each report, parental brutality and cruelty toward the youth or toward the spouse was observed. Spouse abuse, child abuse, and various forms of psychological abuse were repeatedly cited.

2. Seven reports specifically noted that the *adolescents' attempts to get help failed.* Authorities, relatives, and others familiar with the youths' situations did little or nothing to help them when apprised of their situations.

3. *The failure of the adolescents' efforts to escape the family situation* was mentioned in eight studies. Efforts included running away, suicidal thoughts, and suicide attempts.

4. Six reports noted that *these adolescents as a group were isolated from others and had fewer outlets than other youths.*[28]

5. Eight of the nine studies using a clinical case approach noted that the *family situation became increasingly intolerable prior to the homicidal event.*

6. The same eight studies stated or implied that *these adolescents felt increasingly helpless to deal with the home situation* prior to the homicide.

7. In addition, these same eight studies agreed that the *inability of these adolescents to cope with the familial situation typically led to a loss of control.*

8. Adolescent parricide offenders appeared to be *criminally unsophisticated.* Seven studies either stated or implied that the youths had little or no prior criminal history. Only the case reported by McCully and one of the eight patricide and matricide offenders reported by Russell had an extensive history of delinquent conduct.

9. All nine studies using a clinical approach noted the *easy availability of a gun* as a critical factor in the occurrence of the homicide.[29]

10. Six studies referred to *alcoholism or heavy drinking in the homes in which parents were slain by adolescents.* Corder et al. (1976) noted that "all 6 patients charged with murdering their fathers came from homes in which the father was a chronic alcoholic who was severely abusive to both the patient and his mother" (p. 960). As noted above, heavy drinking or alcoholism was found in the homes of six of the seven APO cases in my sample. The two fathers slain by adolescents in Sargent's study were both reported to have been alcoholics. Scherl and Mack also presented data that suggested the mother killed might have had a drinking problem. In one of the five cases presented by Duncan and Duncan, the father was in a drunken rage and was physically assaulting his wife and children when his 18-year-old son killed him. Alcoholism or excessive drinking was explicitly noted by Russell in two of four patricide cases and one of four matricide cases.[30]

11. *Evidence suggesting that the adolescent parricide offender may have been in a dissociative state* during or after the homicide was presented in six studies. Corder et al. found significant differences between adolescents who killed parents and the other two control groups with respect to amnesia for the murder. Five of the 10 youths who killed their parents had amnesia, compared to none in the two control groups. Scherl and Mack's account left a question regarding the APO's memory and experience of the homicide immediately following the crime. The authors noted that after the homicide the youth drove in "a confused state" to see a priest, to whom he confessed the crime. However, the authors stated that while undergoing treatment months after the crime, the boy developed amnesia.

12. All of the studies either stated or implied that the *victim's death was perceived as a relief* by the offender and other surviving family members. Some studies (Sadoff 1971; Tanay 1973; McCully 1978; Heide 1988) also commented on the apparent absence of remorse initially observed in the offender.

4 | Youths at Risk

ABOUT 65 natural parents were slain by youths under 18 each year during the ten-year period 1977–86. When this low rate of matricides and patricides is examined in light of the problems of predicting violent behavior or dangerousness,[1] the conclusion is inescapable: It is impossible to predict which youths will kill their parents. Some youths, are, however, at a higher risk. Five factors help target such youths.

1. The youth is raised in a chemically dependent or other dysfunctional family.
2. An ongoing pattern of family violence exists in the home.
3. Conditions in the home worsen, and violence escalates.
4. The youth becomes increasingly vulnerable to stressors in the home environment.
5. A firearm is readily available in the home.

Of the five factors, two are most important: the chemically dependent or other dysfunctional family, and the availability of a firearm. The likelihood that violence will be present, that conditions will worsen, and that youths will become increasingly vulnerable to stressors in the home environment is higher in alcoholic, drug-addicted, and other dysfunctional families than in healthy families. When firearms are readily accessible, the probability that an abusive parent will be killed by a youth pushed too far who sees no other way out is much higher than when guns are not available. Although it would be extreme to suggest that youths whose parents are chemically dependent and abusive run a high risk of killing the abusive or neglectful parent if firearms are available, one fact can be stated with absolute certainty: A few of the many children who are severely mistreated do in fact kill their parents. This chapter aims at understanding why.

Literature on the dysfunctional family began with observation, discussion, and research on the dynamics and effects of the alcoholic family system.[2] Following the groundbreaking work by the founders of the National Association of Children of Alcoholics (NACoA), the definition of the dysfunctional family was broadened to include types of families in which pathology seemed evident besides those affected by alcoholism. Dysfunction was hypothesized to exist in families in which one or both parents are chronically physically or mentally ill. It was expected to exist in families in which one or both parents are addicted to substances or activities other than alcohol—drugs, work, food, sex, gambling, and religion.[3] Dysfunction was also suspected in families that "love too much" or that are highly judgmental and perfectionist.[4] Clinical experience and observation increasingly have suggested that the issues faced by children raised in these other types of troubled families are very similar to those faced by children of alcoholics.[5] This chapter highlights in particular the literature pertaining to alcoholic family systems as one type of dysfunctional family because of the documented role of alcohol in child maltreatment,[6] wife abuse,[7] and wives killing their husbands[8] as well as in adolescent parricide cases.

THE FUNCTIONAL FAMILY

In functional families, parents have a keen awareness of the role that they play in child development and respond appropriately to the child's needs. A functional family, although typically portrayed as consisting of two parents—a mother and a father who are married to one another—may consist of a single-parent unit or an extended family network. In families in which divorce has occurred and the parents share custody, both, one, or neither of the parents' households could be a functional family unit.

Cermak (1988) identified seven characteristics of healthy families: safety, open communication, self-care, individualized roles, continuity, respect for privacy, and focused attention. Although no family contains all seven characteristics all of the time, most healthy families demonstrate these qualities more often than not, particularly during stressful periods. According to Cermak, "What makes these families function well is that they are less likely than alcoholic families to be overwhelmed by stress."[9]

Healthy families attend to their children's changing physical and emotional needs. Parents are sufficiently in control of themselves that children do not have to fear physical harm from them. In functional families, members relate openly and honestly to one another. Parents tailor their communications to the child's level so that their messages are both honest and safe from the standpoint of the child's ability to handle them.

In functional families individuals are expected to take care of themselves as they mature. They are encouraged by other members to pursue activities and goals that keep them healthy, make them happy, promote their growth, and bring them success and satisfaction. Children are recognized as individuals. Parents define expectations according to each child's particular strengths and needs; set boundaries; and impose limits. Healthy parents are flexible and negotiate different boundaries and limits as a child becomes capable of assuming more responsibility.

Functional families provide continuity to their members by meeting regularly to acknowledge the collective nature of the family unit, its strength, and its permanence. In these families, each individual's privacy is respected. Parents in functional families maintain high-quality interactions with their children and are responsive to their children's physical and emotional needs.

THE DYSFUNCTIONAL FAMILY

Research conducted during the last few years has revealed that individuals raised in alcoholic, chemically dependent, or otherwise dysfunctional families typically share certain characteristic ways of thinking, behaving, and communicating. Cermak (1988), for example, has identified five major characteristics of all types of dysfunctional families. Individuals from these families have difficulty with relationships, low self-esteem, difficulty trusting others, an exaggerated need to be in control of events and others, and an inability to determine what is the authentic self in contrast to the self presented to others. Without intervention, the effects of having been raised in a dysfunctional family are predictable: Generally, everyone who is a member of the family acquires, maintains, and perpetuates dysfunctional perceptions and behavior.

In dysfunctional families, parents lack adequate parenting skills and are likely to abuse and neglect their offspring because issues from their own childhoods are unresolved and because of their inadequate personal development. These families are also more likely to be isolated and to discourage family members from seeking help and from dealing with strong feelings. Children raised in families where one parent is chemically addicted and the other is codependent are unlikely to receive help from either parent in coping effectively with problems in the home. Given these dynamics, the children are more vulnerable to loss of control as stressful events accumulate.

Codependency

In an alcoholic family system, for example, the spouse of the alcoholic is seen as coalcoholic[10] or codependent,[11] and also as ill. Experts have defined codependency as "a pattern of relying on compulsive behavior and the approval of others to find a sense of safety, self-worth, and identity."[12] Cermak (1988), who has argued for the recognition of the codependent personality as a specific type of personality disorder, defined codependency as the continued investment of one's self-esteem in the ability to control others in spite of obvious, adverse consequences to the self. According to Cermak's diagnostic criteria, the codependent gets enmeshed in relationships with "personality disordered, chemically dependent, other codependent, and/or impulse disordered individuals."[13] Due to the codependent's heavy investment in the maintenance of these relationships, she or he assumes responsibility for meeting others' needs to the virtual exclusion of fulfilling her or his own needs.[14] The codependent spouse, because of efforts to control situations and to shield the alcoholic from the natural consequences of addiction, often enables the alcoholic to continue drinking.

Codependents have anxiety and boundary distortions in situations of intimacy[15] and typically confuse intimacy with fusion, the inability to separate oneself emotionally from others. For children, as well as for the addicted spouse, this fusion is damaging. The child is not allowed to be angry with the codependent mother, for example, because the woman will interpret the anger as evidence that the child does not love her. The child is told not to be sad, because if the child is sad, then the mother will be sad.

For a diagnosis of codependence, Cermak (1988) maintained that more must be present than an excessive need to control, an exaggerated sense of responsibility for others, an enmeshment in unhealthy relationships, and anxiety and boundary distortions around intimacy. To warrant the diagnosis an individual must have at least three of these ten characteristics: depression, hypervigilance, compulsions, anxiety, substance abuse, history of recurrent physical or sexual victimization, excessive reliance on denial, constriction of emotions, medical illnesses caused or exacerbated by stress, and staying in a primary relationship with a substance abuser for at least two years without seeking help.

Children in alcoholic families often report feeling more anger and resentment toward the codependent parent than the addicted parent. They seem to recognize intuitively that the chemically dependent parent is ill and may feel some compassion for this parent. Typically, the children experience increasing difficulty interacting with the codependent parent because of this parent's excessive attempts to control the addict and the children.

Rules of Dysfunctional Families

Black (1981) identified three rules that typically operate in chemically dependent families: Don't talk, don't trust, and don't feel. These rules, expanded and amplified by Kritsberg (1988) and particularly by Bradshaw (1988b), apply as well to other types of dysfunctional families. Collectively, they impede normal ways of relating to others and of dealing with life events.

In dysfunctional families, members—whether silent, apparently civil, or openly hostile—generally do not talk about the real issues: What is really going on with you, with me, with us, with the family? Denial customarily flourishes, particularly in relation to outsiders. Problems, if acknowledged at all, are not seen as difficulties faced by each member. If there is a problem in the family, someone else has it. When that person is "fixed," everything will be just fine.

Individuals in high-stress families typically learn not to trust others. Often their trust in themselves is also very tenuous because they have been taught to discount their perceptions since childhood. Persons in dysfunctional families characteristically do not feel because they learned from a young age that not feeling is necessary for psychic survival. Family members generally learn it is too painful to feel the hurt or to experience the fear that comes from feelings of rage, abandonment, moments of terror, and memories of horror. To survive, these individuals have learned to repress feelings. Because they never learned acceptable ways of expressing negative emotions, children from these families often fear that if they allow themselves to feel strong emotion, it might overwhelm them, and they would lose control. These children were exposed to two parents who were often out of control. They watched silently, for example, as the alcoholic drank until he passed out despite the endless entreaties, tricks, and techniques of the codependent.

The Effects of Stress on Family Members

A pioneering study of 115 children with at least one alcoholic parent revealed how stressful living in this environment was for them. The children were much more affected by the parental disharmony and the rejection occasioned by the parent's drinking than they were by the excessive drinking per se.[16] The amount of stress experienced by children growing up in an alcoholic family has been compared to spending time in a concentration camp.[17] Cermak's work in a veterans' hospital led him to conclude that many of the characteristics observed in children of alcoholics were the same as those found in Vietnam veterans suffering from post–traumatic stress disorder (PTSD; see chapter 6).

CHILD ABUSE AND NEGLECT IN THE DYSFUNCTIONAL FAMILY

Children who come from chemically dependent or other dysfunctional families are much more likely to be abused or neglected than children from functional families. Children of alcoholics, drug addicts, and other addiction-oriented parents are at an extremely high risk of being emotionally neglected unless at least one of the parents is in a sound recovery program.[18] Parents who are dependent on drugs or alcohol are usually unable to respond to their children's emotional needs because of their preoccupation with the substance to which they are addicted, as well as changes in their physiological and psychological states. Similarly, parents who are addicted to activities like gambling are often unable to respond to their children because of their absorption in the activities to which they are enslaved.

In a chemically dependent or other dysfunctional family, the codependent spouse is usually emotionally unavailable to the children because of his or her preoccupation with the problems and issues created by the addicted spouse. Emotional neglect was one of the major findings of Cork's study of 115 children with at least one alcoholic parent.[19] Cork's observation about the nonalcoholic mother is unsettling:

Although she usually gives her children adequate physical care, she is frequently no better than the alcoholic at relating warmly or closely to them. As one expert put it, the non-alcoholic mother is usually likely to lose some of her ability to relate closely to her children as she becomes more and more absorbed in her own frustration and anger. She tends, as did most of the mothers in my study, to lose sight of the needs and rights of children beyond such basics as shelter, food, and clothing. By contrast, she often becomes more mothering to her alcoholic husband than she is to her children.[20]

When the mother was the alcoholic, Cork reported similar results. "The children described the non-alcoholic father as too busy doing his own job and the mother's to pay very much attention to their needs."[21]

Children reared in alcoholic or other dysfunctional families are more likely to be physically, sexually, and/or verbally abused by their parents because of the stress that results from the addiction.[22] Psychological abuse, a natural by-product of other types of abuse, compounds the damage. If the nonabusive parent is severely codependent, he or she is often unable to take the action necessary to provide the children with a safe environment. Hence the children are also likely to be victims of physical neglect.

Children in chemically dependent or other high-stress families also run a high risk of being victims of emotional incest. When a father, a mother, or both parents are addicted to alcohol, drugs, or even to some activity, both are greatly hindered in their ability to relate as adequate spouses and as adequate parents. Accordingly, children are frequently expected to assume duties and fulfill roles ill-suited to their needs as children.[23] The wife of an alcoholic, for example, may start to expect her son to shoulder more of the family's responsibilities as her husband's alcoholism worsens. She may exert pressure on the boy to take care of the house and to get a job after school to help with household expenses. The husband of a drug-dependent wife may expect his daughter to get the younger children off to school in the morning, cook the family dinner, and do the shopping and the laundry. He may require her to focus her attention on him after he has returned home from a long day at the office by fixing him a drink and listening while he talks about his day.

Isolation and the Dysfunctional Family

Children from alcoholic, drug-addicted, or other dysfunctional families are at higher risk for killing an abusive parent because these families are likely to be more isolated than other families. As problems associated with addiction increase, family members generally restrict

TABLE 4.1
Weapons Used in Parricides, 1977–86

	Father as victim Offender age categories[a]				Mother as victim Offender age categories[b]			
	Under 18		18 and over		Under 18		18 and over	
	N	%	N	%	N	%	N	%
Firearm								
Type not stated	2	.6	13	1.3	2	1.5	4	.5
Handgun	95	28.4	311	30.3	33	25.2	136	18.1
Rifle	70	21.0	110	10.7	25	19.1	60	8.0
Shotgun	108	32.3	184	17.9	25	19.1	59	7.8
Subtotal	275	82.3	618	60.2	85	64.9	259	34.4
Knife or cutting instrument	38	11.4	229	22.3	26	19.8	226	30.0
Blunt object	11	3.3	83	8.1	7	5.3	103	13.7
Personal weapons	4	1.2	68	6.6	6	4.6	94	12.5
Other	6	1.8	28	2.7	7	5.3	71	9.4
TOTAL	334	100.0	1026	99.9	131	99.9	753	100.0
(Total number of cases)		(1360)				(884)		

[a]*Significant*
Chi square = 85.7, df = 12, p = < .001;
Cramer's V = .25

[b]*Significant*
Chi square = 60.8, df = 15, p = < .001;
Cramer's V = .26

their involvement with the outside world. The chemically dependent husband very often has increasing difficulty meeting demands in the external environment and withdraws into the home to avoid outsiders' detecting his problem. The wife, who may also be chemically addicted, may restrict her involvement because of a sense of helplessness and shame. Children tend to withdraw from friends because they are ashamed of their families and reluctant to bring others into their homes.

As the parents struggle with problems in their relationship and their ability to cope, the likelihood of four events' occurring increases. First, outbursts of violence by the physically abusive parent are likely to escalate in frequency and intensity. Second, the nonabusive parent is increasingly likely to pursue two solutions. This parent is apt to kill the abusive mate[24] or to take psychological and, in some instances, physical flight from the family. Third, if the nonabusive parent selects flight, the children are usually expected to take on more and more household responsibilities. Fourth, as the addiction spirals out

TABLE 4.2
Weapons Used in Parricides, 1977–86

	Stepfather as victim Offender age categories[a]				Stepmother as victim Offender age categories[b]			
	Under 18		18 and over		Under 18		18 and over	
	N	%	N	%	N	%	N	%
Firearm								
Type not stated	1	.5	3	.8	1	6.3	1	2.6
Handgun	44	22.8	114	31.1	3	18.8	13	34.2
Rifle	54	28.0	47	12.8	4	25.0	2	5.3
Shotgun	46	23.8	62	16.9	1	6.3	2	5.3
Subtotal	145	75.1	226	61.6	9	56.4	18	47.4
Knife or cutting instrument	31	16.1	91	24.8	5	31.3	6	15.8
Blunt object	3	1.6	22	6.0	0	0	7	18.4
Personal weapons	9	4.7	21	5.7	0	0	2	5.3
Other	5	2.6	7	2.0	2	12.5	5	13.2
TOTAL	193	100.1	367	100.1	16	100.2	38	100.1
(Total number of cases)		(560)				(54)		

[a]*Significant*
Chi square = 36.15, df = 10, p = < .001;
Cramer's V = .25

[b]*Not Significant*
Chi square = 14.04, df = 10, p = .18;
Cramer's V = .50

of control, the family situation may well become increasingly intolerable to its members. If a gun is readily available, the chances of the adolescent's killing the abusive parent rise.

AVAILABILITY OF A GUN

Analysis of the FBI Supplementary Homicide Report data for the ten-year period 1977–86 revealed that juveniles who killed parents typically used guns. About 82 percent of fathers, 75 percent of stepfathers, 65 percent of mothers, and 56 percent of stepmothers murdered by juveniles were killed by a firearm of some type (see tables 4.1 and 4.2). Important differences emerged between the offender age groups in weapons used in the killings of fathers, mothers, and stepfathers. Juveniles who killed biological parents or stepfathers were significantly more likely to use guns than were adults.[25]

These data underscore the findings of the clinical case studies that identified the ready availability of firearms as a characteristic of adolescent parricide cases. The data strongly suggest that the number of parricides committed by juveniles in particular could be reduced if their access to guns were curtailed. All seven of the APOs whom I assessed used firearms. Few, if any, of these situations would have been lethal had guns not been readily available in the youths' homes. An adolescent, typically smaller than a parent, would be much less likely to be able to commit parricide if restricted to knives, blunt objects, bare hands, or other weapons.

5 | Legal and Psychological Issues

WHEN AN ADOLESCENT kills a parent, the legal system focuses first on whether a crime was committed. The prosecutor's office may file charges ranging from first-degree murder to manslaughter. Determining whether the youth intended to take the life of another human being is decisive in determining whether first- or second-degree murder is an appropriate charge. The state attorney's office typically seeks to charge the adolescent with murder in the first degree if the parricide appears to be the result of a premeditated design to kill the parent. The state may seek to charge the youth with murder in the second degree if premeditation to kill was lacking, but the youth behaved with callous disregard for human life. In such cases, the parent's death results from the adolescent's committing an act imminently dangerous to another human being.

After examining the circumstances, the prosecution may conclude that murder in the first or second degree is not an appropriate charge and may consider filing less serious charges, or none at all if the killing appears justifiable (e.g., self-defense). A homicide committed in response to adequate provocation has traditionally been defined as lacking "malice aforethought" (actual or implied intent to kill) and has been considered voluntary manslaughter. The provocation must have caused the defendant to kill the victim, and it must have been such that it would have caused a reasonable person to lose control. In addition, the passage of time between the provocation and the homicide must not have been sufficient for the passions of a reasonable person to cool, and the defendant must not have cooled off during the period between the provocation and the killing. A killing has customarily been viewed as involuntary manslaughter if it occurred during the commission of an unlawful act not amounting to a felony or if it was the result of criminal negligence.[1]

DEFENSE STRATEGIES

In adolescent parricide cases, defense counsel will typically investigate two avenues of defense when charges are filed by the prosecutor. Was the APO acting in self-defense when the youth killed his or her parents? Was the youth insane under the existing state statute? If either defense succeeds, the youth will be excused from criminal responsibility for his act. Other defenses focusing on the APO's mental status at the time of the homicide that may be available under state laws include automatism, diminished capacity, and intoxication.[2]

Self-Defense

Generally, a person may lawfully use deadly physical force against another in self-defense only when under the reasonable belief that the other is threatening him or her with imminent death or serious bodily injury and that such force is necessary to prevent the infliction of such harm. In most jurisdictions, an honest belief on the part of the defendant that he or she was in imminent danger is not sufficient, although some evidence exists that this requirement may be changing.[3] Self-defense usually requires that the appearance of danger must have been so real that a reasonable person, faced with the same circumstances, would have entertained the same beliefs.[4]

Some jurisdictions require that the defendant have exhausted all possible avenues of retreat before responding to force with force. In jurisdictions that impose a duty to retreat, an exception is often made to permit one to stand one's ground and to use force when threatened with imminent harm in situations where one is attacked in one's home. When both the assailant and the victim share the same residence, however, society's expectations appear to be different: "In cases in which the battered woman kills her abuser, the burden of proof falls on the woman to show why she could not leave the relationship, even though legally she need only demonstrate that she was in danger and was legitimately standing her ground in her own home."[5]

Convincing a judge or a jury that an adolescent acted in self-defense when he or she killed a parent is difficult unless (1) the parent was attacking the youth; and (2) the possibility of the youth's retreating at that moment without sustaining serious injury or death was extremely remote.

The doctrine of self-defense as formulated almost a thousand years ago was designed to address combat situations between men. It did not take into consideration differences in physical size and strength between men and women[6] and between parents, particularly fathers, and their children. In addition, it did not address circumstances related to psychological injury and psychic survival. A compelling argument has been made that the doctrine should be broadened to include psychological self-defense.[7] Children and adolescents who have been severely abused, like battered wives, may believe based on their experiences that they are in danger of being severely beaten or killed in the near future if they do not take lethal action when it is possible. Abused adolescents who do not believe their physical survival is threatened may feel their psychological survival compels them to attack the abusive parent. Perceiving that they are unable to engage in physical battle as an equal with the abusive parent, these adolescents may strike when the abusive parent is physically defenseless.

The Insanity Defense

The insanity defense is currently recognized in federal courts and in all states except Idaho and Montana, which recently abolished their insanity defense laws through legislation. Numerous tests have been formulated by courts over the years to guide judges and jurors in deciding whether defendants should be acquitted because they were insane at the time of the crime. These tests fall into three broad categories according to their primary focus: defects in cognition (understanding), defects in volition (ability to control behavior), and defects in mental or emotional processes or behavioral controls.[8]

The procedures required to raise the defense are not uniform across jurisdictions. The defendant who asserts this defense has the initial burden of going forward with evidence suggesting that he or she was insane at the time of the crime, because a presumption of sanity exists in all jurisdictions. As illustrated in table 5.1, after the defendant has raised the issue, jurisdictions vary, typically in accordance with the insanity test used, regarding who has the ultimate burden of proof.[9]

The decision whether an APO will be held legally responsible for his or her behavior would seem to rely at least to some extent on which test is used to determine sanity and on which party has the burden of proof as to the accused's frame of mind at the time of the crime. Some scholars take the position that when juries acquit defendants on the grounds of insanity they generally do so because they believe it is unfair to convict the mentally ill rather than because the applicable

TABLE 5.1
Comparison of Insanity Defenses

Test	Legal standard	Final burden of proof	Who bears burden of proof
M'Naghten	"didn't know what he was doing or didn't know it was wrong"	Varies from proof by a balance of probabilities on the defense to proof beyond a reasonable doubt on the prosecutor	
Irresistible impulse	"could not control his conduct"		
Durham	"the criminal act was caused by his mental illness"	Beyond reasonable doubt	Prosecutor
Brawner-A.I.I.	"lacks substantial capacity to appreciate the wrongfulness of his conduct or to control it"	Beyond reasonable doubt	Prosecutor
Present federal law	"lacks capacity to appreciate the wrongfulness of his conduct"	Clear and convincing evidence	Defense

[a]Adapted from "Insanity Defense" by Norval Morris, *National Institute of Justice Crime File Study Guide*, 1986. Washington: U.S. Department of Justice, National Institute of Justice/Criminal Justice Reference Service.

insanity defense standard prescribes a particular result.[10] Data presented by Simon (1967), however, indicate that the instructions given to jurors may influence the verdict in an insanity trial.

Despite the attention the insanity defense receives, it is seldom used and rarely successful.[11] When it is successful, the defendant is hardly ever set free. Instead, he or she is almost always committed to a mental hospital for assessment of his or her present psychological condition.[12]

State statutes vary in the procedures required to commit a person found not guilty by reason of insanity. In most states and in the federal system, the trial court or some other judicial body retains jurisdiction over those who have been so acquitted after they have been committed to a mental hospital. Release is usually contingent upon the former defendant's proving to the court that confinement for mental illness or dangerousness is no longer appropriate under the governing statute.[13]

Defenses Based on Other Mental Status at the Time of the Offense

Automatism, a defense recognized more in the United Kingdom and in Canada than in the United States, denotes "unconscious involuntary behavior over which the defendant has no control."[14] When successfully litigated at trial, this defense excuses the defendant from criminal responsibility. The rationale for acquitting the accused is that, if the defendant did not have conscious control of his or her body at the time of the offense, no act has occurred sufficient to impose criminal liability.

Automatisms that result from internal factors such as a dissociative disorder would qualify as a disease of the mind and would be labeled "insane automatism" under Canadian law. The defense of automatism is more frequently used in cases involving unconscious behavior that appears to be caused by such external factors as concussion, medical administration of drugs, and hypoglycemia.[15] Other classic examples of automatism include epilepsy and sleepwalking.

Other defenses, when successfully pleaded, may not completely exonerate the APO. But they may reduce the grade of the offense or mitigate the punishment in consideration that the APO, while partially responsible, should not be held fully accountable. Diminished capacity or responsibility and voluntary intoxication are examples of defenses of this type.

Not all jurisdictions recognize the concept of diminished capacity. In those that do, the types of evidence that mental health professionals may testify about during the trial stage vary extensively.[16] The most conservative approaches allow evidence pertaining to the defendant's mental disease or defect to be admissible at trial to show that the offender lacked the capacity to form the requisite mental state to commit the crime. More liberal approaches advocate that the defendant's personal characteristics, such as his or her intelligence, excitability, personality development, and other dimensions that bear on the ability to control actions and understand wrongfulness, should be admissible to the jury in determining the defendant's culpability. The most radical approaches maintain that any factors that may predispose a person to antisocial behavior, such as growing up in a violent home environment, having an abusive childhood, or living in abject poverty, are all relevant in establishing a defense of diminished responsibility.[17]

The voluntary use (or abuse) of alcohol or other drugs to the extent that they arouse passions, lower inhibitions, or cloud reason and judgment does not excuse a defendant from responsibility for the commission of a criminal act or lead to his or her acquittal. In some jurisdictions, however, voluntary intoxication is recognized in the context of establishing diminished responsibility.[18] In other jurisdictions it is considered a defense in its own right to crimes that require specific mental states.[19] Evidence presented by a medical or mental health professional that an APO was so intoxicated at the time of the crime that he or she was incapable of forming the specific mental state required (say, premeditation) may be introduced to show that the youth did not commit that particular crime (e.g., murder in the first degree). The defendant may be convicted instead of a lesser charge.

MOTIVATION

Society is rarely satisfied with simply establishing legal nuances of degree and type of homicide in charging and processing adolescent parricide offenders through the criminal justice system. The public seems driven to know why a youth killed a parent.

Although motivation is not a legal element of crime,[20] it is often used by the prosecution to establish intent. It can also be used by the defense to engender sympathy for the APO so that, even when intent to kill is clearly established, the youth is not held accountable to the fullest extent of the law.

I use two psychological dimensions, *intention to kill* and *desire to hurt the victim*, to identify different motivational dynamics in homicidal events.[21] There are differences in culpability, recommendations for intervention, and assessment of future risk to the community between adolescents who very much want to kill and/or hurt their victims and those who do not.

The distinction between intention and desire is important. Intention denotes "a determination to act in a certain way"[22] and is basically a cognitive concept. Rating adolescents as high or low with respect to intention to kill the victim requires only an assessment of whether the youth intended to cause the death of the victim at the onset of the incident or at some point during the interchange (high intention to kill) or whether the juvenile's reactions to situational events led to homicidal behavior without his or her consciously intending to cause the death of the victim (low intention to kill). High intention to kill means the homicidal behavior was purposive; low means it was reactive.

The taxonomy presented in this section was originally published as "A Taxonomy of Murder: The Motivational Dynamics behind the Homicidal Acts of Adolescents" by Kathleen M. Heide, *Journal of Justice Issues 1* (1986): 3–19. The account in this chapter has been abridged.

Desire refers to "a conscious impulse toward an object or experience that promises enjoyment or satisfaction in its attainment"[23] and includes an emotional component. Rating an adolescent's desire to hurt the victim necessitates an evaluation of whether the individual enjoyed hurting the victim (high desire to hurt) or whether he or she engaged in the attack without experiencing pleasure (low desire to hurt).

Table 5.2 presents the four types of criminal homicides that result when intention and desire are taken as distinguishing characteristics. The names given to these—*intentional, situational, emotionally reactive,* and *nihilistic*—reflect the motivational qualities of the APO.[24] Understanding of these motivational dynamics is important because the legal ramifications may differ.

A murder is intentional when intention to kill is high and desire to hurt the victim is low. If a girl killed her mother because she perceived the woman as a nag and as interfering with what she wanted to do, the murder would be classified as intentional. Similarly, if a boy killed his father because he wanted the man's money and car, the killing would be intentional. If a juvenile conceived of a plan to kill his father to end the father's abusive behavior toward his mother, his siblings, and himself and followed through with it, the homicide would still be intentional. In most states, any of these situations could and would result in charges of premeditated murder if the youth were prosecuted as an adult.

In contrast, a homicide is situational when intention to kill and desire to hurt the victim are absent at the onset of the interaction. An adolescent would be considered to have engaged in a situational homicide if he or she had no intention of killing his or her parents before it happened. The case of Terry Adams presented in the preface illustrates this pattern particularly well. Terry was 16 years old when he decided to leave home to escape his parents' physical and psychological abuse. While he was attempting to flee in the middle of the night, his father woke up and confronted him. Father and son moved from one room to another as the father tried to strike his son. Eventually they came into the parents' bedroom, and the youth, trying to ward off blows, fell into the closet and literally landed beside the murder weapon, a shotgun. At that point he grabbed the shotgun and fired at his father. The mother, who was in bed, woke up when the gun went off. Terry looked at her and fired immediately.

Although he was charged with two counts of first-degree murder, circumstances suggested that both killings were reactive. At the time

TABLE 5.2
Types of Criminal Homicides

Desire to hurt victim	Intention to kill	
	Low	High
Low	Situational[a] Murder 1 Murder 2 Manslaughter	Intentional Murder 1
High	Emotionally reactive Murder 2 Manslaughter	Nihilistic Murder 1

[a]A situational homicide, if found to be justifiable, would not be criminal.

of the homicides Terry was terrified and responded accordingly. He was convicted of two counts of murder in the second degree.

This conviction, which was the result of a negotiated plea, reflects a very punitive approach. It is conceivable that the father's murder could have been justified on the grounds of self-defense, had the lawyer been able to establish these facts convincingly at trial to show that the boy was in imminent fear of death when he killed his father. Alternatively, the charge could have been reduced to voluntary manslaughter if the battery by the father was so violent and painful as to constitute adequate provocation.

In an emotionally reactive homicide, the adolescent's desire to hurt the victim is the paramount consideration. In this type of homicide, actual intention to kill the victim at the beginning of the incident is low; the youth achieves satisfaction from hurting the victim because of his or her emotional involvement with the victim. Strong emotions that cannot be dissolved or successfully contained cause the youth's behavior to be out of control. A female adolescent would be considered to have engaged in an emotionally reactive homicide if she killed her stepmother in a jealous argument that escalated in intensity because the girl perceived that her father had transferred love and affection to his new wife. In a situation of this type the girl would not be seeking the victim's death. She merely wants to vent emotion and to hurt her stepmother as she has been hurt. Similarly, a boy or girl can kill a parent because he or she is furious at that parent for particular behaviors that impact directly on the youth. Here again the homicide would be classified as emotionally reactive if the youth reacted in anger and frustration, wanting the victim to suffer as the victim had caused the youth to suffer, but neither foreseeing nor intending the victim's death at the onset of the explosive incident. Arguments could be made that the homicide was murder in the second degree or possibly voluntary manslaughter, assuming that the provocation was sufficient to evoke a homicidal response from a reasonable person under similar circumstances.[25]

In the last type of homicide, both intention to kill and desire to hurt the victim are high. In this situation, the youth not only intends murder, but also expects to derive satisfaction from hurting the victim. This type of homicide is referred to as nihilistic because death and destruction are desirable in and of themselves. *Nihilism* has been defined as a doctrine or belief that conditions in the social organization are so dismal as to make destruction desirable for its own sake without advancing any constructive program or possibility in its wake.[26] If a youth intended to kill a parent and felt satisfaction and enjoyment in delivering each blow and watching the parent suffer, the killing would be nihilistic. Most, if not all, states would file a case of this type as premeditated murder. In the 37 states whose death penalty statutes allow the execution of those under 18,[27] some would consider seeking the death sentence.

In my sample, three of the homicidal events involving APOs who fit the profile of the severely abused child were classified as intentional homicides. One of these cases involved Patty Smith, whose story is told in chapter 9. In another case a 16-year-old boy shot his father four times while the man slept. Twelve-year-old Timmy Jackson, who initially planned to kill his mother and himself (see chapter 2), is the third case. The other three cases involving APOs who were classified as severely abused children were situational homicides. The case of Terry Adams was discussed in the preface; the cases of Peter Jones and Scott Anders are presented in chapters 7 and 8. From remarks made during the assessment interview, it was clear that the one APO who fit the profile of the severely mentally ill child also seemed to enjoy acts of destructiveness and fit the profile of the nihilistic killer.

IMPORTANCE OF TAXONOMY

If the four types of homicidal events are scrutinized dispassionately, the motivational dynamics behind all but the nihilistic are readily comprehensible in many situations. Although the classification scheme in table 5.2 names the motivations in the first three types of homicidal events, it tells us little about the individual murderers or how they feel about their acts. The three hypothetical examples of adolescents who intentionally killed a parent illustrate this point vividly. Recall the daughter who killed her mother because she was a nag and interfered with what the girl wanted to do, and the boy who murdered his dad because he wanted his father's money and car. These cases look very different from that of the son who killed his father to end years of abuse of the boy's mother, himself, and his siblings. All three children would be intentional killers. But the girl and the boy in the first two cases might have murdered casually and experienced no qualms about their behavior later, whereas the boy in the third case might have killed out of a sense of desperation and felt a great deal of guilt and remorse after the event. Some juveniles who kill a parent intentionally pose a continuing risk to society; others present virtually no risk. The label "intentional killer" neither characterizes a group of people nor prescribes a course of judicial action.

Similarly, one can imagine myriad scenes in which adolescents might kill a parent situationally or in an emotional outburst. Some of these youths will experience guilt and remorse; others will feel little or no self-reproach. Some of these juveniles will represent a continuing danger to society; others will not. Like the label "intentional," the labels "situational" and "emotionally reactive" killer alone reveal little about the individuals committing these acts. Such, however, does not appear to be the case with the nihilistic killer.

It seems unlikely that the potential for amusement in killing another resides in the heart of every person. Rather, the opposite appears true—a human being who enjoys killing, even the first time around, would seem to be a particular type of individual who presents a continuing threat to others. Fromm (1973) argued persuasively that an individual can attempt to satisfy his or her existential needs through destructiveness. Fromm's theory of malignant aggression is concerned with the identification of various "passions" within a person's character that are associated with constructive and destructive responses to existential needs.[28]

The nihilistic motivational pattern corresponds to the media depiction of "a new breed" of child murderer, who appears to kill intentionally, remorselessly, and even gleefully.[29] This pattern also characterizes the adult serial murderer, who kills many victims over time for no apparent motive other than satisfaction and release of tension. Some serial murderers' first victims were family members. Henry Lee Lucas, for example, was arrested for killing his mother when he was

23 years old.[30] After serving 14 years in prison and in a mental hospital, he was released. He claimed that he spent the next several years killing hundreds of people across the United States with his accomplice Ottis Toole.[31] Edmund Kemper, whose last victims included his mother, had killed his grandparents when he was fifteen. Soon after being released from a psychiatric hospital, he abducted and killed six college women.[32]

From the standpoint of social defense, it is imperative that the APO with this motivational pattern be identified. For him or her, the killing of the parent is not a desperate conclusion to a lifetime of terror and horror. Rather, it may be the beginning or perhaps the continuation of a cycle of destructiveness that is likely to bring suffering and possibly death to others. If human lives are not actually claimed, human spirits will be destroyed unless and until this pattern can be eradicated.

CASE STUDIES

| 6 | # Assessment and Its Implications

UNDERSTANDING WHY a particular youth killed a parent requires knowledge of the adolescent, his or her family, and the home environment. Although many of these data can be obtained by a mental health professional[1] from the APO during the clinical interview, collateral sources of information are often invaluable in verifying information, evaluating competing theories, determining the credibility of the youth, and coming to a conclusion about the motive for the homicide. Sources include police reports, offender statements to law enforcement officers and defense counsel, witnesses' depositions, mental health reports, school records, and previous social services investigations.

Thorough assessment in each case involving an APO is critical regardless of the factual situation. It should not be cut short just because severe abuse is apparent, since a severely abused child could adopt a nihilistic response pattern. Assessment should not be limited to the identification of a conduct disorder or the presence or absence of psychosis. An APO who meets DSM III-R's criteria for a conduct disorder and is classified as a dangerously antisocial child may fit the profile of the nihilistic killer, who is at the farthest point along the continuum of the dangerously antisocial.

The identification of psychosis in and of itself is insufficient to understand the youth and the motive for killing a family member. At the very least, some determination must be made whether the severely mentally ill child's communications, the content of his or her delusions and hallucinations, or behavior are indicative of the nihilistic killer. Identification could serve as a warning signal that these youths pose an increased risk to society and warrant more incapacitation, whether in a mental hospital or a correctional facility, than other youths who kill a parent, unless and until the nihilistic pattern is eradicated. Identification of the pattern has the potential result of saving some lives.[2]

A comprehensive assessment is also important because mental health experts are increasingly called upon by defense attorneys to testify about the APO's state of mind at the time of the killing. Consideration of the mental status of the youth during the crime may persuade a judge or jury to excuse the defendant from whole or partial responsibility. The mental health professional may also perform other important services. Armed with a favorable report from a mental health professional prior to trial, defense counsel may succeed in persuading the prosecution to dismiss or reduce the charges, or at the very least to forgo seeking the death penalty. If the APO is convicted of homicide, defense counsel may use the mental health evaluation to convince the court to depart from statutory guidelines. Death penalty statutes typically contain specific psychological mitigators. For example, it is a mitigator in certain states if a homicide offender, although legally sane during the commission of the crime, was "under the influence of extreme mental or emotional disturbance." Testimony by a mental health expert that an APO was unable "to appreciate the criminality of his conduct or to conform his conduct to the requirements of the law" when committing the homicide is another mitigating circumstance.[3] The mental health expert who has done an in-depth evaluation could also testify to nonstatutory mitigators—child abuse, child neglect, spouse abuse, dysfunctional family, and so on.

In part 2 three clinical case studies of adolescent parricide offenders are presented. Clinical case study has several advantages.[4] It involves studying actual people with real difficulties and, unlike laboratory experiments, is not contrived or artificial. In addition, the clinical case history can investigate phenomena that are so rare or peculiar that it is unlikely that they could be studied using any other standard method of investigation. Clinical case studies are also essential in generating hypotheses about the causes of and solutions to particular problems and, on occasion, in providing disconfirming evidence for a prevailing hypothesis.

The clinical case history method has an equal number of disadvantages, however.[5] Such studies are almost always retrospective, so the data on which interpretations are based may be distorted or selective. Moreover, each case history is unique and cannot be replicated. One cannot predict how far the findings in a particular case study generalize to the larger population. In the three case histories of APOs chosen for the next three chapters, for example, there was severe abuse. But to what extent similar types of severe abuse exists in adolescents who do not kill their parents is unknown because not all cases of abuse are reported, nor do available data classify reported cases by severity. Accordingly, causation cannot be determined with this method. The case study method investigates only individuals who have a particular problem or fall into a particular category, and does not focus on those who do not.[6]

The semistructured interview I conducted with each APO allowed assessment of level of personality growth and moral reasoning.[7] Its format also permitted the exploration of the youth's perceptions of the killing, processing through the adult criminal justice system, and sentencing. In addition, the interview examined other areas of importance, including family relationships, school, work, friends, drug and alcohol involvement, handling of problems and affectivity, and prior delinquent activity.

The interviews provided extensive data on the adolescents' perceptions of themselves, others, and the world around them, and on their characteristic ways of responding to events. This information made it possible to evaluate the plausibility of the youths' statements about the killings, to understand the dynamics behind them, and to make recommendations about the disposition of their cases.

PERSONALITY ASSESSMENT

An assessment of the adolescent's personality or ego development is essential. Personality assessment reveals how an individual makes sense of the world. In addition to helping interpret behavior, knowing the youth's personality level can aid in determining the credibility of his or her statements. It is also critical in evaluating issues related to the likelihood of continued criminal behavior and in charting treatment strategies and prognosis.[8]

Several frameworks to measure personality or ego development currently exist.[9] The youths whose stories are told in this section were classified by the Interpersonal Level of Maturity Theory (I-level).[10] This theory of personality development, which originated with a group of psychology students in Berkeley in the early 1950s, has its underpinnings in child development, psychoanalytic theory, Lewinian theory, phenomenological theory, and social perception. Over the last 30 years, it has been widely researched and used with both juvenile and adult offender populations for treatment and management.[11]

I-level classifies people into one of seven categories according to the complexity with which they perceive themselves, others, and their environment. Very few individuals, if any, reach the ideal of social maturity associated with the highest level, 7. If the developing child has a very stressful or threatening experience, he or she may resist change and make desperate attempts to remain at his or her present level of development because it seems safer.[12]

By maintaining that individuals are accountable for their actions, the criminal justice system implicitly assumes that defendants are at level 4 or higher. The maturity levels that have been empirically identified in the offender population range from level 2 to level 5.[13] The APOs whom I assessed perceived at levels 3 to 5.

Persons classified at level 3 are primarily concerned with identifying who the powerful people are in any given situation. They do not yet appreciate that other people have needs and feelings different from their own, instead viewing others in stereotypic ways. These individuals try to get their needs met by conforming to the demands of the person in power at the moment or by controlling others through attack or intimidation. They frequently deny that they have strong feelings or deep emotional involvements. They do not feel guilty or perceive a need to make amends for their misbehavior because they typically perceive others as objects to be manipulated.[14]

Individuals at level 4 wish to make something of themselves and be recognized for their ideals or interests, their potentialities or accomplishments by those they admire. They are capable of making long-range plans and of delaying their response to immediate stimuli. Unlike individuals at earlier stages, they are able to evaluate their behavior and that of others against an internalized set of standards and have some perception of the role that needs and motives in themselves and others play in behavior. They are aware that behavioral choices are available to them and may experience guilt when they fail to behave in accordance with their values. They are capable of entering into a reciprocal relationship with another person whose needs, feelings, ideals, or standards of behavior are similar to their own.[15]

Persons at level 5 are increasingly aware of different ways of coping with events. They begin to distinguish roles appropriate for themselves and others for different occasions. Although individuals at this level may sometimes wonder which of the roles is "the real me," they are aware of continuity in their own and others' lives. Individuals classified at level 5 are able to appreciate people who are different from them and to understand what they do and how they feel. They are capable of putting themselves in others' roles because they can compare their impressions of events and activities with those of others.[16]

POST–TRAUMATIC STRESS DISORDER
AND THE ABUSED CHILD

When an adolescent kills a parent, a mental health expert should investigate the possibility that he or she suffers from post–traumatic stress disorder (PTSD). PTSD has become associated in the public's mind with the difficulties experienced by some Vietnam veterans in readjusting to civilian life. These individuals report episodes when they feel as though they are reexperiencing the stressful events of the war. On rare occasions, veterans, believing that they are back in combat, will attack others, sometimes seriously injuring or killing them.

In DSM-III-R the American Psychiatric Association gave four examples of events that would be expected to evoke significant distress in almost anyone who encountered them. Children raised in homes where they and/or their mothers are severely abused often experience such events:

1. Serious threat to one's life or physical integrity
2. Serious threat or harm to one's children, spouse, or other close relatives and friends
3. Sudden destruction of one's home or community
4. Seeing another person who has recently been, or is being, seriously injured or killed as the result of an accident or physical violence [17]

In considering the appropriateness of the diagnosis of PTSD in the case of the APO, the three factors discussed below must be present for at least one month.

Reexperiencing the Traumatic Event

In the case of the APO, there is unlikely to be one traumatic event, particularly if the parents are chemically dependent. Instead, the youth has probably been a victim or a witness to a series of incidents in which extreme physical violence was perpetrated by the deceased parent. In addition to the traumatizing effect of the repeated incidents of serious harm or threat, the homicide itself is very likely to be another traumatic event which the APO will reexperience.

The traumatic event or events can be reexperienced in a number of ways, including through recurrent and intrusive recollections of the abusive and threatening episodes, a sense of reliving the event, illusions, hallucinations, and dissociative or flashback episodes. The reexperiencing of traumatic events is often critical to understanding the motive for killing the abusive parent. Intrusive recollections of past trauma can provide the impetus to pull the trigger even at a time when the youth is not physically threatened. The youth's reexperiencing the trauma associated with being abused and witnessing another, often his or her mother, being threatened and injured can lead the youth to kill in a dissociative state (an altered state of consciousness in which the youth may have been unaware of his behavior and its consequences at some point during or around the time of the homicidal event). After the parent is dead, the APO often expresses the fear that the parent may not be really dead. The youth frequently reports dreaming that the parent is coming after him or her, and that the homicide is recurring.

Avoidance and Numbing of General Responsiveness

Individuals avoid dealing with trauma by avoiding thoughts, feelings, situations, or activities that cause them to recall traumatic events. They may develop psychogenic amnesia, the inability to recall important aspects of trauma. The APO's reluctance to discuss details of the trauma that he or she endured for years prior to the homicide often takes the form of a general unwillingness to discuss the abuse and neglect in the home. After the homicide, the avoidance of thoughts or feelings associated with the history of severe abuse may persist even when silence is self-defeating. Patty Smith, for example, was extremely reticent in describing the trauma associated with her and her mother's victimization. She was ready to plead guilty to first-degree murder rather than recount the past.

Individuals numb themselves by losing interest in significant activities, feeling detached or estranged from others, dissociating from their feelings or bodies, or having a restricted range of affect that precludes, for example, loving others. They may believe that their future will be foreshortened and may not expect to have a career, marriage or children, or a long life. The numbing of general responsiveness occurs after the trauma. For the APO, this numbing typically begins years before the homicide as a response to ongoing trauma in the home. This symptom of PTSD, which enables the APO to survive deplorable conditions often for years, is frequently misinterpreted after the homicide as an indication of callousness. When the APO relates episodes of abuse that he or she has witnessed or endured, the youth may seem detached from them. A listener without clinical training may question whether the youth really experienced the events described.

Frequently the APO is alleged to have no remorse. At the time of the homicide and for some time thereafter, remorse may not be accessible to the youth, who has shut down his or her capacity to feel.

Increased Arousal

Individuals may experience increased arousal in a number of ways, including difficulty falling or staying asleep or concentrating. They may have an exaggerated startle response or react physiologically to events that symbolize or resemble an aspect of the traumatic event. Before the homicide the APO is likely to be hypervigilant because his or her life depends on it. Even after the homicide, however, heightened arousal is likely to continue unless there is therapeutic intervention. The APO may know that the threatening parent is dead but still fear the parent. Terry Adams and Scott Anders, for example, reported in follow-up interviews more than six and four years, respectively, after the homicides that they still experienced nightmares and on occasion had difficulty falling and staying asleep because of fear associated with the past.

7 Peter Jones

PETER JONES, a 17-year-old white male from a lower-middle-class background, was arrested within five hours of killing his father. He shot his father twice in the back of the neck and once just behind the ear with a .22 caliber rifle as the man sat watching television in the middle of the night. Peter told a law enforcement officer when he was arrested that his father had constantly beaten him and his mother and had threatened to kill him the evening of the shooting. Shortly after Peter's arrest, Mrs. Jones corroborated her son's statements that the father had repeatedly beaten them both.

In the state in which this homicide occurred, charges of first-degree murder could be brought only by the grand jury; in this case, it refused to do so. The prosecutor was forced to reduce the charge to second-degree murder.

THE CLINICAL EVALUATION

My assessment of Peter Jones, conducted at the request of defense counsel about five months after the homicide, is based on a six-hour clinical interview and a review of numerous case materials. The interview was conducted in private in the adult county jail without interruption and was tape recorded with Peter's consent.

Before evaluating him I reviewed Peter's medical records, a psychiatric evaluation done three months after the homicide, news articles reporting the homicide, and Peter's handwritten responses to a reporter's questions. Additional materials reviewed prior to trial included the autopsy report, the police incident and arrest reports, and eight supplementary reports prepared by the police during their investigation. I also had the opportunity to review four statements made to the police by Paul, an 18-year-old unemployed boarder at the Jones home, a sworn statement made to police by the friend to whom Peter fled after the homicide, and depositions by four law enforcement officers, three neighbors, and the boarder. Finally I perused two statements Peter prepared for defense counsel describing the homicide, public defender investigative reports summarizing interviews with three relatives, two neighbors, and the boarder, and reports prepared by two other court-appointed mental health professionals.

BEHAVIORAL OBSERVATIONS

Peter was alert and cooperative throughout the assessment interview. His responses to questions indicated that he was actively processing them. He did not refuse to answer questions even when they caused him discomfort or pain.

Peter did not appear to be at all manipulative during the interview. His responses to hundreds of questions and his behavior during the interview strongly suggested that he was being as truthful and accurate as possible. The youth's answers revealed that he was able to handle conceptual material and to consider alternative ways of responding to a particular question. Responses to some questions suggested that he might have an auditory processing problem and might be dyslexic. I noted that Peter might be learning disabled and recommended that he be evaluated by a special education professional.

Peter appeared fairly at ease during the interview. His eye contact was excellent, but he was rarely animated. His mood was somber, and he seemed depressed. A couple of times during the interview, he was near tears. His depression seemed to be in part occasioned by the homicide. Peter appeared, however, to have been chronically depressed for years because of his home environment.

PERSONALITY ASSESSMENT

Peter perceived at I-level 5, which is very high on the continuum of personality development and rarely found among offender populations. He was able to look for and understand the reasons for his and others' behavior. The youth had a set of values against which he judged his and others' actions. He felt accountable for his conduct and could feel remorse when his actions hurt others or he failed to abide by his values. Even more important, he was able to appreciate and respond to others as individuals. He could understand fairly easily what others were feeling. Peter could also view interpersonal situations from the perspective of several others' needs and motives. The youth was aware of assuming a variety of roles (son, parent, boyfriend) and was receptive to change. At the same time, he was able to see his own behavior and that of others as possessing continuity.

SOCIAL HISTORY

Family constellation and relationships.   Peter was the older of two boys born to Mr. and Mrs. Jones. Medical records from six years before the homicide stated that there was "a deep-seated family problem between the parents," who had separated on four or five occasions. In addition, the family doctor recorded that Mr. Jones was addicted to alcohol and that continuous problems existed between the father and Peter.

A psychiatrist who had treated both parents described them as having "severe psychiatric illness." When asked to examine Peter at his parents' request approximately 20 months before the homicide the psychiatrist noted that Mr. Jones had a "severe mood disturbance," was "very tense and irritable," and had been "quite physically abusive" throughout Peter's childhood. According to Mrs. Jones, her husband had also been diagnosed as schizophrenic. Statements made by Peter and Mrs. Jones suggested that other relatives suffered from mental illness. One of the individuals mentioned, the victim's brother, was staying at the Jones residence when Mr. Jones was killed.

At the time of the homicide, both parents were living on Social Security disability payments. The victim, 38, had worked as a corrections officer for about five years but had been unable to work for two years before his death, apparently because of mental illness. Mrs. Jones, also 38 at the time of the tragedy, had not been able to work for more than five years because of Crohn's disease, an intestinal disorder that stress aggravates. During the 17 years of their marriage, the Joneses moved frequently; Peter estimated that the family had moved eight or nine times in less than ten years.

Peter described his mother as a nice person, soft-spoken, sensitive, and caring, with a sense of humor. He chronicled her long history of psychophysiological ailments and suffering with compassion. He explained how he had increasingly come to assume family and household chores as a result of her illness and the heavy dosage of Valium that she took for years to stay calm. The youth related that his father was an alcoholic, had "smoked dope" when he was younger, and had been taking Valium for about a year. Mr. Jones was physically abusive to him and his mother, but not to his younger brother, whom Peter protected. Peter felt that Mr. Jones did not trust him and acted "mean" toward him and others.

The younger brother, Patrick, was almost seven years younger than the defendant. Peter described his brother, 11 at the time of the homicide, as smart for his age, funny, and as a typical little boy who wanted to have fun. When asked about his feelings toward Patrick, Peter stated without hesitation that he loved his brother and would do anything for his brother and his mother. He was upset that Patrick had told his mother that, if he had been Peter, he would also have killed Mr. Jones. This remark really hurt Peter; it was not "a natural thought for an 11-year-old . . . to think of killing somebody."

School.   Peter dropped out of school in the tenth grade and was attending night school at the time of the homicide. He had failed fifth and tenth grades and believed that his failures were due to three primary factors. First, reading and writing were very hard for him, and he had trouble keeping up with what the teachers were saying. Second, as he got older, he became increasingly frustrated with the way his father treated his mother and stopped caring about school. Third, because his mother was continually ill and sometimes even hospitalized, Peter did all the household chores, including cooking, cleaning, and taking care of his younger brother.

Peter stated that he had never gotten into any real trouble at school and had been in only a couple of fights. He did not get close to any teachers because his workload at home left him no time to stay after school to talk to them. He expressed his intention of getting his high school equivalency diploma.

Work.   Peter had a job at a fast-food restaurant for nine months while he was still in high school. He got along well with his coworkers and with his boss. He worked overtime, was fast, and did what he was told, including cleaning up, closing the store, and helping the boss with the paperwork. Peter quit when he asked for a raise and the boss gave him an additional ten cents an hour. He thought he deserved more.

Alcohol and drug usage.   Despite an arrest for driving under the influence, Peter did not appear to be a heavy user of alcohol. He drank a couple of beers occasionally with his girlfriend, but did not drink to get drunk. He tried marijuana twice, but did not like the feeling it gave him. When asked, he denied using any other drug illicitly, specifically speed, downers, ludes, and coke. He had heard of crack, but no more.

Friends.   Peter's peers were not involved in delinquent activities. He described his best friend, John, as a "caring person" who would not hurt anyone or anything. Boys who were athletic and who liked to do "fun things" were the kind of youths Peter sought as friends.

Activities.   Peter liked to play pool and to take his girlfriend out alone or with his best friend and the friend's girlfriend. He enjoyed sports, including football, track, tennis, weightlifting, racquetball, and swimming. He was on the track and football teams in junior high, and remained on the football team in high school.

Sexual history.   Peter told me that he had a girlfriend, Becky, whom he genuinely loved and with whom he hoped to be reunited. He liked her because they communicated well. Both of them had to work hard in school, and they had fun together. The youth was pleased that she acted like "a lady" because he didn't like girls who "cussed" or "drank a lot." For Peter, sex was an act of love and not something he would engage in with just anyone.

Prior delinquent history.   Peter's involvement with the police was fairly minimal. In the fifth grade he was picked up when he and two of his friends attempted to run away. Three years later the police were called because he was in a fistfight with another boy who called Peter's girlfriend a name and threatened to slap her. Peter was sent to "opportunity school," a school for youths with disciplinary problems, for several weeks as a result of this incident. His third police contact was an arrest at age 15 for driving under the influence. According to him, he had been drinking with two of his friends when four older boys came up and tried to rob them. When one of the older boys pulled a knife on Peter he got into a truck, which he did not know how to drive, and hit two cars. Peter was held in a detention center for a few days, put on house arrest, and ordered to pay $2,000 in damages.

Self.   Peter described himself, after a long pause, as a person who thought of other people and their feelings, and who worried about what other people thought of him. He saw himself as outgoing, athletic, and someone who liked to do things and have fun. He suggested rather shyly that he was a nice person. When asked if there was anything that he might like to change about himself, he mentioned his study habits. He remarked that he needed to push himself more. If he did not push, he would quit when he "got down."

Values and future orientation (goals, interests).   Peter was no criminally sophisticated youth: His values were very conventional. What he wanted most in life was to have a wife and a family and enough money to give them what they needed and wanted. Although he had been exposed to an excessive amount of violence, he did not approve of violence except under extreme circumstances. The youth suggested that he would fight, for example, if his life were threatened or if another man tried to assault him sexually. In less extreme cases, for example, if his home were broken into or his car vandalized, Peter replied that he would "call the cops" rather than take the law into his own hands.

Peter showed no signs of nihilistic traits. What emerged clearly across various content areas were indications of life-enhancing qualities rather than destructive forces. Peter had no need or desire to control people. His accounts of his relationships with others and his fondness for dogs and cats showed that he had no interest in destructive acts or sadistic control.

Health.   Peter, who stood about 5'11" and weighed less than 155 pounds at the time of the assessment interview, described his health as "pretty good." While in jail, however, he lost quite a bit of weight because of his dislike for the food and his depressed state. Medical records supported statements that he had a history of a hearing (auditory processing) problem, enuresis (bedwetting) at age 11, and recurrent migraine headaches.

The doctor who treated Peter at age 11 for his "nerves" recorded his diagnostic impression as "childhood anxiety and depression syndrome manifested by enuresis, attention problems in school and psychosomatic complaints including muscular tension headaches." He prescribed antidepressant and analgesic medications for the boy. When these medications did not prove effective within three weeks he added a beta blocker commonly used to prevent migraine headaches. Six weeks after the initial consultation, the doctor noted that "the boy continues to be in an environment full of stress and continues to complain of headaches." At this point, the doctor prescribed an anticonvulsant in addition to the beta blocker. Six weeks later the doctor recorded that he had spent "a considerable amount of time" talking to Mrs. Jones about the stressful nature of the environment and "advising strongly a consultation with a family counselor." The doctor prescribed the same medication and told the family to return "when they had been for at least one month under counseling."

The next entry in the chart was dated two and a half years later. Mrs. Jones called to report that Peter, now almost 14, was experiencing headaches and chest pains. The doctor prescribed antihistamine and narcotic analgesic medications. Six months later, Peter's mother requested these medications again. She was instructed to make an appointment because the patient had not been seen for three years. Mrs. Jones brought Peter in for his last visit to this doctor a few weeks later.

In the last entry in the chart, made almost three years before the homicide, the doctor noted that Peter had had no significant recurrence of headaches since he started taking antihistamines. "His anxiety and depression [had] improved." The doctor renewed the medication and asked Peter to return in six months. Peter told me that he took "the medicine for my nerves . . . on and off until about the sixth grade."

Adjustment in jail. Peter found jail very unclean and crowded. He did not feel that he could trust the inmates or the correction officers. The boy commented sadly that he had never been in an environment "where the inmates throw shit at the officers." The behavior of the juveniles was "aggravating" to him. He had had things stolen from him and had been jumped on and beaten up. While he had never really had to fight at school, he had to be ready to fight in jail. When asked about the incidence of sexual assault in jail, Peter talked about sexual activity that he had witnessed. He said, "I ain't never seen anything like that." His voice quivered and he started to cry.

MOTIVATIONAL DYNAMICS
BEHIND THE HOMICIDE

This homicide represents the most common type of adolescent parricide—the abused child who has been pushed beyond his or her limits. Peter had been living in a very stressful home situation for years. He became even more vulnerable as the stressors in his environment increased, particularly during the 30 days before he shot his father. At the time of the parricide, Peter, a victim of PTSD, was in a dissociative state, unaware that he was killing his father.

Peter's Environment

Peter's life was both horrifying and terrifying. His recollections of his life before the homicide show that he witnessed spouse abuse, other extreme forms of physical violence, and verbal abuse. He was himself a victim of physical and verbal abuse, physical and emotional neglect, and emotional incest.

In addition to all this, Peter was raised in a home with an alcoholic father. This high-stress environment was a major factor contributing to the psychopathology.

Physical and verbal abuse of Mrs. Jones. From when he was a little boy, Peter recalled seeing his father beat his mother's head and bang it on the floor. He could remember being "so little I can't do nothing about it." Up until Peter was about ten, Mr. Jones would beat his wife "all the time." His mother was afraid of her husband, but "she couldn't say anything or he would bad-mouth her." Peter gave these examples of remarks his father made to his mother: "You don't know nothing, bitch," and "Shut the fuck up."

The physical violence directed at his mother occurred "every day for a long time." "She left him [her husband] so many times," but Mr. Jones would come and get her, promising to reform. The father then would be all right for a couple of weeks. Eventually, however, he would hit his wife again and threaten that it would be worse the next time. Mr. Jones would tell his wife that if she left he would kill her.

When asked, Peter named several people who had seen the spouse abuse (all his father's brothers and his mother's two sisters). He stated that neighbors knew (they heard the arguments) and that he had on occasion summoned John, "a big guy who lived down the street," to help when his father was beating his mother. The police, however, were never called. Peter was too scared to call them; his father had "yanked the phone off the wall" when his mother tried.

Peter remembered seeing many violent acts at a very young age. In one incident his father was in a bedroom in the boy's maternal grandparents' home beating his mother. The father came out and began beating his wife's sister. Peter's grandfather asked Mr. Jones what he thought he was doing and Mr. Jones hit the boy's grandmother, breaking her ribs. Mr. Jones then reentered the bedroom and shut the door. The grandfather shot at him through the door, and the bullet hit Mr. Jones in the mouth. Peter stated that during this incident "I was going crazy . . . I was young." He said that he could still see the incident in his mind.

Physical abuse of Peter.   Data regarding physical abuse abounded. Peter was never hospitalized for any of his injuries, but he had received bruises and welts on his back, legs, and arms from beatings given to him by his father, who would on occasion use "a switch— a stick," which would "sometimes draw blood." His father would sometimes "bust [his] lips" and punch him in the nose, mouth, and stomach. In addition, the man kicked Peter, punched him in the head, and grabbed him by his hair to move him around. His father threw glasses at him and hit him on the leg with a fruit bowl, cutting his ankle. "He tried to ram my head into a wall, stuff like that, punching me and everything, and my mom would try to get him to stop."

When asked if he was ever afraid of more than being hit, Peter said yes, just within the last year. At that point the boy started standing up to his father. He made it clear that he had respect for his father and would try to push his father away rather than striking back.

When questioned about whether he had ever worried about being maimed or disfigured, Peter told how his father had bent his thumb back until he thought it would break and he was on the floor. When asked what was going through his mind at that moment, Peter replied, "Fear . . . he was going to hurt me." The following interchange depicts the extent of this fear.

> *Heide:* What is the worst thing you thought he might do? Feared he might do?
> *Peter:* Try to kill me. Because he is a big man.
> *Heide:* How big?
> *Peter:* 6'3", 250 [pounds].
> *Heide:* That is a big man. What is your own size?
> *Peter:* 155, 5'11". That is now, I was smaller then.
> *Heide:* What made you think that?
> *Peter:* Because of what he would say. "Keep pushing me, [Peter], because I'll lose my cool and I'm going to do something to you" . . . I'd be scared . . . "like kill you."
> *Heide:* Did you think he might do it?
> *Peter:* Yeah, the way he acted, yeah. I'd run from him; he'd corner me.

As Peter got older he began to fear that his father would kill him. When he was 14 or 15, his father would say "You think you are a man" and go on to say "mean" things. When he was 16 and 17, his father actually threatened him. "Last couple of times we left him, he was coming at me, he'd be beating my mom. I'd say, 'You want to kill me, you kill me.' 'All right, I will' and he started coming at me." On the night of the homicide, his father threatened him. "Either he was going to kill me or I was going to kill him. That's what it came down to, I guess."

Verbal abuse and covert sexual abuse of Peter. Mr. Jones would "cuss," "put down," and say unkind things to his son. Psychologically abusive statements made by Mr. Jones included "You ain't worth shit," "You're stupid, just like your damn mother," and "You're nothing but a sorry son of a bitch."

Although Peter related that his father called him "pussy," he denied any overt sexual abuse. When I asked him about indicators of covert sexual abuse (exposure to pornography, taunting with sexual comments or intimations regarding girlfriends by father, and so forth), his answers were generally negative. Some inappropriateness regarding sexuality concerned "off the wall stuff" that Mr. Jones said when drunk. For example, "If you brought a girl into the house, he wouldn't care." Peter suggested only one other indicator of covert sexual abuse: his father's walking around the house in his underwear. This behavior clearly embarrassed the boy. "I didn't think it was right. Put some clothes on."

Physical and emotional neglect and emotional incest. Peter was not allowed to be a child. Like other children raised in an alcoholic family system, from early childhood Peter was largely on his own. Mrs. Jones's deteriorating physical condition and her addiction to tranquilizers made her unable to give her son a safe environment and provide for his emotional needs. In many ways Peter assumed a parental role. He cooked, cleaned, got himself and his brother off to school, and took care of his mother.

Peter deeply loved and cared for his mother. He worried about her while he was in jail and unable to help her. He had been a very nurturing figure to her, far more like a husband than a son. Peter had been his mother's confidant and protector for years.

While Peter's behavior throughout the years might have seemed exemplary, it was not healthy. His mother's dependence on him was a form of emotional incest. She did not protect her son. Instead, her own psychopathology resulted in her physically neglecting her children, and she allowed a highly stressful situation to be perpetuated.

Changes in the Environment before the Homicide

Living in a household with two chemically dependent parents was enormously stressful for Peter. His father would suddenly turn on him: "He would change. You wouldn't know if you could say any-thing. He could explode at any time like a bomb. That's what we were scared about." In this environment Peter became hypervigilant and numbed his feelings, characteristics of those with PTSD.

> When she was at home this last year, he'd start, he'd be off . . . we'd all be in the kitchen . . . he has said it ["I'll kill you"] in front of my mom, but when he says this, I block everything out. I really don't know who's in the room. It's like I keep my mind on him. 'Cause I watch him. He makes a move. I'm gone. That's just the way it is.

Mr. Jones stopped drinking about a year before the homicide in re-sponse to his wife's threats to leave him. From that time on, Mr. Jones took Valium daily to keep himself calm. During the month before the homicide events deteriorated even further, causing additional stress on Peter. Mrs. Jones was again hospitalized and unable to protect him. Peter did not think he would have killed his father if his mother had been home. The youth said, "She could talk him out of stuff. Why don't you [father] just sit down and talk to him [son]?"

Mr. Jones resumed his drinking. Peter reported a difference in Mr. Jones's behavior.

> The medicine would have no effect. The beer kept it out. He'd be like his old self, he would start on us, want to get violent . . . you'd say something wrong and that's it, he'd jump on you, "What did you say?" He had a hearing problem too. Before you could tell him, "You [are] hearing me wrong," he'd say, "I know what I heard." You can't tell him he's wrong.

Mr. Jones argued more with his son during the last month because "he was worried about my mom, he didn't like her to be away."

At the same time he was experiencing difficulties with his father, Peter was increasingly frustrated with the young boarder, Paul. Peter believed Paul was not trying to get a job. "He was living off us. We argued a lot." Peter had assumed a parental role toward Paul as well, getting him up for work when he was employed, washing his clothes, and so on.

Peter had two major disappointments in the month before the homicide. His girlfriend, Becky, who was his first and only significant girl, broke up with him: "She started liking this other guy." Peter took this loss very hard. When asked how he felt, the boy replied, "I cried. I felt like she was all I had."

The second disappointment involved the sudden and mysterious disappearance of a cat Peter loved. Peter was told by his Uncle George (not a very reliable person by the youth's account) that his father was responsible. Although his father denied it, Peter believed Mr. Jones to have been responsible. In earlier years Peter had had two dogs, both of whom also vanished. He suspected that his father might have had something to do with their disappearances.

The Night of the Homicide

Peter told me that he did not remember "a lot of things" that happened on the night of the homicide. He remembered "bits and pieces of that night. I remember some things of what I did. I remember doing it. I don't know if it's in order." His recollection of events had "hurt me for a long time. When I remember it, it would seem intentionally I did it."

Paul and Peter's Uncle George said that Mr. Jones had hit Peter a couple of times while they were in the kitchen because the boy did not have dinner ready on time, and Peter accepted their report. Peter remembered that his uncle and Paul left and that he ran out the door while saying "Fuck you, asshole" to his father. He also remembered that his father went into the house and got something, which Peter assumed was car keys, and drove off. Peter surmised that his father thought he had gone to a friend's house and perhaps intended to come get him.

At this point Peter went back into the house and entered his father's bedroom, where he got a rifle and three bullets. After that he went to his own bedroom and loaded the rifle. About that time his father pulled up. Peter recalled putting the rifle under his bed before taking flight. "He was coming in the door and I was running out of my bedroom door and he started to chase after me and I ran out the back door and ran around the house. He hollered, 'You have to come in some time!'"

Peter saw his father sit down "in front of the window, in front of the chair and TV." As he crawled through a window Peter felt very afraid that his father would catch him. His father had sometimes booby-trapped windows so he could tell if Peter had reentered the house. Peter "vaguely" remembered a board falling as he came in his bedroom door and feared that his father had heard the noise.

> I was looking constantly at my bedroom door to see if it was going to open. And I just grabbed the gun and snuck out my bedroom window and when I went to the front window, he was sitting there. And that's when I aimed the gun up to his head and I just kept thinking about all

the things he's done to my mom and me and Patrick and I was tired of this. Then it's like I blacked out, I just remember, it seemed like my eyes closed, like I closed my eyes, and then the gunshots woke me up, it seems like, I thought I only shot him one time, I thought I shot him one time. I never found out until the police told me that I shot him three times. Then I ran back into the house after I dropped the gun and I saw what I did and I was shocked. I didn't think I had done that. In a way I didn't want to, you know, and I seen the blood coming down all over him and everything and I was hugging him and telling him not to be dead, you know, and I got Paul. I told him to call the cops and the ambulance. I forgot about my little brother. Paul said to get out of here and hide the gun. I left and went to John's [his friend]. I told John and his mom. I don't remember if I went to sleep or anything. Then I remembered my little brother. I was going to the house to get him. Before I got there, the police stopped me.

When he was asked how much time had elapsed between his father leaving and the shooting, Peter's confusion was apparent: "I don't know. I was like crazy. I couldn't say. It seems like it happened so fast. I don't even know how it got so late. I can't remember anything. That's all I can remember." Peter reported having flashes go through his mind at the time of the homicide:

Things I remember, pictures of him hitting my mom, hitting me. It was like I blacked out. Like I was thinking of then [those times in the past], I guess, that I did that. It was like I pointed the gun—that was it. Flashes going through my mind.

My brother tells me he said that he [the father] had to have really scared me . . . to really have got at me in order to make me do that. Because before I would just leave, run away until he calmed down, you know, and come back.

Paul and others had said that Peter had been talking to them that day "like I was freaked out, talking about leaving" apparently because he was scared of his father. His mother said his suitcase had been found packed. "I must have tried to have left and my dad caught me— I don't know. I try to remember. It's like a black in there." Peter mentioned that his friend John had also said that Peter had been "acting weird a couple of days. Different."

"All that week," Peter said, "he was really bad on me . . . that's why I think I was really planning on leaving." He tried to call his aunt Joan (really a cousin), who lived about 300 miles away, because he thought that he could go there.

Peter was pushed to his breaking point after years of living in an environment fraught with stress. At the time of the homicide, the boy believed his life was in imminent danger. Peter's belief that he could be killed by his father was reasonable in view of past beatings and the threats his father made that night and earlier. Given Peter's apparent intention to leave the home and the thwarting of his efforts, his feeling of being trapped would be reinforced, and his behavior would be situationally reactive. I classify the homicide as situational—Peter's intention to kill at the onset of the incident was low, and he derived no pleasure or satisfaction from killing.

The boy's claim that he blacked out and still has gaps in memory is credible. In addition to being terrified by his father, Peter was also horrified by the memories that flashed before him as he stood holding the gun. He was overcome by the terror and horror that he experienced. The adolescent's report that he closed his eyes, lost consciousness temporarily ("blacked out"), and in essence was unaware of his conduct when he fired the gun is consistent with reports of other adolescent parricide cases.

CASE PROCESSING AND DISPOSITION

At Peter's trial, the defense presented numerous witnesses, including Peter's relatives and neighbors, who graphically corroborated the extensive physical and psychological abuse Mr. Jones had inflicted on Peter and Mrs. Jones for years. In the opinion of all four mental health experts who examined the youth, the boy was legally insane at the time of the crime under the prevailing state standard, the M'Naghten test (developed in 1843). I testified that the stress in the home in which the boy was raised was similar to that experienced by soldiers in combat and that the boy's hypervigilant behavior and flight into attack were consistent with a diagnosis of PTSD. The cumulative effect of the abuse and its escalation during the month before the homicide conspired with the events of the evening to push the youth over the edge. All the experts agreed that the boy was in a dissociative state at the time of the crime: He was both reexperiencing episodes of past trauma and terrified by the events that took place on the evening of the homicide.

After resting its case, the defense made a motion for a judgment of acquittal, arguing that the state had introduced no evidence to rebut the position that the boy was legally insane when he shot his father.

Even some of the state's witnesses supported the defense's contention that the boy was legally insane at the time of the crime. The motion was, however, denied at first. Closing arguments were presented, and the case went to a six-person jury. After more than a day's deliberation, the jury stated it was hopelessly deadlocked and could not reach a verdict.

The defense renewed its motion for a judgment of acquittal after a mistrial was declared. This time the judge granted the motion, and Peter was found not guilty by reason of insanity.

Three of the mental health experts who had testified at the trial were again subpoenaed to testify at the disposition hearing two weeks later. We agreed that Peter needed in-depth psychotherapy to resolve the long-standing trauma to which he had been exposed and that a brief period of hospitalization would help him make the transition from jail back to the community. I testified at this hearing that Peter's successful adjustment in the community would depend on the whole family's undergoing treatment. The most important criterion for success was that the mental health professional be knowledgeable about the dynamics and treatment of alcoholic family systems. The deep-seated problems that Peter, his brother, Patrick, and his mother had developed from living with Mr. Jones did not end with his death; unless they were addressed, the family pathology would continue. I recommended that, in addition to intensive psychotherapy, all three attend community support meetings in self-help groups—Al-Anon for Mrs. Jones and Peter, Alateen for Patrick, and Adult Children of Alcoholics for Peter.

The judge ordered Peter to be transferred to a local hospital to undergo at least two weeks of psychotherapy before release. She accepted defense counsel's plan to have Peter treated by the psychiatrist who had seen him on two occasions and who had treated Peter's parents.

Peter was hospitalized for one month. In a follow-up letter written to the court at defense counsel's invitation, I stressed the need for Peter to participate in therapy that would facilitate the release of his emotions. Conflict with his mother was to be expected, and Peter's unresolved anger toward her had to be safely discharged.

About three months after Peter's release, he was arrested and charged with four armed robberies of convenience stores. In statements made to the press Peter said that he had committed the robberies because he needed money to give to his mother. Details provided to me by defense made it obvious that Peter's treatment program had failed to address the deep-seated family pathology. In the absence of meaningful psychotherapeutic intervention, it was not surprising that, as stress in the family intensified, Peter's conduct took an antisocial course in a series of desperate attempts to solve escalating financial problems at home.

Five factors were primarily responsible for Peter's failure to make a successful adjustment to society: (1) lack of change in the home environment; (2) the effect of drugs on Peter; (3) mounting financial concerns; (4) lack of meaningful treatment and failure to coordinate treatment services; and (5) the lack of therapeutic intervention when the family situation had reached crisis proportions.

During the three months Peter lived in the community, there was no change in the problems that existed in the home environment. He and his mother argued frequently. He would leave his mother's home, usually retreating to his cousin's. When Mrs. Jones thought Peter was upset, she would give him some of her Valium to calm him down.

Within a week of Peter's return home, the defendant's 20- or 21-year-old cousin moved in. Peter drank beer and smoked marijuana almost daily with this cousin for about two or three months before his rearrest. Alcohol and drugs allowed him to escape from the pressure he felt his mother exerted on him and the problems of reentry into society. The drugs he took made him even more likely to behave maladaptively. The adolescent explained that he was "different" on drugs and that he would get even more depressed when he thought about the family's problems.

Financial concerns mounted. Peter had difficulty getting a job because of the notoriety of his case. His efforts to secure work on a daily basis through the labor force were partly successful, and he earned $26 per day. He felt compelled to quit, however, after three days, when he received a traffic ticket for driving without a license. He did not have the money to pay for the ticket and for a license, and he could not rely on his mother for transportation.

Mrs. Jones was very worried about finances. She told Peter that she could not pay for the car repairs and was afraid that they would be evicted because she was $100 behind in the rent. Peter asked her to explore different payment arrangements, but she was too obsessed with their financial problems to take the necessary action. His mother told him, "I can't do anything. You live here, too."

Family problems were escalating, but there was no meaningful treatment and no coordination of services. Only one family counseling session took place in the three-month period between Peter's discharge from the hospital and his rearrest. This session, conducted by Dr. Broker, a psychiatrist, and his wife, ended in an argument between Peter and his mother. Following this session, Peter was seen only by the psychiatrist's wife, who lacked appropriate credentials. Peter's younger brother was not seen again. When I visited Peter he told me that he saw Mrs. Broker weekly, and that she knew he was drinking, smoking marijuana, and using cocaine with his cousin—but took no action. He also told me that the social services worker in his case was aware that he was using drugs to cope with his problems.

In the month preceding the robberies, tension in the Jones home came to a head. Mrs. Jones packed up Peter's belongings, and he went to stay with his cousin. The day after he left, the state social services worker met Peter at his vocational school and told him he was in violation of a court order. Peter had to return home until a court date could be set to reevaluate his residence. Despite the obvious crisis, there was little that the state worker could do. The psychiatrist and his wife were out of town for two weeks and had made no therapeutic provisions for the Jones family. The judge who had presided in the case was also unavailable.

Stressors in the home environment bore heavily on the adolescent. Peter knew that the family needed money, and he eventually came to see robbery as a way to get it. About a month before the four robberies, he saw his cousin rob a convenience store by threatening the clerk with a crowbar. Peter remarked that, although he was unaware of his cousin's intentions when they entered the store, he was surprised at how easy it was to commit a successful robbery. When Peter committed the robberies, he had reached the point where he "didn't care anymore."

By the time Peter appeared before the trial judge at the hearing scheduled to discuss a change in residence, he had four new charges pending for armed robbery. Peter committed the robberies two days after he appeared in court before another judge for his traffic ticket and was apprised of the fines that he had to pay.

When he committed the robberies Peter stated that he was feeling "really foggy" due to the ingestion of alcohol and some Valium that his mother had given him. He had used a crowbar to rob two stores and a brick to rob two others in a two-day period. The youth told me that although he had no recollection of two of the four robberies, when the police showed him photographs taken at the scene, he realized that he must have committed all of them.

Each robbery count was handled individually. Peter was found guilty of armed robbery by one jury and convicted of a lesser charge by another. He pleaded guilty to lesser charges on the other two counts of armed robbery. Sentencing guidelines indicated that a seven-to-nine year prison term was appropriate.

At the sentencing hearing, an assistant state attorney argued that Peter be sentenced to a nine-year prison term to be followed by 15 years' probation. Defense counsel summed up the problems Peter had had in obtaining help following his original acquittal. The boy's lawyer then asked the judge to sentence the defendant to probation with two stipulations: (1) Peter would live and work in a community restitution center in a major city located about 40 miles from his home; and (2) he would undergo intensive psychotherapy with a therapist who was familiar with the treatment needs of this type of youth.

The judge, who had also presided over Peter's murder trial, found merit in the defense's contention of mitigating factors. She imposed a four-year prison term to be followed by six years of probation.

Given credit for time served in jail and the accumulation of gain time in prison, Peter served seven months in adult prison. Defense counsel's plan was not implemented upon his release. Peter did not relocate and had difficulty obtaining employment in the community in which he had been raised. Arrangements he made to live with a roommate did not work out satisfactorily, and he was not allowed to live with his mother. Peter's probation officer confirmed that Peter had been offered no meaningful therapeutic help. The probation officer was seeking alternative housing and trying to implement a treatment program for Peter when he absconded. Within ten months of his release from prison, a warrant for Peter's arrest was sworn. When this book went to press, Peter's whereabouts had been unknown for more than a year and a half.

8 | Scott Anders

SCOTT ANDERS, another white youth from a lower-middle-class family, was 15 years old when he was arrested for killing his 36-year-old father. On the afternoon of the homicide Scott confided in some friends who came to the Anders home that "it had been building up," and said, "One day he's gonna come after me and I'm actually gonna kill him." (When Mr. Anders got "real buzzed" on marijuana and cocaine, he would yell and threaten his son, and he had been talking about killing them both for some time.) Later that day Mr. Anders smoked marijuana, argued with his son, and "cussed" at him. Scott left the house for a while, telling his father that he would be back. When he returned, he saw that a 12-gauge shotgun had been propped up against the couch.

> When I got back, I walked in the door and he [Scott's father] looked at me and he started yelling at me, cussing at me and everything and telling me he was gonna beat my ass and everything and that was the last thing I remember and he was just getting ready to light another joint, when I grabbed that gun, I jumped back and he threw the joint down on the floor and I shot him . . . and he went back and he rolled over and he looked at me and he blinked his eye and blood poured out of his mouth and everything and then I shot him and then I freaked out.

Scott told police that he left the house immediately after the shooting and went to see some friends. At first he lied to his friends because he was scared, but later told the truth to Kirk, a good friend. He told Kirk that he intended to shoot himself, "because it, kinda like, took a part of me away when I shot my dad." Kirk took the gun from Scott and accompanied the boy to the Anders house to determine the man's condition. The boy recalled "screaming and crying and everything" while the friend checked Mr. Anders' pulse and called the police.

Scott was taken to police headquarters for questioning, where he gave a complete confession. The state decided to prosecute Scott as an adult and obtained grand jury indictments for one count of first-degree murder and another of possession of a firearm.

THE CLINICAL EVALUATION

My assessment of Scott Anders is based on a clinical interview with the youth and a review of his statement to police. When this case was referred by defense counsel, investigation of the boy's home life was in its initial stages and depositions of witnesses had not yet been taken. I conducted a four-and-a-half hour interview with the boy approximately five weeks after the homicide. At the time Scott was in the jail clinic. He had been removed a few days earlier from the juvenile section of the adult jail when he reportedly became disruptive and potentially suicidal following a ruling denying him bail.

BEHAVIORAL OBSERVATIONS

Scott was attentive and cooperative throughout the assessment. His responses to hundreds of questions demonstrated that he understood what was being asked of him and was trying to answer truthfully. He did not decline to answer questions that caused him discomfort, embarrassment, or pain. At times Scott said he did not know what he thought or how he felt about a particular issue or event. His statements that he could not answer some questions are credible in view of his level of personality development.

Scott seemed anxious during the interview, fidgeting, avoiding eye contact for some time, and laughing nervously. He smoked almost continuously and played with his cigarettes. He spoke very fast and often had to repeat his statements because I could not understand him.

Scott seemed very depressed; at several points during the interview, his eyes welled up with tears. Like Peter Jones, Scott seemed to have been chronically depressed for years. His coping strategies, however, enabled him to mask his sadness.

PERSONALITY ASSESSMENT

Scott perceived at I-level 4, the most common level of socioperceptual development encountered among both adolescent homicide offenders[1] and juvenile and adult offender populations.[2] The youth had internalized a set of values by which he judged his and others' behavior. He saw himself as accountable for his actions and could delay his response to immediate stimuli. Scott had some awareness of the role that needs and motives played in his and others' behavior and was able to empathize with those like him. He was also capable of making long-range plans.

Among individuals who perceive at level 4, four behavioral subtypes have been empirically identified by observing the ways individuals behave in different situations.[3] Scott's usual behavioral response fit the neurotic acting out subtype. He had a great deal of anxiety from his early childhood experiences. His interactions with his father and second stepmother during the seven or eight years preceding the homicide had in particular been a constant source of pain to him. Rather than attempting to resolve these difficulties, he focused his attention on reducing or overcoming immediate anxiety and pressures through direct action. In reflecting on his life with his father and second stepmother, Scott stated that he had been unhappy because "all I ever had was problems . . . family problems, school problems, or somethin'. Always somethin'."

Scott's remarks suggested that he tried desperately to compensate for long-standing feelings of inadequacy by maintaining a strong front and appearing in control. He realized that his manner of coping with an abusive environment by acting "cool" was often self-destructive, and he felt badly when he did things wrong. Antisocial behavior was not an acceptable part of Scott's self-image. Deep down inside, he harbored a great deal of guilt and wanted to be a better person.

> I was stupid at the time. I was always stupid and I just didn't realize it. I never realized nothing . . .'cause if I wasn't stupid, I wouldn't [have] skipped school, you know. I wouldn't [have] made things worse than what things was. Things would be bad at home and what would I do? I would skip school and run away. That's stupid, now that I think of it.

Scott ran away four times with friends but "never got anywhere." Every time he left he was thinking about "taking off for good," but he always came back. "I always felt sorry for 'em [his father and second stepmother]. I figured they were worried and everything," he recalled, but "I'd come back and they'd be asleep."

Scott "got in trouble with the law" only once prior to the homicide. His behavior in that incident was also indicative of a neurotic pattern of coping with anxiety and painful feeling states. He threatened a girl with whom he had run away because he had "a lot of pressure on me." He admitted that he was angry with her because she had gotten him into trouble. As he discussed the incident, the larger picture emerged.

> Well, at the time I was mad at the whole world . . .'cause I'd go home and I'm in trouble. I'd go to school, I'm in trouble. Wherever I went I was in trouble all the time. That's why I said, seventh grade I never had nothing but trouble. But my parents and me, we fought. People in the school and me didn't get along. I was a total ass them days.

These excerpts reveal the poor self-image that Scott had long before the homicide. He had believed for years that he was a "bad person." To the casual observer Scott might have appeared to be a dangerously antisocial child because of his pattern of acting out his conflicts. He was, however, a severely abused child who at various times during his adolescence engaged in disruptive and delinquent behavior as a means of avoiding the pain, anger, and conflict within. This neurotic pattern of coping worked until the month before the homicide, when the family environment became increasingly intolerable.

SOCIAL HISTORY

Family constellation and relationships.   Scott was the only child born to Lily and Chester Anders. Mrs. Anders had two children, a boy and a girl, from an earlier marriage. Scott stated that he never really knew his mother because she left with the boy's half-siblings when he was between three and five. During the three to five years following Mrs. Anders' departure, Scott moved four times. He lived first with his paternal grandparents and his father in the grandparents' home, which was located in a rural area. When his father remarried, Scott moved in with his father and his stepmother, Mary. Following Mr. Anders' divorce from Scott's first stepmother, the boy moved back to his grandparents', where he stayed until he was about eight, when his father married again. For the next seven or eight years Scott lived with his father and his second stepmother (another woman named Mary whom I call Marytwo) in a neighborhood reputed to be a haven for drug dealers. A month before the homicide Marytwo "ran off" with one of Mr. Anders' male friends: "See, we had this guy staying at our house, you know. Hidin' from the law. My dad fed him, gave him food. My dad gave him a home. Washed his clothes, you know. We took care of him. And then he left, [he went] movin' out to the country. He left and, the next thing you know, my stepmother was gone. I came home from school and she was gone." After his second stepmother departed, Scott remained with his father.

Scott remembered virtually nothing about the time that he spent with his real mother and half-siblings. His memories of his first stepmother were warm, and he would have liked to renew contact with her. The years that he lived with his grandparents, however, were the happiest in his life. Scott pointed out that his grandparents were the only people who really showed him love and that he felt close to them, as well as to his cousins. His grandmother, he felt, was a mother to him, and his grandfather was "his real father." From Scott's descriptions of life with his father and second stepmother it is clear that both parents abused and neglected him.

School. Scott was in the ninth grade when he was arrested for homicide. He had spent some time in a school for the emotionally handicapped when he was young because he had a problem in English and "did a lot of fighting" because he did not generally get along with the other children in school. He had skipped school frequently in the seventh grade because he was associating with the "wrong crowd," but his attitude and behavior improved after that year. He rarely did anything wrong in the eighth and ninth grades, and when he did, he usually did not get caught. When asked if he liked school, the youth said that he "never hated it." He was generally "doin' good" and got along with all of his teachers except one. He had some teachers to whom he felt close, "young people . . . the kind that helped you out when you had problems." But he stopped talking to them about his problems after the seventh grade.

Alcohol and drug usage. Scott was not a heavy user of drugs and alcohol. The youth admitted to trying "pot" once under "peer pressure" and stated that he did not like it. Although he sometimes drank with his father, he would not get high because he did not want to be out of control. Scott did not report drinking with his friends.

Friends and prior delinquent activities. Scott liked to watch people when he first met them before deciding if he wanted them as friends. He did not like juveniles who had "a bad attitude," who think that "they're so big and bad." "The wrong crowd" with whom he had associated when he was younger appeared to be more involved in status offenses than in delinquent or criminal activities. When Scott was with these juveniles, he would skip school or run away; he would not rob people or steal their property because he believed these activities were wrong. Although he had been involved in a few gang fights, he did not like to fight.

When Scott threatened the girl, he was charged with attempted rape. He admitted, "I was talking about raping her, cutting her pants off, slashing her with a razor blade," but maintained that he did not touch the girl and would not have carried out this behavior because he wasn't "that kind of person." He said that this incident was the only time that he scared anybody. He felt sorry about it because "it wasn't the right thing to do"; "it was stupid." Following this incident he had about five counseling sessions, which he did not find helpful.

Activities and work. Scott "never got into baseball or nothin'" and was unable to go to Boy Scouts or to do other fun things because he was "always usually busy around the house. Helpin' with the chores or somethin'." He did the housework and other activities as instructed by his father and Marytwo. "I sweeped, maybe mopped, washed dishes, mowed the yard, clean[ed] up the rooms . . . wash[ed] the car, clean[ed] up the garage, and rake[d] the yard." He sneaked out at night to be with his friends because his parents always kept his time occupied.

In addition to the work that Scott did at home, he did yard work for his neighbors. He said that people in his neighborhood would call on him if they needed help.

Sexual history. Scott reported that he had not engaged in sexual intercourse. The adolescent seemed proud as he described a close female friend as a "goody two-shoes." She did not smoke and was the type of person who liked education and wanted a good job. He denied being sexually involved with her. "Sex is something that comes with love," not "something you just go out and do." He maintained that casual sex "ain't right" and that he "never loved anybody that much" to be that involved. The adolescent denied any homosexual behavior or interest.

Self. Scott had difficulty describing himself. When asked how his friends might describe him, the boy said, "Mellow." He explained that he did not typically get "riled" like his friends. He stated that if he could change places with anybody in the world he would be "a little, bitty baby" and "start all over, won't be such an ass."

Values and future orientation (goals, interests). Scott's value system was conventional. His three tattoos (the word *LOVE*, a cross, and his girlfriend's name) suggested that he valued relationships and believed in God. Scott wanted to get an education and a good job, and expected when he became older to get "a happy lady and a happy family." Scott did not approve of violence except under extreme circumstances. The boy said that he would fight if his life were threatened or if another man tried to assault him sexually. If his home were broken into or his car vandalized, Scott would rather "get the law into it" than "take the risk of pickin' up a gun." The youth wanted to be everything that his father was not, to live his father's life out in a positive way.

> 'Cause he's in my blood and I'm in his blood and we're blood, and, uh, he lived a bad life. And when I get out, I'm gonna lead a good life. He always wanted me to get electronic, like I said, get a good job. Live happy, you know. And I'm gonna do that. That was his dream. He wanted me to live happy, he wanted me to have a good job. He wanted me to be wealthy. And I'm gonna do it . . . if I can get out of here. . . . And I ain't gonna do no drugs. I ain't gonna do nothing.

Health. Scott was 5'6", weighed approximately 140 pounds, and was on suicide watch status at the time of the assessment interview. The youth had considered taking his life before he killed his father, on the night of the homicide, and after being arrested. When he spoke with me, he did not appear to be contemplating suicide. Instead he was investing heavily in hopes that he would not be sentenced to prison and that he would be able to resume a close relationship with his grandparents and cousins.

Scott's habitual pattern was to stay up most of the night and sleep through the day. He had intrusive recollections of the homicidal scene and frequent nightmares. These flashbacks disturbed his sleep, upset him greatly, and even caused him to punch the wall sometimes. He was receptive to counseling when he spoke with me.

The youth's physical health appeared generally good. Scott reported having had pneumonia when he was younger. He had some minor surgery designed to correct an eye problem, which was apparently not entirely successful, because he remained cross-eyed and had learned to compensate for it.

Adjustment in jail. Scott found confinement, whether in his home or in jail, virtually intolerable. During his month in jail prior to the assessment interview, he had fared rather poorly. Although he thought of himself as capable of self-defense when housed in the juvenile section of the jail, his statements revealed that he had already been physically assaulted, threatened, sexually harassed, and exploited by other juveniles. Other inmates stole all of his "stuff" on his first day in jail and took his meals for several days. Believing that fighting would jeopardize his chances to be released on bond, Scott tried for a time to placate the inmates by giving them cigarettes instead of standing up to them and fighting if necessary.

Scott at first vowed that he would fight if other inmates tried to exploit him again, but upon further reflection doubted that he could even "hold his own" with some of the other juveniles. Scott emphasized that if he were sentenced to adult prison for any appreciable amount of time, he would try to escape, realizing that he might be shot and killed: "I'd rather take the electric chair than take two years of prison . . .'cause I know once I get in that prison, I know something's gonna happen. I'm gonna get another charge on me, and get more time and more time and more time. I've been in this place right here almost two months now and I'm about to go crazy."

Scott was also worried about the possibility of being sexually assaulted in prison. He was certain that he would not willingly engage in homosexual behavior. When asked what he would do if someone tried to rape him, the adolescent was adamant that this event would never occur: "They would get no advantage over me . . . 'cause I wouldn't quit fightin' until I was dead. . . . They ain't, I ain't let no one make a woman out of me. . . . They'd have to kill me."

MOTIVATIONAL DYNAMICS
BEHIND THE HOMICIDE

The Scott Anders case closely resembles the Peter Jones case in terms of home environment, increased stress before the homicide, and events on the night of the homicide.

Scott's Environment

Scott Anders, like Peter Jones, had been exposed to a broad array of psychopathology. He had witnessed extreme violence and excessive alcohol and drug use by his father and second stepmother. He had been abandoned by three mothers—his natural mother and two stepmothers. His father had physically abused him, and he had suffered psychological abuse from his second stepmother. Each of his parents—father, natural mother, and first and second stepmothers—had emotionally and physically neglected him.

Physical and verbal abuse of women. Mr. Anders was an explosive man who had a history of both physical and verbal abuse of women. The boy recalled that his father used to refer to women as "sluts": "He [his father] used to beat the shit out of 'em [women]. No reason. He wake up grumpy and go to bed grumpy. That's how he was, 24 hours a day. All he ever was, was grumpy. . . . You make his coffee wrong, he'd throw it in your face. You spend too much money at the store . . . he'd . . . show 'em not to do it no more."

Scott stated that Mr. Anders had threatened Marytwo with a gun several times and beaten her more than a hundred times. She had sustained many black eyes and black-and-blue marks and had suffered a broken arm from a fall caused by Mr. Anders.

Additional forms of extreme violence. Scott's description of his father and of the man's friends suggested that violent responses were commonplace among them. He also feared that his father would commit suicide, as he had threatened to do so. Scott talked about how his father would slaughter rabbits and then skin them for food. One memory still stirred strongly within the adolescent.

> I seen him stab a dog. The dog jumped, it was a German shepherd and, you know, the dog was messed up. You know, they got winos, sick people here, you got sick dogs, too. And the dog come chasin' him [Mr. Anders] and he [dog] jumped [through this guy's truck into his father] and my dad shoved it [a machete] right through his head and just held it here. And I was sittin' there—whoa!

Physical abuse of Scott. Scott reported that his father routinely beat him, "more [times] than I can count, a hundred [times], more than that." Upon further reflection, the boy volunteered this information: "Well, I ain't saying good beatings and I ain't saying bad beatings, but I always had 'em. . . . Yeah, he always slapped me around. All I know I got, I know he hit me at least three times a week. At least." Scott was aware that various reasons existed for the beatings. The boy reported that Marytwo would blame chores she had not done on Scott and Mr. Anders would beat his son in anger. The adolescent admitted that he sometimes deserved what he got; that is, he could relate the beating to something that he had at least done, "like skippin' school or running away." When Mr. Anders beat his son in response to something that the boy had done, the beating was apt to be disproportionately severe. The majority of the beatings, however, had little to do with Scott's behavior: "Any little bitty thing that my dad got fired up [could lead to a beating]. You know, you just spit wrong and he'd get mad. You could fall down and he'd get mad."

The extent and the severity of the beatings were related to his father's drinking. "When he was sober he would hit you, but when he was drinkin' . . . that's when he lost his temper and blew up. And that's when he started swingin'. When he was sober, well, he'd hit you a few times and quit."

Scott did not sustain any broken bones or serious injuries from the beatings. The worst beating occurred when he ran away and then returned home because he was concerned that his parents would be worried. His second stepmother and his father both participated in this beating. Marytwo beat "the shit out of me until about one o'clock that morning. . . . She was swingin' and punchin' and slappin' me and everything else." The following morning Scott's father "beat the shit out of me, too." Scott claimed that his father hit him "everywhere . . . stomach, face, and head." The beating was so severe that his father would not let him go to school for a few days because the boy had "knots" on his head.

Scott stated that friends and relatives knew about the beatings. The youth explained that Mr. Anders would rarely hit him in front of the man's friends because his father was "proud." When Scott went to the school authorities to tell them of his problems, he exaggerated his physical injuries so that they would take action. His desperate attempt to engage their help by making it look worse than it was backfired. When the school authorities contacted the boy's parents, they denied hitting him, and the school never went on to contact the social services agency. Until the seventh grade, Scott tried to get help by telling his friends and his grandparents about the physical abuse, but "nobody ever got involved." Later, he told little even to his friends because he didn't want people to know the truth. Scott said he hated the term *child abuse* because he was concerned about what it implied about his father.

Verbal and psychological abuse of Scott. Although Scott maintained that his father loved him, he stated that his father did not respect him and would say that he was "no good" and that he was "with the devil." When the adolescent first mentioned Marytwo's name, he said that he "despised her" because "she treated me like a dog." In addition, he felt that her demands on him were excessive and unfair: "Do everything. Do this. Do that. Get me a beer. Wash the dishes. Clean the porches. Sweep the house. Cut up potatoes. You know, she told me to do everything. Tell me this. Tell me that. I ask her to do something for me. No. She didn't want to do it."

Scott said that Marytwo was the only person who ever really got him angry because she "blamed stuff" on him and took all the credit for chores that he did. When she left, she called to tell Scott's father that Scott's behavior was the cause. Scott blamed her for "just about everything." He thought that Marytwo had his father "wrapped around her finger" and made the man a "nervous wreck." The youth believed, for example, that his second stepmother made Mr. Anders get rid of Scott's dog because she preferred little dogs to the one that Scott had. Scott saw Marytwo as greatly responsible for the unhappiness he had felt for years. At the time of the assessment interview, he felt threatened by her because he feared what she might say about him if his case were to go to trial.

The chemically dependent family system. Scott was raised in an environment of physical and emotional neglect. He reported that his father and Marytwo were both alcoholics. On an average day his father would start drinking at about one in the afternoon and keep drinking until he passed out. Heavy drinking was a common pattern among his relatives, and the alcoholism might have been multigenerational. In addition to excessive drinking, both his father and Marytwo smoked "pot" daily and used other drugs, including cocaine.

Weekends were worse from the boy's perspective. On these days his father and Marytwo "partied" or went to bars, leaving Scott outside in the car. When he was younger he had been scared. As he got older he was no longer afraid, but he still did not like his parents' lifestyle: "Well, all I know is they never had time for me, and I didn't like that. Always too busy . . . just always out partying, having fun, getting stoned, too busy."

Scott noted that excessive drug use had taken its toll on both his father and second stepmother: "He [his father] had told me he was burnt. 'Cause he'd tell me one thing, 20 minutes later he'd forget it. Well, that's what he always say, 'Oh, I forgot.' 'Oh, Dad, do this for me.' 'Oh, I forgot.' Ha." The boy remarked further that Marytwo "always had bad nerves. She was always shakin'. She'd drink more beer and smoke more pot than I ever seen anybody do."

When asked about demonstrations of love and affection in the home, Scott reported that neither his father nor Marytwo ever hugged him or acknowledged that he was loved. The home he shared with them was more of a workplace than a home. When asked if he would raise his children the same way, he answered: "I would raise them with affection and love and I would get them into things, you know. 'Cause if you get somebody into baseball, football, and that, they won't have time to worry about drugs and violence and stuff."

Scott reported no contact over the years between him and his natural mother and first stepmother. If Mr. Anders had been physically abusive to his first two wives, as Scott stated was his general pattern with women, their lack of contact with Scott indicates physical as well as emotional neglect. A reasonably responsive parent maintains contact with the child after a divorce to ensure the child's physical and emotional well-being and takes the measures necessary to protect the child from being harmed by an assaultive former mate.

Changes in the Environment before the Homicide

Remarks made at various points in the interview indicated that Marytwo's departure a month before the homicide was a catalyst in the lives of Scott and his father. Scott's father blamed him for Marytwo's flight and told the boy, "Things are going to get a lot worse." The youth perceived his father as a proud man who blamed everything that went wrong on either his wife or his son. When Marytwo left, "He blamed everything on me."

In addition to getting all the blame, Scott was expected to do all the housework and the cooking. Mr. Anders, who was unable to work and to drink because of physical disability, became more involved with drugs. He smoked marijuana "continuously" and snorted cocaine regularly.

> *Heide:* Did things . . . when [Marytwo] left, did they get better or worse?
> *Scott:* Worse.
> *Heide:* Worse? How did they get worse?
> *Scott:* 'Cause I had to do everything.
> *Heide:* Yeah.
> *Scott:* Cleaning and everything. And my dad grumped at me. Grumped at me 24 hours a day. Expected me to do good in school and he yells at me all morning before I go to school. And he's on drugs and the way he was. It'd get worse. He'd threaten my life and everything else. I didn't want nothing to do with him. I was wanting to leave. Then he'd just get stoned and talk about killing me

> and him both, and getting us out of this world. Now, I ain't ready to die yet. . . . And you know what it is, he got depressed, he been depressed, he's depressed, you know, that's how he was . . . was depressed.
>
> *Heide:* Do you have any idea why he was so depressed?
> *Scott:* Why not? He can't work. He can't drink. He couldn't, he was sick. My mother left him. What else is there?
> *Heide:* Sure, O.K.
> *Scott:* And then he started on me and I couldn't handle it.

The Night of the Homicide

On the night of the homicide Scott's father argued with him first about school grades and then, "It was just one thing after another. Everything . . . he'd been griping." The youth admitted that he was really tired of the constant arguing and that he had been upset for a while. At one point in the assessment interview Scott suggested that he had been "mad" before Mr. Anders started arguing with him because he had to wait outside until his father returned home—the boy was not allowed in the house alone. The youth said later in the interview that he really did not mind waiting outside.

Scott's response to his father's yelling at him was to run out of the house, something that he had never done before and believed at the time of the assessment interview that he should not have done. "When he got mad, all I wanted to do was get the hell away from there, but he wasn't going to let me. 'Better not go nowhere.' That's why I hauled ass that night. I was scared, I guess. I just hauled ass, I was upset. My dad was angry and everything else, I just hauled ass."

When he returned to the house a little later, he noticed immediately that "the shotgun was sitting there beside him [boy's father]. He [the father] was smoking a joint," and said, "You shouldn't of done that. I'm gonna have to beat your ass." Scott's response was almost instantaneous. "I just grabbed the gun and shot it." When asked during the interview what was going on in his mind, the youth stated that he didn't know then and didn't want to know.

> *Scott:* That was all he said. That's the only thing he said. You know, I didn't even give him time to flinch. 'Cause he was lighting the joint and I grabbed it [shotgun] and shot him.
> *Heide:* How did he react? Do you remember?
> *Scott:* Well, I thought he was still alive and I thought he was suffering, and he raised me up when I used to go hunting and you shoot a bird or something, he raised me up, don't let nothing suffer.

And I felt bad 'cause he was suffering, you know. They said that first shot killed him. Maybe it did, but he was still suffering in my mind, and I was still . . . I was messed up. I was crying and everything, and I reloaded and shot him again and I grabbed the bullets and the gun, and just took off. But I still don't understand why I shot him. Maybe it's like everybody is saying, you know, 15 years of what kind of life I had. The way he treated me. Everybody said, well, maybe there is just a point, you know. They say everybody got a point that breaks. I don't understand it though.

Scott's description of the family environment was consistent with the portraits presented by other severely abused APOs. Statements he made throughout the assessment interview indicated that the boy placed a high value on telling the truth. He did not try to present himself in a glowing light, openly admitting that he did things wrong and sometimes even aggravated situations by his behavior.

Scott's remarks during police questioning and the assessment interview provided convincing evidence that he was afraid of what his father might do to him as he fired the first shot. He did not claim that he thought at the time that his father was going to shoot him, but he did believe a severe beating was imminent. Scott was terrified of his father, particularly when the man was drunk or "stoned."

The homicide appears to have been an impulsive act committed by a momentarily terrified adolescent who had reached his breaking point after being subjected to years of various types of abuse and neglect. References that the boy made at several points to his changed behavior after the seventh grade, approximately a year and a half before the homicide, were evidence that the murder was an act of desperation. He stopped talking about the abusive family environment after the seventh grade because his attempts to get help from family, friends, and school authorities had failed. Although Scott claimed he had become "proud," it was apparent that he was ashamed of his family life and could no longer bear to discuss it. After four unsuccessful attempts to run away with friends, Scott stopped trying. He also stopped hanging out with the wrong crowd and was trying to be a "better person." He switched from playing an active role to a more passive one, returning home after school to do chores.

When Marytwo left, Scott's situation became increasingly intolerable and depressing to him. On the night of the homicide, after having argued with his father, the boy knew he had no place else to go. When he entered his home, saw the gun, and heard his father's threatening remarks, he felt that he was in imminent danger of bodily injury. He picked up the weapon and immediately shot his father. Afterward he felt remorse.

> *Scott:* If I was gonna plan first-degree murder like everybody's saying, I would have made it look like he killed himself. Or I would have made it look like somebody else killed him. I wouldn't have been at home.
>
> *Heide:* O.K. When you shot him the first time and you still thought he might be alive . . .
>
> *Scott:* He was moving; his head was moving. His body or nothing wasn't moving, but his head was. And he was making a gurgling sound.
>
> *Heide:* Yeah. Did you think of . . . that maybe he could have gotten to the hospital or something like that? Did you ever think of calling the ambulance?
>
> *Scott:* No. I never thought of nothing like that. I wish I did. If I was thinking stuff like that, I would never have picked up the gun.
>
> *Heide:* The second time, you mean?
>
> *Scott:* No, I would have never picked up the gun the first time, if I . . .
>
> *Heide:* I don't understand.
>
> *Scott:* 'Cause you're saying if I was able to think of calling the ambulance and all this I should have been able to think and not pick up the gun!
>
> *Heide:* Period?
>
> *Scott:* Right! And that's what I'm saying, I wasn't able to think to pick up the gun and I wasn't able to think about the ambulance. Maybe he could have been saved the first time.
>
> *Heide:* O.K., I don't think that that's the case, so don't think that I'm suggesting that. I'm just kind of trying to cover all bases.
>
> *Scott:* Yeah. I know what you mean.
>
> *Heide:* Yeah . . . Hey, it's O.K. if you, you're upset. I don't mean to upset you, but that is O.K. All right?
>
> *Scott:* That's all right. I been upset more than once.
>
> *Heide:* If you cry, that's O.K.
>
> *Scott:* No. I'm not gonna cry.

Scott's statement that he fired the second shot to put his father out of his misery was interpreted by the police and the state as evidence of premeditation. Although the youth's explanation was completely consistent with remarks he made later about killing animals for food, it is unclear what he was actually thinking when he fired the second shot. The youth was bewildered by his homicidal behavior and appeared to be searching for a reason to explain it to himself as well as to the police. Scott's remark, whether or not it was an accurate depiction of his thoughts when he fired the second shot, was a very important one. It provided convincing data that this homicide was not characterized by a desire to make his father suffer.

Close examination of Scott's confession made it hard for me to believe that he had consciously planned to kill his father when he fired the second shot. Scott seems to have experienced some dissociation about events surrounding the homicide and may have been in an altered state of consciousness during the killing. The motive for this parricide, like that for Peter Jones's, was more likely to have been situational (low intention to kill at the onset of the interaction) than intentional (high intention to kill).

In light of the boy's previous episode of violent behavior, it was particularly important to ascertain whether Scott had nihilistic traits. What clearly emerged during assessment were indications of life-enhancing qualities rather than destructive forces. One theme that Scott mentioned several times was the importance of love to him in his current and future relationships. Scott did not approve of scaring people, another indicator that he did not derive pleasure from exercising sadistic control over others. The excerpt about kindness quoted below occurred toward the end of the assessment interview. It provided convincing evidence, when examined in light of material presented throughout the entire four-and-a-half-hour period, that Scott was not a nihilistic killer.

> *Heide:* How would you treat girls?
> *Scott:* Oh, I treat 'em nicely.
> *Heide:* Would you? What does "nicely" mean?
> *Scott:* I'd treat 'em like a regular human bein'. Treat 'em kind, you know. Everybody needs to be kind. Damn sure wouldn't call her nothin'. I wouldn't hit 'em.
> *Heide:* O.K. Why is kindness so important?
> *Scott:* 'Cause everybody likes kindness.
> *Heide:* O.K.
> *Scott:* Life is supposed to be kindness.
> *Heide:* Um hmmm.
> *Scott:* Animals, you know.
> *Heide:* Sorry?
> *Scott:* You know, little animals, you know?
> *Heide:* Yeah.
> *Scott:* They kind. You could be an animal, you know. We are animals.
> *Heide:* Yeah.
> *Scott:* Really, we are.
> *Heide:* O.K.

Scott: You know, we can make people go out there and kill rats and stuff like that. But what if you was a rat? You want somebody tryin' killin' you? You know, rats gotta live. He gotta eat.

Heide: Um hmmm.

Scott: And they gotta raise little babies.

Heide: Yeah. O.K.

Scott: It's stupid to call it a rat, but, you know, look at it—look at it that way, you know. Everybody say, "Ah, you're crazy. A rat's a rat. Kill 'em." I ain't gonna kill no rat.

Heide: Yeah. I think that makes sense to me.

Scott: This is the way I feel about it.

Heide: Uh, that's good.

Scott: Now here I'm telling somebody I feel sorry for all the rats and everybody, and I already killed somebody myself.

Heide: O.K.

Scott: Can't bring him back so what can I do? Nothin' I can do. Only thing I can do is try to live right. Start all over.

CASE PROCESSING AND DISPOSITION

At the beginning of the assessment interview, Scott asked (without being solicited) if what he told me could be used against him. Subsequent discussion led me to question his understanding of the Miranda warnings when he waived them on the night of the homicide.[4] He said that the police had "really messed me up that night for something I totally misunderstood, which I thought I understood at the time but I misunderstood it." He explained that when he confessed, he thought anything that he said could be used *for* or against him. Not talking, he thought, would be akin to an admission of guilt.

The boy felt alone that night and did not want a "parent" or other family member with him because "I didn't think I was liked by none of 'em anymore." There was no one whose help or support he felt he could enlist because all his relatives were on his father's side. In addition to feeling alone, he was in shock from the traumatic event. Although he never suggested that the police lied to him or did not read him his rights, he did say that he did not remember hearing them, and he could not recall exactly what he had said to the police in his confession.

Scott's statements at various points indicated that he had negative perceptions of police officers based on personal experience or on what he had seen. Although he did not report that the police that night in any way tried to intimidate him, his negative perceptions of police in general might have induced him to waive his rights. Perhaps the most convincing data about his ignorance of his rights came from his responses to subjects in school. When asked what he had learned about the Constitution in his social studies class, the youth asked if I meant "the Bill of Rights and all that?" His answers to further questions proved that his statement, "I never paid too much attention to it," was all too accurate. Scott knew none of the amendments and did not understand what the privilege against self-incrimination was.

Before the trial defense counsel attempted to have Scott's confession suppressed on the grounds that he was not competent to waive his rights when he confessed. The court denied the motion. Counsel was concerned that statements Scott had made to the police, particularly about firing the second shot, could lead the jury to conclude that the youth was guilty of first-degree murder.

There were two viable defenses in Scott's case—insanity and self-defense. Defense counsel was worried that the jurors might not find arguments under either defense compelling enough to acquit and might convict Scott of murder in the first degree. Defense counsel was reluctant to pursue an insanity defense for two reasons. In the ten years preceding the Anders case no insanity defense had been successfully litigated in this jurisdiction, and in this case the two defense psychiatrists who examined the boy disagreed about his sanity. It seemed unlikely that the evidence would persuade jurors of Scott's insanity at the time of the homicide.

The self-defense strategy was also fraught with problems. Defense counsel would have needed to establish that, at the time of the homicide, Scott was in imminent fear of death or serious injury and that he believed the use of deadly physical force was necessary to protect himself. It seemed unlikely that jurors would find it acceptable for an adolescent to stand his ground and use deadly physical force against his father in the man's home unless it could be shown that safe retreat was impossible.

Documenting the history of abuse to which Scott had been subjected was considered essential to establishing the reasonableness of Scott's belief that he would be seriously injured or killed when he reentered the home, saw the shotgun propped up near his father, and heard the man's threatening words. While defense counsel and the examining mental health experts believed that the boy had been both physically and emotionally abused, the nature and the scope of the physical abuse were difficult to corroborate. Family and friends who had witnessed some acts of physical abuse were reluctant to testify because they were not sure if these incidents were that extreme.

On the advice of defense counsel Scott Anders pleaded to murder in the second degree. He was sentenced to seven years in prison to be followed by ten years' probation. The court ordered that Scott receive psychiatric counseling during his entire probationary period.

Scott served three and a half years of his sentence. He was housed in a maximum-security prison for youthful offenders for about two years. Although he got in trouble twice, staff rated his overall adjustment at this facility as above satisfactory. He completed his GED, attended recommended psychological counseling sessions, and completed many self-improvement programs, including ones in substance abuse, human relations, and positive thinking counseling. He also completed three vocational training programs, attended two others, and held two jobs. Scott was recommended and accepted for transfer to a minimum-security facility after two years.

Scott also made a good adjustment at the second facility, getting into trouble only once. He continued to participate in vocational programs and to work. After he had served two years and eight months of his sentence, the classification team concluded: "This young man has gained a considerable degree of maturity since his initial incarceration and [the team] considers him a good candidate for early termination of sentence." Ten months later, Scott began serving the ten-year probation part of his sentence, which included psychiatric treatment.

Scott initially returned to the southern city where he had lived at the time of the homicide. Shortly thereafter, he relocated to the Midwest to live with his mother, who had visited him for the first time in more than ten years while he was in prison. After experiencing difficulties living with his mother, he considered returning south, but had trouble getting into school. He decided to return to the Midwest. When this book went to press, Scott had completed more than two and a half years of probation without incident.

9 | Patty Smith

PATTY SMITH, a 17-year-old white girl from a middle-class background, was arrested about 32 hours after killing her father. Police charged her with first-degree murder. Within 24 hours police also arrested four of Patty's friends, ages 17 and 18, and charged them with being accessories after the fact. Three—Mary, Tom, and Jim—were charged for disposing of evidence and withholding knowledge of the crime; the fourth, Joe, for lying to police to provide an alibi for Patty.

Investigation by the police and statements by Patty and her co-defendants yielded the following sequence of events. Patty was having difficulty with her father. At one point the idea of killing him occurred as a possible solution, and she asked her friends, "Who would be stupid enough to shoot my father?" Mary said that she would, and Tom and Jim offered to dispose of the body and other evidence. Mary stayed over at Patty's home, and in the middle of the night, as planned, went into the victim's bedroom with a handgun, only to emerge a few minutes later to tell Patty that she could not shoot the victim. Patty said that she would do it herself, but her first attempt was unsuccessful because the handgun jammed. She quickly secured another handgun and shot the victim in the head at about 4 A.M. on Saturday morning, as he lay sleeping. After the shooting the girls went to Tom's trailer, then to a park in search of other friends. There they located Jim, Joe, and another youth, Curtis, and invited these boys back to Patty's house to verify that the victim was actually dead. After observing the body, Curtis and Joe wanted to go back to the park. While Patty was driving them back, Jim and Mary remained behind, showered, and had sex in Patty's bedroom while Mr. Smith lay dead in his bedroom.

When Patty returned (it was still morning), Jim fixed pizza and drinks for the three of them, and Patty made three phone calls. She told her father's secretary, Joy, that she had gotten in a fight with her father and he had left. Patty asked Joy to handle the payroll and said she would come by the office later to pick up her car and her driver's license, which her father had taken away from her recently as a disciplinary measure. Patty called the real estate agent next because the house was listed for sale and Patty did not want it shown. Finally she called her mother, who had been divorced from Mr. Smith for several years and lived about a thousand miles away. Patty told her mother that her father had left following a fight with her and that she was O.K. Jim also assured Mrs. Smith that he would take care of Patty.

The three retrieved the house key from the realty company, then went to Tom's trailer. Tom accompanied Patty, Mary, and Jim to Mr. Smith's office. Within a few minutes the four drove off in Mr. Smith's two cars. The youths gassed up the cars and spent Saturday afternoon picking up or checking on friends and driving around. They returned to Patty's neighborhood to discover that it was swarming with police. As evening passed into night, Patty took refuge in Tom's trailer, leaving only to drop Mary and another girl off at a party. When Mary returned Jim advised Patty to take the back roads out of the neighborhood and go to a nearby city. He gave her the phone number of a pay phone on the corner and told her when to call in. Jim and Tom disposed of Mr. Smith's wallet, the murder weapon, and the empty casings.

Patty and Mary checked into a motel in the city and made a series of phone calls to friends from 11 P.M. to 3 A.M., when they went to bed. The following morning, the girls ordered room service, and Patty made a few more calls to friends to see what was happening back home. Patty was talking on the phone when the police knocked on the door.

The grand jury indicted Patty as an adult on first-degree murder charges. Two months after the indictment the assistant state attorney prosecuting the case announced the state's intention to seek the death penalty. About three and a half months after the five youths were arrested, the state prosecutor filed new charges of conspiracy to commit first-degree murder against Mary. Mary had faced a maximum sentence of five years for being an accessory after the fact, with state guidelines calling for a "non–state prison" penalty, but she now faced a maximum of 35 years including prison time. At the same time that the state was upgrading her charges, the three boys, who had also been formally charged as accessories to the murder, were given the opportunity to testify in Patty Smith's murder trial in exchange for one-to-three-year probation terms to be decided by the judge after the trial. The boys accepted the state's proposal. One month before Patty's trial, Mary agreed to testify against her in return for the state's recommending that she serve only one year of prison time.

THE CLINICAL EVALUATION

The assessment of Patty Smith is based on clinical interviews with the defendant and her mother, plus review of hundreds of pages of pertinent materials. My seven-hour interview of the adolescent, conducted at the request of defense counsel, occurred over the course of two consecutive evenings. It was almost five months after the homicide when I interviewed Patty in private in the adult women's jail. Within a week of examining her, I spent five hours following up with her mother.

Before speaking with Patty I studied 14 police incident reports and ten supplemental investigation reports containing police interviews with the codefendants and 35 other individuals. These 35 people included Patty's friends and classmates and a few of their parents, relatives of Mr. and Mrs. Smith, Mr. Smith's employees, staff at the realty company, one of Mr. Smith's former girlfriends, service personnel who had contact with the youths after the homicide, the newspaper delivery girl, bank personnel, an employee of the diet center where Patty was enrolled, a man who had recently sold Mr. Smith a camper, two neighbors, and a psychic who advised Mr. Smith about financial affairs.

In addition to police reports, I examined statements Patty made to jail deputies and to defense counsel staff and defense notes from interviews with six of Patty's relatives, two of her classmates, and two former neighbors. I also perused her medical records, the psychological self-report data collected by the weight management center, and a report of a child abuse incident dated approximately one year before the homicide.

Prior to the trial I was able to review photographs and correspondence between Patty and her mother both before and after the homicide; correspondence between Mr. and Mrs. Smith; and defense counsel notes from interviews with six individuals who had worked for Mr. Smith. Before drawing final conclusions and making recommendations, I reviewed Patty's high school records, Mrs. Smith's medical records, and depositions from Patty's four codefendants.

BEHAVIORIAL OBSERVATIONS

Patty was about 5′6″ tall and somewhere between 50 (her estimate) and 100 pounds overweight, and had a severe case of acne at the time of the assessment interview. She had a speech impediment that made her a little difficult to understand at times and appeared to cause her mild discomfort. The girl's answers to questions showed that her long-term and short-term memory processes were good. There was no evidence of hallucinations or delusions.

Patty was alert throughout the two evenings and took the interview seriously. Her concentration was generally good. She was, however, occasionally distracted by passersby, voices outside, ants crawling on her towel, and the need to call her mother. Patty gave the impression that interviews by her attorney, a psychologist, and myself were an imposition.

Patty appeared fairly relaxed throughout the interviews. Rapport was easily and quickly established, and she related in a warm and trusting way. Her eye contact was typically very good, and her mood generally good throughout the interviews. At times, however, she seemed angry, particularly when describing her father and her home situation.

Patty made some attempt to answer every question that was asked. She was reluctant to discuss abuse by her father at length, and her discomfort increased when questions focused on determining whether she had been sexually abused.

PERSONALITY ASSESSMENT

Patty perceived at I-level 3, which is relatively low on the continuum of personality development. Of the 75 adolescent murderers I have assessed, about 40 percent perceived at I-level 3. Patty was, however, the only APO among the six who fit the profile of the severely abused child to perceive at that level. Her low level of development was critical to understanding motivation in this case.

Patty thought very concretely and in terms of external dimensions (places, events, and surface characteristics). Her self-definition was restricted and her self-esteem low. She was relatively unaware of the role that such internal dimensions as needs, feelings, and motives played in her life and in the lives of others. She had little motivation to integrate, interpret, or resolve information about herself and others, and was unable to empathize with others. Patty was not capable of long-term planning.

Patty did not see herself as really responsible for her behavior. She had not internalized a set of values that she used to evaluate her behavior. Because she did not see herself as having choices, she did not typically feel guilt or remorse for her behavior. She was essentially concerned with power fields, viewing herself and others in relation to who had power and searching for rules, formulas, and techniques to get what she wanted. For example, she saw her father as a very powerful man. She believed that he had an "in" with the police and could influence other people and institutions in the community.

Among level 3 individuals, there are three behavioral subtypes.[1] Patty's behavioral response was that of the passive conformist. She saw herself as inferior to others and had a high need for social approval. She tended to overestimate the power of others, conforming to people who made explicit demands of her. Patty described herself in conventional, socially desirable terms and saw her involvement in antisocial behavior as the result of peer pressure, not as acceptable behavior. She was responsive to adults and authority figures and wanted to do right. The range of her emotions was restricted to anger, sadness, hurt, and fear; the relationship of emotions to behavior was minimized.

SOCIAL HISTORY

Family constellation and relationships. Patty was the only child born to John Smith and his second wife, Theresa Baxter Smith. Mr. Smith had five children from his first marriage. Patty's half-siblings (one brother and four sisters) ranged in age from about 33 to 37 at the time of the patricide. Patty was not close to any of them and had very negative feelings for all except the youngest, Joan, who apparently made some effort to keep in touch with Patty before the homicide.

When she was a young child Patty's half-brother, Harold, lived with her and her parents. She described Harold as just like her father —physically and psychologically abusive to her mother. Patty believed that all her half-siblings were aware of the spouse abuse.

Patty's memory for dates was fuzzy. She described living in the Midwest until she moved to the South. She thought that her parents may have separated when she was in the sixth grade (she was about

11 or 12) and been divorced when she was in the seventh grade (12 or 13). She remembered that her father went to another state for about two months and that he moved out to establish a residence with Judith Thompson, a woman he met while away. After Mr. Smith moved out, Patty lived with her mother in the Smiths' beautiful home with a pool until Mr. Smith stopped paying the mortgage, when they moved to "a poor apartment." They remained there until summer 1984 (between Patty's eighth and ninth grades), when Mrs. Smith moved to one of the Mid-Atlantic states. Patty spent about a month of that summer with Mr. Smith, returned to her mother's residence to get her belongings, and moved back south to live with her father and his girlfriend.

Patty explained that she decided to leave her mother's residence because her mother had already had open-heart surgery once and was "due to have a second one with no chance of coming out of it." She moved in with her father to give her mother more time to live. "In your mind and different people talking to you, raising a teenager would give her too much trouble, too much stress, maybe you could add more time to her life."

Patty remained with her father from 1984 until she killed him in 1987. Judith Thompson left Mr. Smith in October 1985, about 16 months before the homicide. Although Patty and Judith did not get along, her home life got worse when Judith left. Patty had to do the cooking, and Mr. Smith blamed Patty for Judith's leaving and "took it out on [her]." Patty reported that her father sexually assaulted her, drank more, and got more into one-night stands with women after Judith's departure.

Despite her father's abuse, Patty did not return to her mother because he had threatened to kill them both if she did. She had not even told her mother about the abuse because she believed her father's claim that such news would kill the sickly woman. She also worried that her mother might not believe her.

School. Patty liked school and her teachers and had had problems with only a few. In the tenth and eleventh grades almost all her teachers were male, and she claimed that she could learn better from them because they were stricter. She said she got along fine with "the other kids."

Patty reported that her grades were B's and A's "if I tried," and tended to go down when there were problems at home. She claimed that she got F's in physical education because she did everything to get out of it. She didn't like wearing shorts because she had bruises on her legs, but didn't tell her attorney "the truth" about her reason for avoiding physical education because she found it hard to talk to him. The tone of his voice made her think he didn't believe her at times.

Patty's statements suggested extensive extracurricular involvement. She was the basketball manager for both the junior varsity and varsity teams for both boys and girls. As the basketball manager, she had two assistant managers working with her. In addition, Patty was the head track manager, with ten assistant managers below her. Her four codefendants were all assistant managers.

Patty noted that before eleventh grade she was rarely in trouble. She was suspended for three days in ninth grade for forging her teacher's name on a pass and in tenth grade for skipping school. In eleventh grade she stopped going to homeroom and regularly skipped her sixth-period astronomy class.

Work. Patty worked for about three months at her father's water treatment plant. As a phone solicitor she worked from after school until about nine o'clock and received minimum wage and a bonus when she "sold" a free water test. The work was unpleasant because her father would bring their personal life into the office. He would not allow her to work at another job; it was "his office or nothing."

Alcohol and drug abuse. Patty stated that she did not drink often, "maybe twice a year," and had never been drunk. She was about 14 or 15 when she first tried alcohol, at a party she gave in her mother's absence. She denied any drug usage.

Friends. Throughout the interview Patty defined scores of people as her friends and did not discriminate between friends and acquaintances. She saw her codefendants Mary, Tom, and Jim as the "wrong crowd." When Patty started hanging around with them in eleventh grade, she started skipping school and getting into trouble. Patty described Jim and Mary as leaders; Tom as a leader, but "in some cases, he can be a follower." She saw herself and Joe as followers. According to Patty, Jim was lying when he said that the whole murder plan was done to her command.

Activities. Patty enjoyed art and had acquired some skill in oil painting, particularly painting animals and nature scenes. She liked going to the mall, watching sunsets on the beach, going for a drive, sitting and talking (especially with Jim), managing and coaching the basketball and track teams, watching soap operas, playing video games, and going to the movies with her friends. Action-packed movies and books in particular interested her. Her interest in romance books waned after her incarceration.

Patty had played the organ when younger. She enjoyed listening to music, including heavy metal as well as soft rock and country. She did not feel that the lyrics had any negative effect on her. In heavy rock, artists were "really singing about life, about what goes on in the world, what drugs can do to you, having boyfriends and breaking up."

Sexual history. Patty claimed she could take sex or leave it alone. Sex was "something you enjoy," "you and him have a commitment, he cares about you and you care about him, a small commitment." She reported first having sexual intercourse when she was in eighth grade, with "a guy I liked." She explained that "you're curious the first time." She reported having had sexual intercourse with about 12 partners, though only one was before her father began sexually assaulting her.

Patty told me that she had not received formal instruction about sex. She learned about sex from her friends. She did not use birth control, but claimed the boys used "rubbers." She stated that she had never been pregnant. Although Patty stated that all of her sexual encounters except with her father were "consensual," at least one involved a person who was considerably older than she. This man, who was in his twenties, was the chaperon at her fifteenth and sixteenth birthday parties and her best friend's brother.

Prior delinquent activity. Patty had never been arrested before the homicide. She had run away on five or six occasions but had always been caught and returned to her father. The girl recalled getting into trouble and being disciplined by her father (grounded) for "doing do-nuts" in the car on the beach with Jim and damaging the motor mount on her car. The girl also acknowledged truancy and attempted forgery of her father's checks.

Self. Patty described herself as someone who "can help people," is "good to be friends with," and "can hand out advice to those who need it." When asked to discuss the things that she really liked about herself, Patty said, "I'm easygoing, have a good spirit . . . you can come to me and tell me your problems." The girl suggested that her mother may have confided her problems to her. She named three people, none of them codefendants, to whom she could open up. When asked about what she did not like about herself, Patty said, "I don't like that I am a follower" because that's how "you get yourself

in trouble" and "sometimes you have to take the lead in your life."
She also said, "I'm scared to speak my opinion, to say what I think is
right," because she was afraid of losing people.

Future orientation (goals, interests). Patty had wanted to pursue art
as a career, but since the homicide has become increasingly interested
in counseling as an occupation and presently dreams of opening up
a residential counseling center for abused kids in California. She intends to get her GED, take college courses, and major in counseling
so she can have her "place on the beach where teenagers (under 17,
problem people) can sit out with their friends," with an "art shop on
the side."

Patty did not see herself as getting married because it seemed to
her that "all of them end up in hurt" and divorce. She did wish to have
children and wanted a girl and a boy. She believed that she would be
a "pretty good parent" because of what she had gone through. She
would raise her children differently from the way she had been raised,
making sure that they had guidelines.

Health. Patty had relatively good health. She had trouble with
her ears and a back injury, both documented. She sustained the back
injury when her father kicked her.

Patty had contemplated suicide before the homicide and had once
attempted suicide by taking an over-the-counter drug to induce sleeping. While in jail she tried to kill herself with an office staple. She did
not pose a serious suicidal risk at the time of the assessment interview.
Patty believed that her suicide would kill her mother, about whom she
cared deeply. If correctional staff continued to pay her some attention
and be supportive, her half-hearted gestures toward self-destruction
would cease.

Adjustment in jail. Patty was not afraid of the inmates and considered most of the guards her friends. Patty's mother shared my belief
that she seemed relatively happy inside the facility.

INTERVIEW WITH PATTY'S MOTHER

Mrs. Smith, whom I interviewed six days after my
assessment interview with Patty, was on antidepressant medication
but was very alert and cooperative throughout the interview. Her

good memory was helpful in reconstructing some of Patty's history. She appeared fairly at ease and in control of herself, although she did smoke about seven or eight cigarettes and cried twice.

Before interviewing Mrs. Smith, I doubted the extent of Patty's alleged victimization and her depiction of her father. After talking to the girl's mother, virtually no doubt remained in my mind that Patty's allegations were truthful. Mrs. Smith remained in an abusive relationship with Mr. Smith for 17 years before she divorced him. Her statements corroborated Patty's stories that Mrs. Smith was a victim of physical, verbal, sexual, and psychological abuse. She described her former husband as follows:

> [John] was a very violent man, a very physical man, verbally very abusive, he used every filthy word that was known. . . . Every other word was "Fuck," you were a "whore," you were a "tramp," you were a "slut," every other word, "F you." . . . Also with his hands, I have been beat up several times, more times than I care to remember, last time, probably the worst, I was black and blue from knee to hip, he damaged my sciatic nerve, I went and had shots . . . until I couldn't have any more, so I could walk.

Mr. Smith had pulled a gun on her "I don't know how many times. He always went for a gun, very easy, very quick, he cocked it and only shot at me once." She sustained injuries after Mr. Smith kicked her because "I didn't get a pair of shoes out of the closet fast enough." On another occasion, her former husband had backed his car up against hers to prevent her escape and appeared intent on killing her.

> [John] backed me up in a corner. He had already slit my hand with the keys to the car, laughing because he had backed me in. He cut my hand open with the car keys, he literally sliced it up. He backed me in a corner with a knife above my head and he was coming down with it. I came up with my knee and I kneed him. He did back off. Patty at the . . . time was out on the street screaming for help.

Mrs. Smith spoke at length of the difficulty of placating her former husband. She related, for example, that Mr. Smith wanted his supper on time, but that she never knew when that would be. "If he came in, and it wasn't ready, you got it. If it was, and he wanted to relax with a drink, then he was upset too."

Some data indicated that Mr. Smith may have been an alcoholic who had long periods of sobriety interspersed with periods of heavy drinking. When he drank, he "always drank pretty regular to the point of getting drunk" and would get "very mean." She recalled his making a "funny statement" after his common-law wife Judith left. "You don't think I could ever be an alcoholic?" Mrs. Smith thought that Mr. Smith might have used tranquilizers from the time of their separation, approximately four years before his death. Sedatives were found in the body.

Mrs. Smith's description of her former husband was consistent with Lowen's depiction of the narcissist.[2] Lowen, a psychiatrist and psychoanalyst by training, identified five types of narcissists. Mrs. Smith's description of Mr. Smith placed him as a psychopath who sometimes slipped over into the paranoid personality—the two furthest points along the continuum of narcissism. The psychopath considers himself superior to others and often expresses contempt for them. His lack of feeling toward others is extreme and he has a tendency to act out antisocially. His ability to manipulate people is keen; his ability to tolerate frustration is minimal. The paranoid personality distrusts others and is suspicious of them, often believing that others are conspiring against him.

The narcissist is absorbed with his image and invests himself in maintaining an image rather than in being who he is. Mrs. Smith made the following observation about her husband: "[John] did everything for looks. Big house, nice furniture, nice cars, boat, if he never went out on the boat—fact was, it was for show—this is what he was and, you close those doors, he was a terrific salesman, he was good at selling himself until you got to know him."

The narcissist denies his feelings and puts an exaggerated emphasis on winning. The denial of feeling gives the narcissist the license to do whatever he desires because of his insensitivity to others' rights and needs. By exercising power and control over others and situations, the narcissist protects himself from sadness and fear, which make him feel particularly vulnerable. Mrs. Smith described her former husband as "a very strong man over weak people, not strong people." She said her husband kept her isolated from others to ensure his dominance and her dependence. He always carried both a gun and a knife on his person. She saw him as a coward because he would not fistfight someone unless it was somebody he could beat. "If [John] drank, he wanted sex. He would then demand it. I used to try and get him like to pass out. I'd watch TV or I would stay out in the family room. One night he slammed the TV off. 'This is my house, my TV, and you'll go to bed when I say so.' . . . It was more like I submitted."

Mr. Smith's obsession with controlling others included his employees. If he could not control an employee, he did not want that worker around. "If you worked for him, he wanted you around 24 hours a day. He cross-checked on people. He would spend all evening calling [his employees to check up on them]."

Mrs. Smith was terrified of her husband from the early days of their marriage. Her methods of coping were endurance and the use of tranquilizers. Sometimes she fled from her husband, taking Patty with her if she could get to the child, and stayed at her sister's house.

Mrs. Smith had had a serious heart problem from childhood. Medical records confirmed the gravity of her illness and the limitations it imposed on her. When Patty was about six years old, Mrs. Smith had her first open-heart surgery. After returning home for four weeks, the woman was hospitalized again with hepatitis. At this time her husband was barred from the room, according to Mrs. Smith, because she had attempted to swallow "a bunch of Valium because he wouldn't leave me alone." A few weeks before the homicide Mrs. Smith was again hospitalized for open-heart surgery; its prognosis was uncertain.

The home environment was so stressful that at one point Mrs. Smith had "a mental breakdown" and had to be hospitalized for a short period. She used Valium extensively from the time Patty was 6 until she was 13. Mrs. Smith's addiction to Valium made her unresponsive to Patty's emotional needs. She said Patty's third- and fifth-grade teachers had thought that Patty was an unloved and unwanted child. After meeting Mrs. Smith, these teachers did not understand what was going on, because it was apparent to them that she did want and love her little girl. What these teachers didn't know was that "I was not there when I was on Valium." Hence Patty was raised by one, if not two, parents who were chemically dependent.

Mrs. Smith had been aware of her husband's emotional abuse of their daughter. She described it as constant. "He took something you cared about and then destroyed it." Mr. Smith had bought Patty a phone and a radio; one night he got angry and smashed them. The verbal abuse is clear from this statement: "If anybody was around, it was, 'This is my baby girl,' and 'I am proud of her.' As soon as they walked out the door, he would switch, 'you pig,' 'you fat slob,' 'you slut,' and 'fuck,' every other word."

Patty's mother had also seen some of the physical altercations between father and daughter. She described an incident that occurred a few months before the homicide in which Mr. Smith became angry because a car hose had sprung a leak and "raised a wrench as if he were going to hit her [Patty]." Although he did not actually hit the girl with the wrench, "he did slap her with both hands and hard."

Mrs. Smith related that she knew a complaint about physical abuse had been made to the state social services agency. The woman remarked, as her daughter had previously, that Mr. Smith always made friends with the sheriff or local police authorities and "made you look like an idiot" if you said anything against him.

Mrs. Smith had no trouble believing that her former husband could have sexually assaulted their daughter to punish Patty and, even more so, to punish Mrs. Smith "because he couldn't control me any more." Patty's description of the circumstances leading up to her father's raping her vaginally and anally sounded to Mrs. Smith like her husband's style. Mrs. Smith portrayed her husband as a promiscuous man who hated women. Other remarks she made convinced me that Mr. Smith was capable of committing the acts that his daughter alleged he had committed. Mrs. Smith related that Mr. Smith made love "to" her rather than with her, and used explicit and degrading language when performing sexually. He was obsessed with anal sex, interested in such sexual instruments as vibrators and dildos, and absorbed in pornography. Toward the end of their marriage, he became increasingly "masochistic."

Mrs. Smith said that Patty's material needs were not adequately met by her husband. She bought all of Patty's clothes because her husband would not. Even though her former husband and daughter lived in an expensive home, and Patty had her own car at 16, Mrs. Smith maintained that Patty had very little and was not "a rich kid" at all.

Mrs. Smith was unaware of the extent of the abuse inflicted on her daughter because Patty did not talk about it. It seemed to Mrs. Smith that Patty had come to assume the chores of a wife in the Smith household in recent years—cooking, buying groceries, and so on. When she visited during the holiday season, approximately two months before the homicide, Mrs. Smith felt an eeriness in the house; Patty and Mr. Smith would not stay in the same room.

Mrs. Smith's relationship with Patty was good when Patty was young, but deteriorated during the years when her Valium usage was high. As a teenager Patty adopted a protective stance toward her mother. Mrs. Smith said that Mr. Smith would not allow Patty to come live with her and used their child to maintain control over her. Patty told her mother about two months before the homicide that she intended to leave home as soon as she turned 18, an event that was only eight months away.

Mrs. Smith did not believe that her daughter was the mastermind behind this crime and had some question as to who really shot Mr. Smith. Patty's mother was perplexed that her former husband did not wake up during the incident, because she knew him to be a very light sleeper.

Mrs. Smith was supportive of Patty. After the homicide she made arrangements to relocate to the city where her daughter was incarcerated pending trial. She talked with Patty daily and visited weekly. Her willingness to testify was never in question, and she saw her testimony as critical. Mrs. Smith claimed that she was recovering from open-heart surgery despite the homicide, but expressed concern that because of the stress she might not survive the trial.

MOTIVATIONAL DYNAMICS BEHIND THE HOMICIDE

In this homicide we again see an abused child who has been pushed beyond her limits. The involvement of one friend as a coconspirator and three others as accessories makes the case of Patty Smith different. Patty's behavior, though at first shocking, is understandable in the context of this adolescent's level of personality development and the deteriorating conditions in the home environment.

Patty's Environment

From the time Patty was born her life was both horrifying and terrifying. Patty's recollections, corroborated by her mother, show that she had been exposed to a broad array of psychopathology. She had seen the physical, verbal, and psychological abuse of her mother by her father and half-brother and other extreme forms of violence; she herself had been a victim of physical, verbal, and psychological abuse, and of forcible rape perpetrated by her father. Her father's possible alcoholism and her mother's drug addiction and debilitating illness made Patty the victim of emotional neglect and emotional incest as well. Physical neglect was also present because of the mother's failure to protect Patty from her abusive former husband.

Physical and psychological abuse of Mrs. Smith. Patty remarked that from the time that she could remember she had seen "Dad kicking Mom, Dad hitting Mom, Dad throwing glass at Mom, Dad shooting at Mom." Her half-brother, Mr. Smith's only son, had also physically abused her mother: "What I lived through, either my brother would start a fight with my mom, start hitting her and all. My dad would finish, and my brother would go to his room, shut the door, turn the stereo on so he couldn't hear, or my dad would start and my brother would join in and they both would finish on my mom."

When asked how she felt when her father was beating her mother, Patty replied, "Helpless, because I knew I couldn't do anything." The girl believed that, if she went into the room where her mother was being assaulted and tried to help her, she would also be beaten.

Patty witnessed other episodes of extreme violence. Mr. Smith's business building was firebombed and burned to the ground. According to Mrs. Smith, an investigation suggested that the arsonists "were more after the man than they were the business," and Patty was put on restrictions at school for her protection.

Physical abuse of Patty.   Patty had been physically "abused on and off most of my life." If Mr. Smith's common-law wife was late, she said, he would beat his daughter up, "start slapping me around. Start kicking, hitting."

Patty had lived in fear ever since she could remember because her father carried a gun or had one nearby 24 hours a day. "It makes you scared. Scared if you do something really wrong; any time he can just whip the gun out and shoot you." He pulled the gun on her once.

Patty felt that there was nothing she could do when her father verbally abused her or accused her falsely. If she protested, "All I would get was a backhand across the mouth or a fist in the mouth or end up getting things worse 'cause I knew what was coming," referring to physical abuse and sexual attack. Her friends witnessed some of the physical abuse, as did her mother.

On one occasion Patty reported her father's physical abuse to the state social services agency. Her remarks indicate her loss of faith in the ability of the system to help her and in her own ability to escape the situation.

> I went to [the agency] once and that time all I had was a cut over my eye, and they said there was no evidence. But I found out later that before [the agency] worker talked to me, she had talked to my dad, even before she saw and talked to me, she talked to my dad. As soon as I walked in, she sat me down and she goes, "There is no evidence" and she goes, "You have to go back with your dad." And she said, "By the way, your dad will be here to pick you up after school." And I was really scared, if I went and tried to find help that would always get back to Dad, and Dad would always be free. He would always be able to find me and I would just end up going back to him, and it would end up being worse than it ever had been. Every time I ran away he always found me. And every time I ran away it wasn't ten minutes after he found out that I was gone,

there was always a APB out on my car. I have like, five or six runaways on my juvenile record.

Patty ran away more often once she got her car, but her father would always find her. When asked where she would go, the youth said that she would go to a friend's house because she really did not know where else to go: "I couldn't go to my mom's. He said if I ever went back up to Mom's, he would kill me and Mom both, and Dad is the type of guy to do it."

Verbal and additional psychological abuse of Patty. Instances of Mr. Smith's verbally abusive remarks abounded. In addition to cursing her, Patty said her father would say things "that would tear down your confidence, tear you down, make you feel like you weren't worth doing anything." Mr. Smith told her that she was nothing but "fat and sloppy," that all she did was lie around on the couch and eat chocolates. "He told me I was sleeping with everybody in my class and how I was nothing but a whore, a slut, and all that." The girl said that her father would tear down her friends, insisting that they were only using her. He would also belittle her paintings. Once he scoffed at a painting that she did, telling her it looked like something a little child had done, and threw it in the trash.

Patty as a victim of incest/forcible rape. Patty was reluctant to talk about sexual assaults by her father. The first assault that she related occurred when she was 14 and living with Mr. Smith and his common-law wife, Judith. Her father became angry because she had been on the phone too long, an argument ensued, and the two wound up fighting in Patty's bedroom.

> *Patty:* He pushed me down on the bed, and he kept on saying it's all my fault for everything that's been happening, the divorce with Mom and all. Sometimes I would think it was my fault. Sometimes I would. Then he kept on saying it was my fault that the way Mom was, she's taking so much Valium and all. He kept on saying he'd have to teach me a lesson, so I won't be destroying people's lives anymore. And he pushed me down on the bed, and I was wearing jeans, I kept on asking what he was doing, he said, "I'm going to give you your punishment for breaking up our marriage, and trying to ruin my life" and all that. And I just looked up at him, kept on trying . . . every time I tried to fight him off, he kept on hitting me and slapping me. And the next thing I knew, he had my pants off, even with me fighting him. And it seems like even if I was going to fight with him, it wouldn't do any good. It

got worse if I kept fighting. And the next thing, he didn't have his pants on, and he just had sex. He kept on hitting me and repeating, "This is your punishment."

Heide: How long did the whole thing last?

Patty: I don't know, I didn't keep track of it.

Heide: At that point, aside from thinking, how could he do this to his own daughter [a statement that Patty had made in reference to the sexual assaults during the assessment interview the evening before], is there anything else that went through your mind?

Patty: I was real scared and didn't know what to do. I just laid there after he got done, he left, and I just laid there on the bed crying.

Heide: And then what did you do?

Patty: I stayed in my room almost all of the night, didn't come out for dinner, didn't come out for anything. Then he came in, him and Judith came in, and was lovey-dovey like nothing happened.

Heide: To you?

Patty: Yeah.

Heide: Did he tell you not to tell anybody?

Patty: Yeah. He said that, if I ever told anybody what was going on, that he would kill me, and if I went to Mom, that he would make sure Mom got killed.

Patty reported that the sexual assaults did not happen often at first, but occurred more frequently after Judith left because Mr. Smith blamed Patty for Judith's leaving. It seemed to Patty that at some point Mr. Smith began raping her "once a week or something like that." Patty indicated that intercourse with her father, unlike sex with her boyfriends, hurt. She stated that her father had anal intercourse with her three or four times, and that these acts were "really painful."

He wanted dinner on the table as soon as he walked in the door, he could walk in any time, and I almost had supper ready, couple of minutes until it was done, he came in, and he was mad that I didn't have supper on the table. We got into a big argument, and he started hitting me and all. I had a pair of handcuffs. He had a couple of like leather straps and all he had kept in his bedroom [Mr. Smith had a box in which he kept sexual paraphernalia]. And we were fighting, fought and fought, an hour yelling back and forth, he kept on slapping me, and I kept fighting him that night, kept hitting him back, telling him to leave me alone. I guess because I was fighting him, I really got it bad. He pushed me in my bedroom . . . he put the handcuffs on my hand so I couldn't move, and he had my feet strapped down to the bed to the end of the bedpost. He ripped my shirt off. He took my pants down and he had sex with, intercourse, and he kept on saying, "This is your punishment, this is what you get for not having dinner on the table when I come into the house." And I kept on hitting him and he goes, "Well, since you're going

to fight me this time, I guess I'll have to make your punishment worse."
And he undid my hands, handcuffs, and so he flipped me over, I was
twisted. I was lying on my stomach halfway and my back halfway. My
feet were still strapped, and he put my hands back up on the bed, and
he bent my feet, and the next thing, I felt real sharp pain and having anal
[inter]course. I kept on trying to kick him, but my feet were not doing
it because they were strapped. I kept on trying to buck him off, nothing
would, nothing would get him off. So I finally gave up. I decided that if I
quit fighting, then I wouldn't get it so bad.

The chemically dependent family system.   Patty's mother was chemi-
cally dependent and emotionally unavailable to her from the time
Patty was about six. Both Patty and Mrs. Smith characterized Mrs.
Smith as a "zombie" during the seven years she was addicted to
Valium. "She [Mrs. Smith] would sit there and watch TV and that was
it. She would fix dinner, but you couldn't talk to her."

With Mr. Smith, the evidence of a problem with alcohol and perhaps later with tranquilizers, as discussed earlier, though not de-
finitive, was strongly suggestive. Test responses given by Patty were
consistent with the responses of children of alcoholics.[3]

Changes in the Environment before the Homicide

When Mr. Smith's common-law wife left his house, approximately
16 months before the homicide, conditions went from bad to worse.
Patty's father had kept a tight rein on Judith, as he had on his former
wife. When she left, Mr. Smith tightened his hold on Patty.

It was like she [Judith] was all there was in his life. There was no outside
activity and that was what he expected from me. Just go to school and
come straight home and that was it, have no friends or anything else because that's what he had. When she took off, they had a fight one night,
and she took off while he went to go calm down, and I couldn't hardly
go to school during the first three months she was gone. He didn't want
me out of his sight. He didn't want me to have friends over or call anybody. He was calling the house every ten minutes. And he really got bad
after she left. He really got worse after she left, more than I have ever
seen him.

The Environment at the Time of the Homicide

At the time of the homicide, Patty's mother had just had open-
heart surgery and was recuperating far away. Before the surgery, there

was considerable doubt whether Mrs. Smith would survive or how far she would recover. Although Patty made several efforts to secure help from others, each one failed. Her attempt to get help from the state agency was unsuccessful, and her claim that she had received no help from a weight counselor to whom she reported sexual abuse was verified. Two of Mr. Smith's employees indicated that Patty had told them of incidents of covert sexual abuse and they had done nothing to help her. Patty had told these two women that Mr. Smith used to converse with her in the bathroom while she was in the shower and had once made her watch while a woman performed fellatio on him.

Patty's efforts to escape the family situation had also failed. Her attempts to run away had been futile, her attempts at suicide half-hearted. With Judith's departure she became increasingly desperate and isolated. In the week before the homicide her feelings of isolation intensified when Mr. Smith took her car away as a punishment for misbehavior. The car symbolized a temporary freedom from an increasingly intolerable environment. Her father called her repeatedly at home, met her at the bus, and made it clear that her friends were not welcome at their house.

Of critical importance, given Patty's personality development, was the fact that her friends were willing to support the idea of patricide. When Patty asked her friends, "half-joking, half-serious," "Who would be stupid enough to kill my father?" she was desperate. There seemed no other way out but murder. If her friends had laughed and told her to forget such a stupid idea, she probably would have.

On the basis of Patty's 45-minute description of the homicide, there was indeed a plan, although a poorly conceived one, to kill Mr. Smith. Guns were readily available; Mr. Smith was a gun enthusiast and had many firearms throughout the home. Much was left to happenstance, as was consistent with Patty's level of personality development. The homicide appeared to be almost farcical. Patty had given no thought, for example, to disposal of the body—she figured the boys would do it. She had no plans to get away and had not thought about getting caught. She figured that she would just "let the house go" and live in her car, taking some food from the house for her and her dog, until she could save up some money to get a place for her and her friend Mary.

When Mary, who had agreed to shoot Mr. Smith, "chickened out," Patty was flooded with anxiety. She seemed to feel a need to go through with the plan out of desperation, "to end the hurt," and also to get the social approval that she so badly wanted from her friends. As she stood in her father's bedroom the second time, after an aborted first attempt to kill him with a malfunctioning gun, she reported flashbacks of what he had done to her and to her mother and pulled the trigger, shooting him in the head.

> I stood there for seven minutes, cause he didn't get shot until 4:07, . . . and I thought what he did to Mom, I thought of all the trouble he caused me, pain he has put me through, and actually I don't remember pulling the trigger. I just remember the shot firing and the sound that he made. I don't remember my hand pulling the trigger. All I remember, what I was thinking and the time on the clock.

Patty remembered pulling the trigger on the gun that jammed, but not on the one that actually killed her father. While the escalating stress may have in fact produced a dissociative reaction, the facts did not suggest that she was insane at the time of the homicide under the state standard, the M'Naghten test. The attempt to shoot the first time was dispositive on this issue. She intended to kill her father, clearly knew what she was doing, and, from all available evidence, knew that this conduct was against the law.

Interviews with Patty and her mother provided a consistent picture of the victim, Mr. Smith, and of the home environment. There was clear evidence corroborated by Patty's mother to indicate that Patty had witnessed events to which no one, and especially no child, should be exposed: physical and psychological abuse of her mother and other forms of extreme violence. Her statements and her mother's described a child who had been a victim of physical, verbal, and psychological abuse by her father, and emotional neglect by both parents. Her statements about sexual victimization were credible because they were consistent with other sexual assault victims', with the portrait Mrs. Smith painted of her former husband, and with others' reports about him. Patty's sexual victimization could be more appropriately characterized as brutal rape than sexual abuse.

This homicide would be classified as intentional, defined by high intention to kill and low desire to hurt the victim. Patty's intention was to have her father killed on the night of the homicide, but there was no evidence that she derived satisfaction from making him suffer.

Patty seemed to be overwhelmed by life and survived for years by passively conforming to whoever had power. She perceived herself as helpless to control her life. At the same time, she viewed her friends, whose approval she desperately sought, as the "ones who call the shots." That Patty's friends were willing to entertain the idea of killing her father was crucial to Patty's going through with it. Patty comes closest to fitting a composite of the situationally trapped kid and the helpless child.[4] Although she did fit the profile of the most commonly encountered APO, the severely abused child, her lower level of personality development made her even less able to handle the psychopathological home environment than was Peter Jones or Scott Anders.

CASE PROCESSING AND DISPOSITION

There was no question about who killed Mr. Smith. Patty's guilt or innocence rested on one point: Was the 17-year-old a dangerously antisocial youth, as the state argued? Or was she a severely abused child, a victim herself, who killed out of desperation, to ensure her psychological and perhaps her physical survival, as the defense contended?

The state attempted to portray the adolescent as a sociopathic youth who killed her father because he disciplined her for getting bad grades, skipping school, and other misbehavior. In the words of the prosecutor, Patty was "a vicious, mean, spoiled young woman" who murdered her father in cold blood because he kept her on a tight rein and took her car away as a punishment. Patty's codefendants all testified against her. In recounting the events following the homicide, Tom, Jim, and Joe suggested that Patty was untroubled by having killed her father. Jim indicated that Patty seemed amused as she related the details of the killing.

Mary testified that when Patty had asked her whether she would sleep over at the Smith household and really kill Patty's father as he slept, she replied, "Yeah, whatever." Mary testified further that Patty said that she could live with Patty in the Smith home after Mr. Smith was dead. According to Mary, Patty had promised to give her an unspecified amount of money and some rock concert tickets for killing Mr. Smith. On the night of the homicide Mary dressed herself in black, entered Mr. Smith's bedroom, stayed there for about a minute, and pointed a gun at him for at least 15 seconds. She then left the bedroom, claiming that she was just playing out the final segments of a joke and had never intended to kill Mr. Smith. Upon reentering the living room, Mary told Patty that she could not carry out the plan. Patty said then that she (Patty) would have to do it herself.

The defense contended that Patty was a child trapped in an intolerable home situation, where she suffered continuous "mental, physical and sexual abuse" from her father. The public defender argued that

Patty killed her father because he was slowly killing her and she could find no other way out. Defense counsel buttressed its position by calling former employees of Mr. Smith, his former in-laws, the defendant, and two mental health experts. Several of Mr. Smith's employees described him as an employer who publicly berated his workers and never seemed to be satisfied by their job performance and efforts. The victim's former father-in-law and former wife painted a picture of Mr. Smith as a violent and abusive man. They recounted specific incidents of Mr. Smith's violence against family members. Mrs. Smith vividly portrayed her former marriage as one filled from the beginning with fear, threats, and physical and mental abuse. She testified that Mr. Smith always carried a gun and usually kept brass knuckles and a switchblade nearby.

Patty Smith testified about the physical and mental abuse and sexual assaults to which her father had subjected her. She explained that classmates who testified were unaware of the physical abuse because she wore long-sleeved shirts and long skirts to hide any marks. She told the jurors about the two occasions when she sought help to no avail and reported that she had tried to run away on several occasions, but her father always found her. Her attempt at suicide failed, she stated, because she failed to take enough pills to kill herself. The defendant related the events on the night of the homicide in a detached way, admitting to the jurors that she came to see killing her father as the only way out.

The other mental health expert who examined the defendant, a psychologist, shared my opinion that Patty was sane and suffering from PTSD because of the conditions in which she had been raised. I testified about the abuse and neglect that had existed in the Smith household for years, explaining each of the areas of victimization discussed in this chapter. The wide array of materials made available to me proved to be invaluable in substantiating that Mr. Smith was a person who had used sex as an instrument of power and who could have sexually assaulted his own daughter. Statements made by former employees to defense counsel revealed that Mr. Smith used sexual remarks and demands to intimidate them at work. Mr. Smith fit the profile of an extremely narcissistic individual whose behavioral style most closely resembled the psychopath's. Such an individual, I testified, would be capable of raping his daughter.

My testimony also focused on how conditions in the household worsened after Mr. Smith's common-law wife left. The pivotal role played by Patty's friends in bringing her to the point where she stood with a loaded gun pointed at her father's head as he lay sleeping, believing that there was no other way out, was explained to the jury. Evidence that Mr. Smith's continued abuse, committed verbally, psychologically, physically, and sexually, might have caused Patty to have been in a chronic state of fear and to believe that he was capable of killing her at any time was presented to the jury.

The jury deliberated for more than ten hours before finding Patty Smith guilty of murder in the second degree. The jury's selection of the verdict of murder in the second degree appeared to have been a compromise. This verdict precluded Patty's being sentenced either to death in the electric chair or to life imprisonment, with a mandatory 25-year sentence to be served before parole eligibility. The defense had hoped that the jury would return a verdict of excusable homicide or manslaughter, believing it unlikely that jurors would conclude that Patty acted in self-defense.

Sentencing guidelines called for a 12-to-17 year period of incarceration for an individual convicted of second-degree murder who did not have a significant prior record. The prosecution asked the judge to impose a 30-year sentence, arguing that aggravating factors in the case warranted a longer term. During the sentencing hearing the prosecutor attempted to read into the record portions of the adolescent's diary that detailed her sexual encounters with two boys and a pamphlet of Patty's that apparently showed various sexual positions. From comments that the assistant state attorney made to the press prior to attempting to introduce these materials in court, it appeared that he believed promiscuous behavior to be evidence against being a victim of sexual abuse. The fact that sexually abused children frequently act out sexually is well known among those who work with this population.[5] This fact was specifically noted during the trial by the other mental health expert when he mentioned the characteristics of the abused child. Patty's sexual history was also discussed at length in my report.

The defense asked the judge to suspend the prison sentence and order confinement in a facility that offered intensive psychiatric treatment. I testified at this hearing that Patty was not a criminally sophisticated youth. She needed a structured environment where she could get psychiatric help. If Patty were sentenced to adult prison or to a youthful offender facility, she would encounter more criminally oriented individuals, homosexual play, and "familying," a process where women set up make-believe families, sometimes including sexual affiliations, to survive the physical and emotional deprivations of imprisonment.[6] Because of Patty's personality development, she would be at considerable risk of detrimental influences from more hardened inmates. Despite her size and age, Patty was still a little girl who craved attention and wanted to be liked. Her desires clearly affected her judgment.

Patty needed intensive therapy in three main areas. In-depth psychological intervention was needed to help her deal with the trauma she had experienced. She needed to confront feelings of rage, betrayal, abandonment, and powerlessness safely and to rebuild her self-concept. Therapy was also necessary to help Patty develop healthier, more mature coping techniques. In addition to discussing Patty's passive way of responding to others, I alerted the court that the adolescent had signs of an eating disorder, underscoring that an addictive pattern was already in place and could be life-threatening if not checked. Finally, Patty needed professional help to facilitate more mature ways of perceiving. Counseling could help Patty see herself as responsible for her behavior, increase her awareness of feelings and their relation to her behavior, and foster empathy. I recommended placement in one of three psychiatric hospitals instead of prison because each had programs that could benefit Patty.

The court sentenced Patty Smith to 17 years in the women's prison, noting that a life had been taken. In pronouncing sentence the judge commented that, independent of the mental health testimony, the court believed that Patty had a problem and needed treatment. He strongly urged the state corrections authorities to put Patty in a facility where she could receive some counseling, stating on the record that he was aware that there was little in the way of treatment available in prison. He specifically noted that it was a "great failing in our system" that people who need help do not receive it in the prison environment. He expressed dismay that our society did not recognize this fact and that the legislature had not seen fit to change this state of affairs.

When this book went to press, Patty had been incarcerated in adult prison for almost four years. Initially, she lost about 50 pounds, looked good, and seemed happy in prison. She had a "whole family." Her "mom" was an 18-year-old woman who was serving a 15-year sentence for murder. Her "dad" was "like a dad I never had . . . she's older, 23–24, she's serving 16 years, she was gay on the street." Patty met her "brother" in county jail: "She's not like a female to me, she plays more of a dominant role." She had four uncles and four aunts, and a grandma who is a "nut, she's crazy, my mom's mom." Patty said, "They help out a lot."

For the first couple of years, Patty was invested in learning what she could. She completed her GED and finished courses in graphics, computers, and nursing aid. She had jobs in the warehouse, on the grounds, and in the library. In the first nine months, she said that she got eight disciplinary reports for breaking rules and lost gain time. After two years, staying out of trouble was still difficult, but she had found a formula to help her. "All what I do is go to work and stay at work all day. Then I go to the dorm at night and stay on my bed. . . . All the stuff I learn in here can help me when I get out of here. So I try to learn all what I can while I'm in here. And when I do have spare time I crochet. I learned how to crochet about a month ago. . . . As long as I keep my hands busy, I keep my mouth shut. And if I keep my mouth shut, I stay out of trouble which is what I am doing."

After almost four years of incarceration, Patty's attitude and mood had changed. She was unhappy and angry that she was still incarcerated and felt that she was being treated unjustly. Prison "family" members had been released, and she decided it was better for her to stay by herself. She decided to take a dorm job and stop pursuing further training because learning more did not seem to help her and she did not like having people over her. She spent her days hanging out in the dorm and did not even go outside for exercise. She said she rarely visited the prison psychologist although she liked her, never attended any support group meetings, and was never contacted by the local rape crisis center who agreed to see her. She had more than gained back the weight she lost and had little interest in her health or appearance.

With the exception of Patty's mother, family members and friends did not keep in touch with Patty. Patty's mother accepted weekly telephone calls from Patty; she lived a thousand miles away and had become too ill to visit Patty during the last year.

IMPLICATIONS, PRACTICAL SUGGESTIONS, AND FUTURE DIRECTIONS

Intervention after the Tragedy
with Don McCann and
Eldra Solomon

IDEALLY, INTERVENTION COMES before problems at home escalate into homicide, but unfortunately, society often does not intervene until a family's problems can no longer be ignored. When murder occurs, society has no choice but to respond.

Society's first response to parricide is a legal one; the determination of the adolescent's guilt or innocence may take a year or more. During this period, the youth is likely to be held in a juvenile detention center or, in some states, in an adult jail. Only after the youth's conviction (or rare exoneration) is therapeutic intervention typically considered.

Therapeutic intervention should begin immediately after the tragedy. Delay in addressing the issues that led to the homicide is undesirable. Because APOs are usually not criminally sophisticated, they often have a hard time adjusting to incarceration. Confinement aggravates depression, and the youth may attempt suicide.

The professional literature has not addressed in depth the type of intervention or treatment strategy most effective in dealing with various types of adolescent homicide offenders.[1] Only four studies of adolescent parricide offenders have addressed treatment. Sargent (1962) advised that children who acted out the unconscious wishes of one parent by killing the other be advised of the role that the surviving parent played in encouraging the youth to kill. He advocated family therapy if reunification of the child with the family was desired. Scherl and Mack (1966) described the posthomicidal symptoms and behavior of one adolescent matricide offender and noted that he was not receptive to beginning treatment until almost two years after the homicide. After a year and a half of therapy, they noted that, although the prognosis was guarded, the youth seemed able to control impulsive acting out and to consider the consequences of his behavior. Duncan and

Duncan (1978) maintained that the APO must be institutionalized until he can regain self-control. They stressed that nonpunitive staff who refuse to validate the offender's justification for his violent acts must provide external structure. Russell (1984) recommended that youths who kill family members be confined for one to two years in a secure juvenile facility that functions as a therapeutic milieu. He cautioned, however, that treatment is particularly difficult because these youths have deficiencies in emotional and personality development that the commission of the crime affects. He recommended that the youths be given much emotional support while being confronted with reality.

The prognosis for successful reintegration into society for these youths is generally good. Duncan and Duncan (1971) noted that four cases for whom follow-up data were available had not committed further crimes during the ten-year period following their release. They drew the following conclusion: "It appears that in cases where the murderer is sane, where the victim is the original hated parent and not a surrogate, and where immediate apprehension and control are established, then the chances that the offender will kill again are minimal."[2] Long-term follow-up data on three APOs (more than ten years in two cases) provided by Tanay (1973, 1976b) indicated that each made a successful adjustment after release. Corder et al.'s (1976) analysis of follow-up data, which averaged 4.5 years, revealed that adolescents who killed their parents adjusted well outside prison, requiring minimum psychiatric intervention and treatment. Only one of the ten parricide offenders remained in prison, as opposed to 19 of the 20 youths who had killed strangers, acquaintances, and relatives other than parents. Post's (1982) limited (length of time unspecified) follow-up data on two APOs indicated that they adjusted successfully after release; neither had been rearrested. Long-term follow-up data provided by Russell (1984) for two APOs (nine years in one case, more than ten in the second) showed that one APO had made a successful adjustment; the other was violently explosive and "wonders if he isn't going to get someone to kill him just as he killed his father; or will he kill himself first?"

APOs frequently maintain relationships with surviving family members.[3] Corder et al. (1976) noted that all eight of the APOs for whom follow-up data were available had been accepted by their families; seven maintained frequent contact; four returned home to live with them.

Our discussion of effective ways of treating the most commonly encountered APO, the severely abused child, is based on our assessments of parricide offenders as well as effective intervention with hundreds of clients who have been abused and have entertained homicidal thoughts about their parents. It appears that with proper treatment most APOs can be successfully treated and eventually return to society to lead productive lives. Therapeutic intervention is desirable both to reclaim the individual offender as a productive member of society and to protect the public.

We invite other therapists who deal with this population to join us in testing the treatment methods we describe below. The conclusion of Benedek, Cornell, and Staresina (1989) following their review of the literature on the treatment of adolescent homicide offenders underscores a critical need for additional evaluation of intervention strategies: "The appropriate psychiatric/psychological treatment of the homicidal adolescent is a critical area that leaves much room for further research. . . . Treatment planning for the violent juvenile is only in an experimental stage."[4]

This discussion of treatment strategies is intended to serve as a guide to mental health professionals who may encounter clients who have been severely abused as well as parricide offenders. It is our hope that social services agency providers, state attorneys, defense attorneys, and judges will acquaint themselves with the issues discussed in this chapter to facilitate their making sound recommendations regarding the treatment and disposition of adolescent parricide offenders. Guidance counselors, teachers, and other school personnel are encouraged to become familiar with this material to help them make appropriate referrals in cases where child mistreatment has not resulted in homicide. Students and general readers may also find treatment issues and strategies of interest.

TREATMENT OF THE SEVERELY ABUSED CHILD

This chapter focuses attention on treatment of the severely abused child because this type is the most common among adolescents who kill their parents and the one with the most favorable prognosis. APOs have typically experienced a lifetime of dysfunctional parenting. Their poor self-esteem, distorted thinking, inability to express emotion in a healthy way, and self-defeating, destructive, impulsive behavior are the product of years of neglectful, inadequate, and abusive parenting. Our therapeutic framework is *integrative therapy*, a process of cognitive, emotional, and physical restructuring. The therapist serves in the role of a healthy, supportive adult for the abused adolescent. Slowly these clients are shown how to provide for themselves the support and nurturing that they did not receive from their parents. Old, destructive parental messages are replaced with new, constructive ones.

Cognitive restructuring involves building more rational and congruent thinking and developing a positive self-image. Emotional change includes learning healthy strategies for accepting, experiencing, and releasing feelings. Physical change consists of breathing more effectively, learning relaxation techniques, and being more in touch with bodily sensations and needs.

In the integrative therapy model, we take an eclectic approach, using traditional therapeutic strategies associated with psychodynamic and humanistic approaches, cognitive therapy, and behavioral techniques as appropriate.[5] Clinical experiences have led us to conclude that the awareness and discharge of emotions is basic to resolving issues related to child abuse and neglect. An experiential approach facilitates clients' confrontation and resolution of feelings associated with early childhood mistreatment.[6]

So pronouns would not be confusing, the APO has been designated male and the therapist female in the following discussion. The chapter focuses on three phases of treatment and the issues that accompany them. First, the APO's current crisis must be addressed. The youth must deal with the homicide and its consequences for himself and other family survivors. Second, issues that arise in day-to-day life must receive attention to enable the youth to learn to cope more effectively with current events. Third, the youth's past history of victimization in the home must be unraveled and resolved.

BASIC ISSUES

At the beginning of therapy, the client's level of personality development must be assessed. Knowing how the youth perceives himself and his relation to others and to outside events is often critical in understanding the dynamics that led to the homicide. In general, the higher the level of personality development, the better the prognosis. Knowing the client's developmental level is also very important in charting realistic and effective treatment goals and objectives.[7] In addition, obtaining as complete a psychosocial history as possible is essential to ensure that family history and dynamics can be effectively studied and addressed.[8] The client's psychosocial history is of paramount importance in reexamining the past, dealing with the present, and projecting the future.

If the APO will be reentering the family unit, therapy must involve all family members. Family therapy can help family members become aware of their roles in the tragedy. Without this awareness, the unhealthy patterns that characterized family interactions will be repeated. Until the problems of codependency are resolved, the APO may engage in further antisocial behavior. Each family member should also undergo individual therapy. Individual therapy for the APO should be designed to help him resolve issues relating to his abuse and to the homicide.

Whenever possible the adolescent parricide offender should not be imprisoned; prison psychological services are rarely adequate to deal with the depth of his problems. Consistent with the recommendation made by Benedek, Cornell, and Staresina (1989), we suggest that the APO be placed in a structured therapeutic environment for a period of stabilization. This environment might be a psychiatric hospital or clinic specializing in child abuse or the dysfunctional family, or a group treatment home with professional mental health staff. In some cases the APO will need several years of treatment before he can return home.

The APO must decide that he wants to recover. Six factors must be addressed in therapy. First, a therapeutic relationship must be developed between the therapist and the APO so that he feels safe enough to participate fully in the therapeutic process. The APO will come with a firmly established pattern of withholding trust from another human being. The therapist must be patient and take the time to prove her trustworthiness. Only when the APO feels safe will he reveal himself.

Second, the youth's current crisis must be recognized and handled. The fact that the youth killed a parent must be squarely addressed. If the APO is in prison or headed there, life in a correctional facility must also be faced. The youth must be helped to develop strategies to cope with threats of sexual assault, ridicule, or banishment by other inmates, continued deprivation of goods and services, loneliness, and further abandonment by society.

Third, the youth must understand the family dynamics that provided the backdrop for the tragedy. Attention must focus on helping the youth to understand the family psychopathology and to consider that the killing may have been a family conspiracy, as suggested by Sargent (1962). Because of familial circumstances, he may have had to take on responsibilities and duties that children are not normally expected to fulfill. As a result, his life may have become increasingly and inappropriately outer-directed. This pattern may have resulted in his becoming particularly empathic toward the surviving parent and siblings. He needs to understand, however, that his outer-directedness has typically come at enormous cost and has often robbed him of his childhood.

Fourth, the youth must acknowledge that he and his parents betrayed each other. Betrayals by the parents center around issues of trust: mistreatment of the child, age-inappropriate expectations, psychological abandonment, and, on occasion, physical abandonment by the nonabusive surviving parent. The adolescent also must see that he has betrayed his parents by striking out at the abusive parent. In killing a parent he broke one of society's strongest taboos and destroyed the family myth that the family was still a viable functioning unit capable of meeting the needs of its members. If the parent was the primary breadwinner, the youth's actions also threatened the family's continued survival.

Fifth, the child must come to understand the lack of congruence between his real self and the self that he was encouraged to adopt. Central to recovery is the APO's understanding that he has certain basic rights as a human being, including the rights to feel, see, hear, think and the right to the security of his own body. The abuse and neglect to which his parents exposed him have led the child to abrogate the self. He was probably told not to cry, not to be angry, and not to express any other negative emotions. He may have been assured that problems like alcoholism did not exist in the family. He learned to deny his own experience in order to receive his parents' approval. As this incongruence developed between what he knew to be reality and the distorted perception he adopted to gain parental approval, he abandoned his core self.

Sixth, the APO needs to take an inventory of himself and identify his personal successes as well as his failures. The youth must count his survival among his successes. By focusing on his strengths the youth can accept that he is not a "bad person." He needs to be encouraged to take credit for what he did to help the family unit survive as long as it did. In taking on such adult responsibilities as cooking, maintaining the household, and looking after and protecting younger siblings, the youth did what he believed would help.

The youth must become aware that he made mistakes and engaged in destructive and unhealthy behavior. He must face the fact that he killed his own parent. If he acted out in school or in the community to deal with the stress at home before the homicide, this behavior must also be evaluated honestly. The youth must come to see that his behavior, while understandable, is generally not acceptable by societal standards.

RELEASE AND MANAGEMENT OF CORE EMOTIONS

The APO may feel numb when he enters therapy and may suffer from PTSD. During therapy the APO may come to experience feelings typically associated with the grieving process, such as anger, sadness, and fear,[9] just as if the slain parent had died of natural causes.

When he is terrified or enraged, he may sense that his body is out of control due to his autonomic reactions. When an individual attempts to control the expression of intense emotions, his body becomes an armor of defense: The rigidity of the body defends the individual from experiencing the intensity of feeling. The therapist must help the APO release the emotions being held in the body slowly and safely. The therapeutic environment must be safe for the therapist and APO to get in touch with the adolescent's feelings and to discharge them.

Creating a Safe Environment

A sound-proofed room with a one-way, unbreakable mirror installed for observation and protection of the therapist is recommended. Therapy for the APO can proceed more comfortably and quickly if the adolescent knows that he is in a safe place with the therapist and that interference from others is unlikely. He will be more at ease discharging strong feelings by screaming or crying if he knows that no one other than the therapeutic team will see, hear, or interfere.

To be able to confront the adolescent and facilitate the expression of his emotions, the therapist must be comfortable with the expression of her own emotions. If the youth tries to remove himself psychologically from the situation, the therapist must be willing to confront him about his behavior. If he tries to remove himself physically or to harm himself, she must be able to contain his flight and his attempt to injure himself or others. The youth may try to bang his head against the wall, punch, scratch, or cut himself.

The APO, particularly if he is relatively high in personality development,[10] may try to hurt himself as therapy progresses because he believes that he ought to be punished and made to suffer for having killed or for the anger that he feels. This behavior may be the result of thinking that it is safer to turn anger inward to avoid further death and destruction. In addition, he may have learned to direct anger toward himself rather than toward the abuser.

Emotional Discharge

Emotional discharge is not a simple verbal venting of emotion such as "I am angry." It involves the physical acting out of intense emotions screaming, kicking, hitting, and deep sobbing. The therapist performs three tasks in the emotional discharge process: facilitating the experience, encouraging expression, and validating the expression. Strategies must be implemented to ease the experiencing and release of anger, fear, and sadness. As recovery proceeds, other feelings such as happiness and love, which the APO may have felt particularly unable to express, can be addressed. Shame and guilt must also be systematically explored.

Anger

After the client has acknowledged and mobilized his feelings, the therapist instructs him in their direct expression.[11] The adolescent must be given validation by the therapist for expressing his anger. In essence, the therapist must support the APO in expressing anger, continually validating his right to feel what he feels and to express his feelings safely.

The client must learn to discriminate between blasting his anger out in the therapeutic environment by shouting or hitting a punching bag and screaming "Fuck you" to a teacher or beating up an employer who angers him. The therapist must make it clear to the APO that he will continue to experience anger as events arise, and the adolescent must realize that the therapist can and will help him release his anger gradually. As anger is released, the youth may experience a lessening of depression.

In addition to working on current anger, the therapist must also address past anger. This anger is typically a response to having been abused, not having been protected, and not having been supported as a young child. It can be a catalyst for recovery. Anger from the abuse can be elicited by having the client recall and reexperience the abuse.

The client must learn how to express anger outside the therapeutic environment. Therapy should focus specifically on the development and improvement of communication skills, and the client should also be asked to identify specific ways of discharging anger safely.[12] The APO has to be encouraged to stand up for himself when attacked or insulted. He must be taught to defuse the threat at inception so that the situation does not escalate into violence.

Fear

The APO, like many people, may have difficulty acknowledging fear and be resistant to admitting that he is fearful. He probably will be unwilling to experience his fear because he might lose control again. For the APO to recover, he must realize that fear, even panic, can and must be expressed safely.

Once the client acknowledges his fear, the therapist guides him in the direct expression of this emotion.[13] After the expression of the fear, the client may need the therapist to comfort him. She must help the APO realize that his being afraid did not result in annihilation or loss and that his expression of fear did not result in further death and destruction.

As with anger, early therapy focuses on issues closely associated with the homicide and its aftermath. Questions of the client's physical and psychological survival are likely to surface immediately after the tragedy. The youth may be confronted with the possibility of execution or life imprisonment. In addition to fears for his physical safety, the APO is likely to fear abandonment by surviving family and friends and being the victim of more psychological or emotional abuse because he has killed. The youth may be afraid to trust those close to him. He often fears that the deceased parent is not really dead or will come after him in supernatural form.

Fear associated with the past, some of which may be tied to specific incidents of abuse, must be confronted. All his life the APO may have denied and repressed thoughts and memories of situations that evoked various types of fear. He must be assured that if he allows himself to be afraid in the therapeutic environment, the therapist will be there to support him. The psychosocial history can assist the therapist in identifying past events that may have contributed to the present crisis.

As the process of releasing fear progresses, denied memories of the past and the fear associated with them will begin to surface. Recollection leads to increased awareness of the abusive environment and the releasing of more fear and other emotions. The process of unraveling and dealing with the past may be very extensive. When the most severe abuse situations and fear responses have been processed, the youth will be ready to deal with new fear-producing situations (e.g., meeting new authority figures) as they arise.

Sadness

After the homicide, sadness may not predominate in the youth's grieving process. As therapy progresses, however, he will come to experience and express sadness for himself, his parents, and other familial survivors. When he enters therapy, he may not be able to cry. He may have learned to hold in tears rather than express pain. If so, the therapist will give him permission and encouragement to cry.[14] After sadness has been acknowledged and mobilized, the therapist will help the youth to express it directly. Expression may include deep sobbing and crying, screaming, gagging, and hysterical laughing.

The therapist must help the client to understand that feelings of sadness and their release will continue, while assuring him that he will not be consumed by sadness. Sadness initially follows from the realization that the parent is dead, that the family is broken, and that the youth's life is dramatically changed. The youth will grieve the loss of his immediate and possibly long-term future. He needs to acknowledge the loss of his high school days, his college plans, his relationship with his girlfriend, his friendships, his dreams of a career.

As the youth experiences the loss of his adolescence and young adulthood, he realizes the losses that he sustained during his childhood. Some of these painful events may include, for example, having been discounted, humiliated, beaten, abandoned, hit, or having had possessions taken away. Mourning needs to take place for experiences that the client never had, such as possibly never having been told that his parents loved him, and for the loss of self and self-worth.

While therapy is progressing from the past into the present, the therapist needs to reassure the client that it is all right to be sad and to communicate sadness. As sadness is expressed, depression may lessen. The youth has to be supported in realizing that life is a continuing process of losses and new beginnings. Each loss needs to be acknowledged, mourned, and released to allow the individual to focus on emergences and gains. The therapist must assist the client in learning to create safe places where he can mourn.

Shame and Guilt

Shame is among the most important underlying factors in negative self-esteem and is a critical consideration in the treatment of the adolescent parricide offender. Experiencing guilt—externalized shame—is an appropriate feeling when one has in fact committed some transgression. Shame becomes problematic, however, when it is internalized and becomes identified with one's core self rather than with a specific action or series of actions.[15] Those who are consumed with internalized shame typically believe at a very deep level that they are worthless and learn to dissociate from their feelings. However, when they dissociate from their feelings, they cannot know their own needs and hence cannot meet them or allow them to be met. This dissociation from feelings leads shame-based individuals to neglect themselves.

As the therapist assists the APO in releasing anger, fear, and sadness, she will also be helping him externalize internalized shame, feeling that he is defective. Recognition of guilt (externalized shame) for the homicide is a movement toward health. As she supports the adolescent who has internalized the message of unworthiness, the therapist must communicate to the APO that the denial of his basic rights has resulted in his adopting a confused and negative self-image. The therapist must encourage the youth to identify and meet his needs and to exercise basic rights. These rights include the right to feel, see, hear, and think freely, the right to privacy, and the right to make choices.[16]

In the early and middle stages of therapy, internalized shame ("I am no good") becomes externalized ("I have made some mistakes") as feelings are acknowledged and released and permission is given to exercise basic human rights. In later stages, situations in which the adolescent experiences guilt will be examined in the light of past and present behavior. A key factor in helping the youth recover is addressing the appropriateness of his feelings. An important goal at this point is to assist the youth in acknowledging responsibility rather than persisting in experiencing guilt for past, present, and anticipated future behavior. The therapist must assist the APO to shape his behavior so that it is consistent with an emerging positive self-image.

DEVELOPING A POSITIVE SELF-IMAGE

The APO generally enters therapy with a negative self-image, the result of abusive and neglectful parenting. In the early stages of therapy, internalized shame is at its peak. The youth who has killed a parent feels as though he has betrayed his family and himself and has exposed himself and his family to public scrutiny and judgment. From the beginning the therapist must give the APO positive affirmations (e.g., "You are a good human being," "You have a right to your feelings") and heighten his awareness of his fundamental rights as a human being.

The therapist serves as a positive adult figure. Responding with understanding and support to the adolescent's younger self is critical because regression to early childhood behavior and feelings is part of the recovery process. Like a good parent, the therapist sets limits and teaches problem-solving skills.

When the adolescent regresses emotionally, he becomes aware of the depth of early needs not met by his caretakers. The therapist validates the client's unmet needs and explores the effects of this neglect. She teaches the APO how to begin to satisfy his needs in a healthy, adult manner. With the therapist's assistance, the youth learns to give himself more self-nurturing messages. For example, he learns to give himself messages like "I am OK," "I'll be OK, no matter what," and "I love you."

Application of effective intervention strategies with adolescents who have killed parents is vital. Given the home environments in which APOs were raised, they are often victims as well as offenders. While they are confined by the state, it makes sense to help these individuals let go of the past, learn to express feelings in a more appropriate way, and behave more adaptively.

One goal of the integrative therapy model, a positive self-image, has benefits that transcend the individual. People who have positive self-images make healthier choices for themselves. Because many of these choices affect others, society benefits when individuals are guided toward greater emotional health and maturity. Abused and neglected individuals who have worked through the anger, fear, sadness, and shame associated with years of maltreatment are more likely to break the intergenerational cycle of abuse than those who remain untreated.

11 | Society's Role

THE UNDENIABLE REALITIES and effects of child abuse and neglect in our society are being recognized increasingly as everyone's responsibility. Although few severely abused children actually kill their parents, these children are at a much higher risk of becoming delinquent or socially dependent than are children who are treated well by concerned and loving parents or guardians.[1]

Despite the increased public attention given to child mistreatment, many people are unclear about what to do when confronted with this problem. Almost seven years after the double homicide, Terry Adams, whose case introduced this book, had a strong message for teachers:

> A kid has a black eye, be inquisitive, don't ask him in front of the other classmates, don't never confront [the child]. You can see the symptoms: black eye, bruised lip, [child seems far away as if he's] just not really there, [may come across as] rebellious, wanting attention. . . . It's hard on teachers to be personal with classmates, because there's, what, 40 to a class. But, you know, if they detect that, try to find out what's wrong, be questionable [question the child], take the kid home one day. If he's got to take the school bus, yeah, you know, that's a little extra time out of your way, but if down deep inside, you really want to help, [then] *help*, you know. Don't think, I don't want to get involved—what happens if the kid dies. Remember, I think that's the biggest thing, if the kid dies, you could be responsible for that. . . . That's how I feel—you are just as responsible for it [death] as the person that did it. True enough, you don't want to get involved in the big, long, drawn-out thing, [but] *that's part of life*.

Scott Anders expressed bitterness in a follow-up interview four and a half years after his conviction when he recalled the number of teachers, neighbors, and relatives whom he had told about the abuse who did nothing to help him:

Just because a kid is young, don't think he's stupid. They don't have to believe him, but at least listen to him. They could check into it. When I told my teachers what was happening, before I got home, they had called my dad, and asked him "Did you beat your son or not?" "I didn't do nothing. I don't know what happened to him." I go to school the next day, I got called a liar. All they had to do is check it out. Neighbors knew about it, but nobody ain't want to call the law and want to get theirselves in trouble.

If one suspects that a child is being abused or neglected, one should at least call the local or state agency that investigates child abuse and neglect cases. The caller's identity is kept confidential. Reports in many states can be made anonymously. If the agency determines that the child is in danger, he or she will be removed from the home and placed in a temporary shelter pending a safe return to the home or other suitable arrangements.

Doctors, teachers, hospital personnel, and law enforcement officers are legally mandated to report suspected cases. Yet even those who are obligated by law are often reluctant to report. I have been contacted by elementary school teachers who have persuasive evidence that children in their classes are being seriously mistreated by their parents. These teachers have pursued school policy by reporting the incident to school administrators and guidance counselors who took no action because of the "sensitive nature of the topic," beliefs that "that is how those kind of people raise their children" or that "nothing will be done anyway," or heavy caseloads. These teachers were frustrated and too fearful to go further. School administrators need to be held more accountable for their responses when cases of suspected abuse are brought to their attention. Meanwhile, teachers who find such a lack of response should ignore school procedures and call either the social services agency or the state attorney in the juvenile division.

In a follow-up interview conducted about one and a half years after the homicide, Patty offered the following advice specifically to teachers: "If you have a student that comes up to you, listen to them, don't turn them away, and talk to them, and call someone—all teachers in junior high, even elementary [schools], and all members of schools should have a list of where kids could go [for help], and automatically, if a kid talks to you, call this center."

When in doubt about what to do, individuals should look to the child's safety and report the suspected case to authorities. In the words of Patty Smith, "Just because there's no [physical] evidence, don't mean the child isn't being abused." As Scott Anders stressed, there are at least two kinds of abuse, physical and emotional. His experience clearly suggested that people seem to want hard evidence of physical abuse and adopt a more complaisant attitude toward emotional abuse, often the more damaging of the two.

Prejudice, inertia, defeatism, or fear of being wrong is insufficient justification for doing nothing and hoping for the best. Terry Adams offered a litmus test regarding when to act: "Would you let that happen to your kid if you weren't an abusive parent? If you wouldn't let it happen to your kid, then why let it happen to someone else's?"

Those who fear causing undue suspicion to focus on possibly innocent parents should realize that social services agencies are required to investigate cases thoroughly and, if no abuse or neglect is substantiated, to consider the case unfounded. Even if the allegation is found to be without merit, some damage may be done, but we should consider the child's safety first. The record of social services agencies in the past indicates that they cannot always be trusted to investigate and exonerate parents who have been falsely accused quickly and to provide help and services to children and families in need. These circumstances need not exist if our society is willing to take two stands. We need to commit the financial resources required to provide quality services, employ sufficient numbers of social services personnel, train them adequately, and empower them to discharge their duties. In addition, we need to remind ourselves constantly that people who have been cleared of wrongdoing are really not guilty. To achieve this end, child abuse laws may need to be reexamined and rewritten in some jurisdictions. Provisions for confidentiality and expungement of records kept on parents who have been investigated for child abuse and cleared may need to be changed.

EDUCATION IN PARENTING SKILLS
AND CHILD ABUSE IDENTIFICATION

Child Development and Parenting Skills

Classes need to be made easily available to help parents cope with the stresses of raising children, particularly children with special needs. Serious consideration should be given to incorporating child development and parenting skills classes into high school curricula for both boys and girls. Research has indicated that increasing the knowledge of present and future parents about home and child management, and enhancing the development of good communication skills, healthy emotional ties, and parent-child bonding help prevent child maltreatment.[2]

Helping individuals learn appropriate parenting skills will reduce child abuse and neglect because many instances of child mistreatment come from ignorance. In a recent case, two 17-year-old parents brought their two-year-old son to the emergency room with a swollen penis. Investigation revealed that the father had tied a rubber band around his son's penis because he believed that the treatment would discourage the child from urinating while sleeping.

Identification of Child Abuse; Appropriate Action

In addition to teaching adults and teenagers about child development and good parenting skills, elementary, junior high, and high schools should develop courses on child abuse and neglect. The curricula should help students recognize child abuse and neglect and encourage them to take appropriate action if victimized or threatened. The programs should aim to foster the development of self-esteem and conflict resolution skills to aid youths in self-protection.

Almost 40 percent of elementary schools in the United States do not offer prevention education.[3] Programs restricted solely to helping children protect themselves from sexual abuse are inadequate; children and adolescents must learn about all types of abuse and neglect. The earlier these behaviors are targeted, the earlier they can be stopped and any accompanying damage can be addressed therapeutically.

Abuse and neglect are not always obvious to their victims. When abuse and neglect are discussed in university classes, some students become aware for the first time that they were abused or neglected as children. Some mothers of APOs and other homicide offenders abused or neglected their children or allowed them to be mistreated because they had never identified or resolved their own victimizations as children.[4] One mother who had been overtly and covertly sexually abused as a child, for example, covertly sexually abused her son. She did much that was damaging to her son because of ignorance, not malevolence. Her ignorance of child-rearing practices provided the springboard for a homicidal rage within her son that, when combined with his subsequent history of brain damage, left ten women dead.

PROTECTING CHILDREN FROM THE EFFECTS OF PARENTAL CHEMICAL DEPENDENCY

The effects of parental alcoholism and chemical dependency on children send a clear message: Immediate action must be taken to educate and insulate children who are being raised in chemically dependent families from potential damage by their parents. The schools are the most appropriate vehicle for this responsibility primarily because they may be the only institutions to have any regular contact with children from chemically dependent families. Available estimates put the number of children of alcoholics under the age of 18 at seven million.[5]

Children and adolescents need to learn the differences between functional and dysfunctional families. They should know that children of alcoholic, chemically dependent, or otherwise dysfunctional families are at a higher risk of being abused or neglected. They should be told explicitly about support groups, such as Alateen, that help youths cope effectively with the problems of living with an addicted parent. These groups should be allowed and encouraged to meet in the schools during lunch, free periods, or immediately following classes. A teacher who had an alcoholic, chemically dependent, or other dysfunctional childhood family would be an ideal moderator if he or she (1) had focused on recovery issues in his or her own life and (2) had sufficient support group experience to know that his or her role would be to facilitate, not to lead or dominate.

The National Elementary School Education Project[6] sponsored by the National Association for Children of Alcoholics (NACoA) is the largest and most significant effort to educate school personnel and students about issues faced by children from alcoholic homes. The project is a collaborative effort of private and public organizations, governmental agencies, and corporations. The Elementary School Principals Association, National Council of Alcoholism, COA Foundation, and Chemical People are among the organizations that have endorsed the project. Project materials mailed to 50,000 public elementary schools in fall 1987 and spring 1988 included resource information and statistics and the publication *COA's: Meeting the Needs of the Young COA in the School Setting* (1986) by Ellen Morehouse and Claire Scola. A comic book about emotional abuse and children of alcoholics' issues published by the National Committee for Prevention of Child Abuse (NCPCA) in collaboration with NACoA and six posters for display in the school were also provided.

© Marvel Entertainment Group, Inc., and the National Association for Children of Alcoholics.

The poster series, developed by NACoA and Marvel Entertainment Group, Inc., and written and designed by Claudia Black and Rockelle Lerner, has a threefold message: observation, assurance, and action. At the top of one poster is the observation, "SOME MOMS AND DADS DRINK TOO MUCH . . . AND IT HURTS." Then the child receives assurance from a Marvel Comic Hero (Amazing Spider Man, the Incredible Hulk, Captain America, Iron Man) telling him or her, "IF YOUR MOM OR DAD DRINKS TOO MUCH, YOU'RE NOT ALONE. THERE ARE MILLIONS OF KIDS WITH ALCOHOLIC PARENTS." At the bottom of each poster, the child is directed to take action: "IF YOU WANT TO LEARN MORE . . . ASK SOMEONE YOU TRUST."[7]

THE SUPPORT NETWORK

Without a support network available to guide children through the process of obtaining help, victimization will continue. As Patty Smith said: "After the person [child] comes up to you, for the kid to keep talking, it will be hard, because once she even starts a little bit, she is going to want to shut the door on it. If she knows that she is going to have someone stand by her all the way, like holding her hand and knew the experience, she could continue opening up."

Currently, the mistreated child in most states is on his or her own unless and until the social services agency investigates and files a petition alleging dependency on the basis of its investigation. Once a dependency petition is filed, some assistance for the mistreated child is likely to be forthcoming in most jurisdictions. The Child Abuse Prevention and Treatment Act enacted by Congress in 1974 required that states seeking federal funds for child protection must enact provisions for the appointment of guardians for children involved in abuse or neglect proceedings.[8] A guardian ad litem (a person acting as the child's guardian in an action) is the child's advocate in court proceedings.

State laws vary regarding whether the guardian appointed must be an attorney. In a growing number of states, the appointment of volunteer lay (nonlawyer) guardians ad litem is permitted in child abuse cases.[9] Lay volunteers in these states typically receive training through the CASA (Court Appointed Special Advocate) program.[10] As of January 1991, there were 412 CASA programs operating in 47 states.[11]

Intervention and assistance by a guardian ad litem at the filing of a dependency petition is good, but it should begin much earlier. Children need an advocate before the filing stage is reached; they need someone to stand by their decision to report the mistreatment. A child advocate program is a means to ensure that children's allegations are properly and promptly investigated and that appropriate action is taken. Such a program could be either a separate entity or an expansion of guardian ad litem programs modeled after CASA.

Florida's Guardian ad Litem Program

Florida took the lead in passing legislation authorizing the development of guardian ad litem programs modeled after CASA.[12] In 1980 Florida began a pilot program to test the effectiveness of using trained volunteers as representatives for abused and neglected children. Within two years the program's success was apparent, and it was funded by the Office of the State Courts Administrator. Currently there are guardian ad litem programs operating in 19 of the state's 20 judicial circuits.

These programs train men and women who volunteer and who

meet criteria to represent the child before the court, social services agencies, and the community. The initial 25 hours of training is followed by regularly scheduled in-service training in areas of need or special interest.[13] Topics featured have included the medical identification of abuse, the use of psychological tests, appropriate techniques for interviewing the sexually abused child, and legal issues and answers.

In Florida, guardians ad litem fulfill five roles: investigator, spokesperson, reporter, protector, and monitor. As investigator the guardian conducts an independent investigation on behalf of the child, both speaking with the child and interviewing those who know the child and the situation to determine the facts. Those interviewed may include relatives, neighbors, friends, teachers and other school personnel, doctors, counselors and mental health professionals, clergy, and law enforcement and social services agency personnel.

As spokesperson and reporter the guardian ad litem makes sure that the child's best interests are represented to the court and to agencies dealing with the child. In addition to speaking in the best interests of the child, the guardian ad litem presents information to the court in a written report. This report, which is entered into the court record, is useful in helping the court determine what is in the child's best interests.

As the child's protector the guardian ad litem shields the child from insensitive and unnecessary questioning and attempts to minimize harmful effects of the adversarial process. The guardian ad litem serves as a monitor of the agencies and individuals ordered to provide services to the child.

Ideally there would be a satellite office of a guardian ad litem program in every school. The person who staffed each satellite office—the school guardian ad litem—could be a full-time salaried employee of the guardian ad litem program in the jurisdiction. The success of existing guardian ad litem programs provides convincing evidence, however, that with coordination and creativity satellite offices could be run completely by volunteers. Under an exclusively volunteer model, five to 12 individuals would be necessary to cover school sessions. This group could meet periodically to share information.

The school guardian ad litem would be the referral person in each school for teachers, parents, guidance counselors, and, most important, children who may be abused or neglected. It would be the satellite guardian ad litem's role to ensure that each child's case was adequately investigated. The satellite agent would be responsible for assigning a guardian ad litem from the pool of volunteers to ensure that each child had support as soon as possible.

The volunteer guardian ad litem would also monitor to ensure that court-ordered services were received. The outcome might have been different for Terry Adams had a guardian ad litem actively monitored Terry's case when three petitions alleging neglect, abuse, and physical abuse were filed in the two years preceding the homicide. Had a guardian ad litem brought to the court's attention the failure of his parents to participate in court-ordered counseling, both parents might be alive today. It is disturbing to realize, as Terry Adams said, that "the judge recommended [ordered] all this stuff, but nothing was fulfilled."

THE ROLE OF THE MEDIA

Public-service advertising through television, radio, and the print media has played a big role in educating the public about the problem of child maltreatment, particularly since the mid-1970s. Initial efforts focused on acknowledging the existence of the problem and the reasons for focusing on prevention ("Child abuse hurts us all"). Later messages emphasized how parents under stress could cope better and how others could help them ("We all have a role to play in preventing child abuse. If you know of a parent having trouble, reach out and offer some help").[14]

Largely as a result of media efforts, a great deal of progress has been made in increasing the public's understanding of and interest in preventing child abuse. As noted by Anne Donnelly, executive director of NCPCA, "By 1990, virtually all adults in the United States were aware of child maltreatment as a major social problem."[15] In spotlighting the reality of child maltreatment in our society, the media need to continue focusing on the most constructive coverage they can provide.

Child maltreatment commonly springs from parental ignorance; therefore, movies, television documentaries, newspaper stories, and magazine articles focusing on the parameters of child abuse and neglect can educate the public. Recent changes in attitudes and behavior linked to the media show how powerful a role the media can play in eradicating child abuse and neglect. In a 1990 survey, 90 percent of the public reported believing that yelling and swearing at children can result in long-term emotional problems; from 1988 to 1990, 15 percent fewer parents reported yelling and screaming.[16]

In addition to information about what types of behavior and words are abusive, the media can publicize where abusive parents can get help and what actions concerned citizens can take to help prevent child abuse. The media can alert the public to the increased risk chemically dependent parents have of abusing and neglecting their children and list support groups and community facilities where they can get help. By advertising community resources available to them, the media can also carry the message to abused children that help exists. Abused and neglected children who are aware that they can get help would be less likely to conclude that killing the abusive parent is the only solution.

CONCLUDING REMARKS

My recommendations look to the future, to a society where the incidence of adolescents killing their parents is reduced because the conditions that make such a deadly state of affairs seem necessary are substantially lessened. In striving for a better world in which to raise our children, our society must look with compassion on adolescent parricide offenders who had the misfortune of being born before such a world could be created.

Our justice system needs to show mercy toward the APO who has been abused and neglected by his or her parents and abandoned by society. Social science evidence depicting the plight of the "battered child" belongs in today's courtroom. The time has come for serious discussion about broadening the definition of self-defense to include psychological self-defense.[17]

There is a pressing need for increased awareness of the devastating nature and effects of child maltreatment and increased public involvement in prevention. "Child abuse . . . is too complex a problem, too deeply engrained in the ways our communities are organized and our families are structured for any one profession or any one sector of society to be in a position to prevent abuse—all sectors need to be involved and do have a role to play."[18]

Child mistreatment is a killer. Often significant damage comes not in human carnage, but in the death of the human spirit. With awareness of the problem comes the opportunity to change the conditions that give rise to child mistreatment and allow it to continue. The words of Terry Adams alert us to the realization that awareness is not the end but the beginning:

> The biggest thing is just being aware. Care, 'cause if you don't, it's not just the little kid you are hurting, you're hurting tomorrow. . . . Because kids are defenseless, they don't have the vocabulary, the mental capacity, the mentality, the strong points to stand up. If somebody won't stand up for them, nobody will. If no one does, then, what's tomorrow?

Each of us, regardless of age or station in life, can make a difference in the lives of children. A story attributed to the Minnesota Literacy Council makes this point graphically.

An old fisherman stood on the beach watching a young boy at the shoreline. As the fisherman approached, he saw that the boy was picking up starfish, which had been washed ashore by the waves, and was throwing them back into the sea. When the fisherman had caught up with the boy, he asked the boy what he was doing. The boy did not stop his effort as he told the fisherman that he was throwing the starfish back into the sea so that they could live. If left until the morning sun, the starfish would die. The fisherman's eyes scanned the beach, revealing thousands of starfish ashore. He said, "But, son, there are thousands upon thousands of starfish on the beach. What difference could your actions possibly make?" As the boy hurled another starfish into the sea, he looked the old man in the eye and said, "It makes a difference to this one."

■ APPENDIX

Analysis of Parricide Offenders
by Juvenile versus Adult Status

SONS WERE RESPONSIBLE for most killings of parents and stepparents during the ten-year period under investigation, accounting for between 85 and 87 percent of homicides involving fathers, mothers, stepfathers, and stepmothers.[1] The proportion of males who committed these types of parricides was approximately equal to their 87 percent representation among homicide offenders in general during this decade.[2] There were no significant differences in the percentages of parents and stepparents killed by juvenile and by adult sons and daughters.[3]

During the period 1977–86, Hispanics rarely killed parents and stepparents. The percentage of Hispanic offenders arrested in these types of parricides ranged from 3 percent for stepmothers to 6 percent for fathers. When the percentages of parents and stepparents slain by Hispanics were examined within juvenile versus adult age categories, the percentages remained small and no significant differences emerged.[4] The involvement of Hispanics in the killings of parents and stepparents was disproportionately low in relation to their involvement in 16 percent of total homicide arrests. Among juveniles arrested for homicide during these ten years, 22 percent were Hispanic.[5]

Mothers and stepmothers who were killed were significantly more likely to be white than fathers (chi square = 21.37, df = 1, p = <.01) and stepfathers (chi square = 4.24, df = 1, p = <.05). The percentage of victims who were white was as follows: stepfathers, 59 percent; fathers, 65 percent; mothers, 72 percent; and stepmothers, 74 percent. A weak relationship was found between the race of the offender and offender age category (under 18; 18 and over) among those who killed fathers (chi square = 10.03, df = 1, p = <.001) and stepfathers (chi square = 10.95, df = 1, p = <.001). Blacks under 18 were significantly less likely to kill their fathers and stepfathers than were white youths and blacks over 18. Approximately 27 percent of fathers and 30 percent of stepfathers killed by juveniles involved a black youth. In contrast, slightly more than 36 percent of fathers and almost 45 percent of stepfathers slain by adults were killed by a black offender.[6] Although the proportion of blacks who killed parents and stepparents greatly exceeded their 12 percent representation in the population, it was still less than their representation among homicide arrestees. Of those arrested for homicide from 1977 to 1986, 49 percent were black. Among juveniles arrested for homicide during this time frame, 48 percent were black.[7]

■ NOTES

1. Heide 1989.

2. Federal Bureau of Investigation (FBI) data are the only national source of homicide data in the United States; the victimization surveys conducted by the Bureau of Justice Statistics as part of the National Crime Survey do not measure homicide. FBI statistics compiled from data submitted voluntarily by police departments across the United States have some limitations (see Black 1970; Skogan 1977; Savitz 1978; Savitz and Johnson 1978). These limitations, however, are much less likely to be operative for homicides because of the seriousness of the crime and its higher clearance rate.

The FBI Supplementary Homicide Report (SHR) data base was used for the ten-year period 1977–86 to analyze parricide cases across the nation. Cases involving biological parents were separated from those involving stepparents. Cases with obvious errors in coding were identified in initial screening and excluded from further analysis.

Analysis concentrated on single-victim, single-offender situations largely because of the completeness of the data and their proportionate representation in the data set. These situations were analyzed separately from homicides involving multiple victims or multiple offenders. Single-victim, single-offender situations homicides involving 1,368 fathers, 887 mothers, 562 stepfathers, and 54 stepmothers were examined over the ten-year time frame. Ninety-two percent of fathers, 86 percent of mothers, and 89 percent of stepfathers were killed in single-victim, single-offender situations. The percentage of stepmothers slain in situations of this type, 73 percent, was not as high largely due to the smaller number of stepmothers slain. For additional information see Heide 1987. In an analysis of homicides in Canada between 1974 and 1983, Daly and Wilson (1988b) also found more fathers than mothers slain.

3. The median ages (scores at the 50th percentile) were slightly less than the mean ages: stepfathers, 45; stepmothers, 49; fathers, 52; and mothers, 57.

4. A strong relationship was found in the analysis of SHR data between the age of the offender and rates of mother versus father victimization. Fathers were significantly more likely than mothers to be killed by offspring under 30. Conversely, mothers were significantly more likely to be killed by children 30 years of age and older (chi square = 114.34, df = 1, p <.01). Differences

that emerged between adult and juvenile parricide offenders are noted in the appendix.

5. The higher percentage of stepparents slain by adolescents is consistent with a sociobiological perspective of family homicide. See Daly and Wilson 1988a.

6. FBI 1978–87.

7. There is no evidence to suggest that youth involvement in the killings of fathers, mothers, or stepmothers increased over the period 1977–86. Close study of the data, however, reveals that the proportionate involvement of youth in the murders of stepfathers has steadily increased since 1982, when it was at its lowest. This suggested escalation in the involvement of juveniles in homicides of stepfathers, although not statistically significant, is worthy of note, as it stands in marked contrast to the percentage of juveniles involved in the murders of fathers. Patricides have become somewhat less common since the 1980s. This relationship, although weak, was statistically significant.

8. This determination was possible only for parents. Figures for stepparents are not published separately in the *Uniform Crime Reports*. For a discussion of the difficulties of analyzing the SHR data set and the rules adopted for analysis, see Heide 1987.

9. Solomon, Schmidt, and Ardragna 1990.

10. Bortner 1988.

11. Ibid.; Heide and Pardue 1986.

12. Bender and Curran 1940; Cornell 1989.

13. Bender and Curran 1940.

14. Bender 1959; Zenoff and Zients 1979.

15. Sorrells 1977; Zenoff and Zients 1979; Heide 1984.

16. E.g., Siegel 1983.

17. *Stanford v. Kentucky; Wilkins v. Missouri.*

18. Heide and Pardue 1986.

19. Wadlington, Whitebread, and Davis 1983.

20. Brief of the American Society for Adolescent Psychiatry and the American Orthopsychiatric Association as Amici Curiae in Support of Petitioner, *William Wayne Thompson v. State of Oklahoma*, October 1986.

21. On matricide offenders, see Scwade and Geiger 1953; O'Connell 1963; Gillies 1965; McKnight et al. 1965; Chiswick 1981; Green 1981; Campion et al. 1985; Lipson 1986; on patricide offenders, Cravens et al. 1985; on offenders who killed both parents, Raizen 1960; Maas et al. 1984.

22. My typology of adolescent parricide offenders is in some ways very similar to the typology of juvenile homicide offenders recently proposed and tested by Cornell, Benedek, and Benedek (1989). But I emphasize the motivational dynamics underlying the offense more than Cornell, Benedek, and Benedek do.

23. Mones 1985; Morris 1985; Hull 1987; Daly and Wilson 1988b; Cornell 1989; Ewing 1990b. Severe abuse has also been found in the histories of violent adolescents and those who have killed nonfamily members (see, e.g., Sendi and Blomgren 1975; Lewis et al. 1979, 1983, 1985, 1987; and Ewing 1990b).

24. Hull 1987.

25. Blais 1985; Morris 1985; Rosenthal 1985; Kleiman 1987f; Hull 1987; L. E. Walker 1989.

26. Janos 1983; Matthews 1983; Prendergast 1983.

27. Foucault 1975; Morris 1985; Benedek and Cornell 1989a; Ewing 1990a, 1990b.

28. APA 1980, 1987.

29. E.g., F. Russell 1979.

30. "A Family's Nightmare," 1983.

31. McGraw 1983.

32. Townsend 1983; "Man Accused in Killing of Mother," 1983.

33. Callaway 1989a, 1989b.

34. Callaway 1989b, B13.

35. C. Alldredge (personal communication [June 22, 1989]).

36. Ewing 1990a, 1990b.

37. Bootzin and Acocella 1984.

38. APA 1980, 1987. In cases where the specific criteria for diagnosis are not met (i.e., the antisocial behavior is not part of a pattern that can be attributed to either a conduct disorder or an antisocial personality or other mental disorder), two V codes in particular may be appropriate—childhood or adolescent antisocial behavior and adult antisocial behavior (APA 1987). Individuals so classified, although not diagnosed as having any mental disorder, may also be labeled fittingly as dangerously antisocial.

39. APA 1987.

40. Ibid.

41. Ibid.

42. Cleckley 1976.

43. "The Daddy's Killer?" 1979.

44. "Writer Murdered," 1984.

45. Ewing 1990b.

46. "Muffin," 1970.

47. Ibid.

48. "Who Killed Grandfather?" 1982.

49. Alexander 1985; Coleman 1985.

50. E.g., Bunker 1944; Freud 1961; Rubinstein 1969; Kiremidjian 1976; Roberts 1985; Daly and Wilson 1988b.

51. Bunker 1944, 198.

52. Ibid., 207.

53. E.g., the Ten Commandments; Tanay 1976a; Forward 1989.

54. Morris 1985; Ewing 1990b.

55. "It Made Terrible Sense," 1982.

56. Ibid., 34.

57. Prendergast 1986.

58. Ibid.

59. The reaction to youths who kill their parents has not been met consistently with sympathy, however. In times of fiscal austerity, the federal government decided that youths who had murdered their parents were no longer eligible for Social Security benefits under final rules published on September 24,

1982. Social Security officials had previously suspended such payments in January 1982, upon hearing of two cases in California where individuals adjudicated in juvenile court for the murder of their parents had collected $21,500 and $8,000 upon parole ("Benefits Frozen," 1982).

The *Financial Times* (January 19, 1982) presented the issue in a rather acidic way in an article titled "Bad Luck for Lizzie Borden." The article indicated that parricide had become an increasingly popular activity for children in Southern California to make some fast money. In response, the federal government recently formulated a policy that effectively put an end to the lucrative game by ensuring that Social Security benefits were no longer available for adolescent parricide offenders.

60. "For Janet Reese," 1987.

61. "Poet Tried," 1986; "Woman Says," 1986; "Witness Says," 1987.

62. May 1986; Kleiman 1987a, 1987b, 1987c, 1987d, 1987e, 1987f, 1987g, 1987h, 1988.

63. "Girl Gets Jail Term," 1987.

64. "Goes Free," 1988.

65. Siegel 1983; Chambers 1986; Hull 1987; Ewing 1990a, 1990b.

66. Cornell, Staresina, and Benedek 1989, 53.

67. Ibid., 174.

68. Hull 1987; Mones 1989.

69. Chambers 1986.

70. Siegel 1983.

71. Ibid., 8.

72. Hull 1987.

73. Kaczor 1989, B1.

74. Ibid.; P. Mones (personal communication, February 24 and July 13, 1989).

CHAPTER 2

1. Miller 1990 shares a similar viewpoint.

2. There are similarities in the ways that abusive parents and spouses behave. The offending parent, like the battering spouse, may feel guilty and remorseful after the abusive act, ask the child's forgiveness, and promise never to assault the child again. Caution is, however, advised in generalizing from the literature on battered wives/husbands and battered children because the dynamics between victims and offenders are not identical. For further discussion of battered women, the battered-wife syndrome, and the problems these women face in protecting themselves and their children from harm by an abusive mate, see L. E. Walker 1979, 1984, 1989; Browne 1987; Ewing 1987.

3. Gelles and Straus 1987.

4. Rosen et al. 1983; Guandolo 1985; Jones et al. 1986; Rosen, Frost, and Glaze 1986; Rosenberg 1987.

5. "Woman Faces Abuse Charge after Dressing Son like a Pig," *Tampa Tribune*, July 6, 1988, Section A.

6. Sargent 1962; Duncan and Duncan 1971; Tanay 1973; Corder et al. 1976; Post 1982.

7. Lowen 1983.

8. Middleton-Moz 1986.

9. Burgess et al. 1978; Groth and Birnbaum 1979; Groth 1981.

10. Bass and Davis 1988.

11. Middleton-Moz 1986.

12. Ibid.; Bass and Davis 1988.

13. Bass and Davis 1988.

14. Covert sexual abuse is a culturally relative concept. The norms operating in a particular culture and time period determine what society interprets as sexually explicit or provocative.

15. Middleton-Moz 1986; Bass and Davis 1988; Bradshaw 1988b.

16. Middleton-Moz 1986; Bass and Davis 1988; Forward 1989.

17. Middleton-Moz 1986; Bass and Davis 1988; Forward 1989.

18. Bass and Davis 1988; Forward 1989.

19. Rotter 1966.

20. Bass and Davis 1988; Forward 1989.

21. P. Weislo (personal communication [July 26, 1989]).

22. Burgess et al. 1978; Groth 1981.

23. Bass and Davis 1988.

24. Groth and Birnbaum 1979; Groth 1981.

25. Assault may provide a way for the parent to project or externalize his own internalized shame. In attacking the child the parent may be attempting to free himself of his fear, helplessness, or rage by acting it out. The parent in this situation seems to be symbolically passing his pain on to the child, who now will have to deal with similar shame-based feelings arising from the victimization (Kaufman 1985).

26. Kaufman 1985.

27. Bass and Davis 1988; Bradshaw 1988b; Forward 1989. The National Committee for Prevention of Child Abuse (Garbarino and Garbarino 1980) addresses emotional maltreatment of children. This concept seems to combine both psychological/emotional abuse and emotional neglect. Competence is used as a focal point to identify four types of caregiver behavior that would be considered emotional maltreatment:

Penalizing a child for positive, normal behavior such as smiling, mobility, exploration, vocalization, and manipulation of objects

Discouraging caregiver and infant attachment

Penalizing a child for showing signs of positive self-esteem

Penalizing a child for using interpersonal skills needed for adequate performance in nonfamilial contexts such as schools and peer groups.

28. Bowlby 1969.

29. Ellerstein 1979.

30. Ackerman 1986.

CHAPTER 3

1. Wertham 1941, 24.
2. Ibid., 26.
3. Ibid., 27.
4. A psychoanalytic orientation is associated with Sigmund Freud, the founder of psychoanalysis. Briefly, the term refers to Freud's theory that human behavior is largely determined by deep-seated conflicts in the unconscious that stem from childhood fixations, and to the therapy that developed from it.
5. Wertham 1941, 225.
6. Russell 1965; Corder et al. 1976.
7. D. H. Russell 1979; Sorrells 1981; Cornell, Benedek, and Benedek 1989.
8. Patterson 1943; Medlicott 1955; Hellsten and Katila 1965; Reinhardt 1970; Malmquist 1971; D. H. Russell 1973, 1979; McCarthy 1978; Solway et al. 1981; Gardiner 1985; Myers and Kemph 1988; Benedek and Cornell 1989a.
9. Duncan and Duncan 1971; Anthony and Rizzo 1973; Mack et al. 1973.
10. A history of psychosis was rarely diagnosed in a recent empirical study of 72 juvenile murderers conducted by D. Cornell, E. Benedek, and D. Benedek (1987) using a three-group typology (psychotic, conflict, crime) and was especially unlikely to be found among youths who killed a family member. Of the 72 juveniles, only five adolescents (7 percent) were classified as psychotic and, of these, only one killed a family member. Thirteen of the fifteen family members murdered were killed by adolescents who were engaged in interpersonal conflict; an adolescent committing another crime killed the other family member.

Ewing (1990b), table 2.1, has noted the relative infrequency of diagnoses of psychosis in 17 studies of juvenile homicide offenders beginning with Bender's study in 1959 and including the recent study of Cornell, Benedek, and Benedek (1987).

11. Scherl and Mack 1966; Mohr and McKnight 1971; Sadoff 1971; Mack, Scherl, and Macht 1973; Russell 1984.
12. Foucault 1975.
13. Schizophrenia is a group of disorders characterized by deteriorated functioning, disordered thought and communications, distorted perceptions, blunt or flat affect, bizarre behavior, and disturbances in motor behavior. Hallucinations or delusions are typically present (APA 1987).

In 1978 clinicians were using DSM II. The borderline nature of the diagnosis given by McCully suggests that, although there was definite deterioration in functioning prior to the appearance of characteristic psychotic symptoms, it was not clear whether the symptoms had been present for the six-month period needed for a diagnosis of schizophrenia. Had DSM III-R been available at that time, McCully might have diagnosed schizophreniform disorder.

The reference to a sociopathic understructure suggests that the youth may have met the criteria for an antisocial personality described in chapter 1. DSM III and the current diagnostic system, DSM III-R, allow the diagnostician to note the coexistence of a mental disorder and a personality disorder.

14. Suinn 1984.

15. APA 1980.

16. Medlicott 1955. Paranoid disorders are psychotic disorders characterized by systematized delusions in which the individual's emotional reactions and behaviors are consistent with the delusional network. Hallucinations, if present, are not prominent as in paranoid schizophrenia. The individual with a paranoid disorder, in contrast to a person suffering from paranoid schizophrenia, typically is not impaired in his daily work, intellectual functioning, and personal hygiene habits. One diagnosed as having a paranoid disorder tends to experience impairment in social relationships and marital life (APA 1987).

17. Benedek and Cornell 1989a.

18. McCully 1978.

19. Scherl and Mack 1966; Russell 1984.

20. Heide 1984.

21. Heide 1988.

22. In the remaining case, that of Patty Smith (chapter 9), the youth saw herself as powerless in relation to others. Her sense of being overwhelmed by life events was the result of her personality development, which was less mature than the other parricide offenders', and not a gender difference.

23. Dissociative disorders involve "a disturbance or alteration in the normally integrative functions of identity, memory, or consciousness" (APA 1987). These disorders may be sudden or gradual, transient or chronic. DSM III-R delineates four types of dissociative disorders: multiple personality disorder, psychogenic fugue, psychogenic amnesia, and depersonalization disorder. The APA has reserved a fifth category, dissociative disorder not otherwise specified, for dissociative states that do not meet the criteria for any of the first four.

24. As discussed in chapter 6, to feel badly for one's behavior, one must see oneself as accountable for that behavior, recognize that behavioral choices are available, and have an internalized value system against which to evaluate behavior. Not all adolescents or adults have reached the level of personality development associated with these perceptions. Hence, these individuals are not truly capable of experiencing remorse.

25. Heide 1984.

26. Inter-rater agreement (percentage agreement between two raters evaluating the same information) in type recognition and identification exceeded 80 percent on six of the seven types. On the type remaining, the nihilistic killer, inter-rater agreement was only 60 percent, indicating that this type needs greater specification.

To determine how valid this clinical typology is, more than 1200 items were constructed to measure 47 different content areas covered during the assessment interviews. A reliability assessment of these items provided convincing evidence that empirical analysis of these data is possible.

27. Heide 1984, 1985.

28. Tanay (1973) talked about the isolation of the nuclear family in society in general, rather than the isolation of families in which parricide occurred, and hence is not cited in support here.

29. Cornell, Benedek, and Benedek (1989), in their study of 72 adolescents charged with homicide, noted significant differences in weapons used by the youths to kill particular types of victims. Although they did not report specifically on weapons used by adolescents who killed parents, they noted that "Adolescents who murdered family members most often did so with a gun, and none of them failed to use some kind of weapon" (71). Nine of 15 adolescents in their study who killed family members used firearms of some type.

30. In studies where the focus has been on juvenile homicide offenders rather than specifically on adolescent parricide offenders, references to the slain parent having been abusive and an alcoholic or prone to episodes of heavy drinking have also been made in the brief case histories presented. These case citations provide further evidence that alcoholism/excessive alcohol consumption, particularly by an abusive parent, is often a significant factor in cases of adolescent parricide. For example, Malmquist (1971) mentioned a case of a 15-year-old boy who killed his abusive stepfather with a gun ("The boy had been a witness to a series of beatings when the father [stepfather] was intoxicated" [464]). Hellsten and Katila (1965) described a case of a 13-year-old boy who also shot to death his abusive father "who used alcohol fairly often" (59). A case described by Benedek and Cornell (1989a) of a 17-year-old boy who shot and killed his abusive alcoholic father was mentioned in chapter 1.

CHAPTER 4

1. Monahan 1981.

2. Cork 1969 (reissued 1980); Ackerman 1979; Black 1981, 1985; Wegscheider 1981; Deutsch 1982; Woititz 1983, 1985; Gravitz and Bowden 1985; Seixas and Youcha 1985; Wegscheider-Cruse 1985; Middleton-Moz and Dwinell 1986; Kritsberg 1988; Wholey 1988.

3. Bradshaw 1988; Bowden and Gravitz 1988; Wholey 1988.

4. Bowden and Gravitz 1988.

5. Middleton-Moz and Dwinell 1986; Bowden and Gravitz 1988.

6. Mayer and Black 1977; Walker, Bonner, and Kaufman 1988; Faller 1990.

7. Walker 1979; Gelles 1987.

8. Browne 1987; Ewing 1987; L. E. Walker 1989.

9. Cermak 1988, 56.

10. Greenleaf 1981.

11. E.g., Wegscheider 1981; Subby 1987; Cermak 1988; Wholey 1988.

12. First National Conference on Co-Dependency, Scottsdale, Arizona, September 1989.

13. Cermak 1988, 223.

14. Cermak 1988.

15. Ibid.

16. Cork 1969.

17. Valliant 1983.

18. Cork 1969.

19. Ibid.

20. Ibid., 51. Cork identified 53 alcoholic fathers and 19 alcoholic mothers in her sample (p. 45). She noted that the proportion of male to female alcoholics in her sample was much lower than in other reports, which generally suggest that there are five male alcoholics to every female alcoholic. While acknowledging that the gender difference might have resulted from her study design, she expressed a belief that much hidden alcoholism exists among the female population.

21. Ibid., 51.

22. Ackerman 1979; Middleton 1984; Seixas and Youcha 1985; Forward 1989.

23. Bradshaw 1988b, 1990.

24. Gillespie 1988; L. E. Walker 1989.

25. Given the small number of stepmothers slain in single-victim, single-offender situations during the decade, 54 total, it is not surprising that the differences in weapons used by juveniles and adults were not statistically significant. The likelihood of noticeable differences reaching the level of significance increases with the number of cases available for analysis.

CHAPTER 5

1. Modern statutes have followed the Model Penal Code's (1962) lead in abandoning the distinction between voluntary and involuntary manslaughter and creating a single manslaughter offense. Under this framework, manslaughter is a killing committed recklessly or one which would otherwise be murder if not committed "under the influence of extreme mental or emotional disturbance" for which there is a reasonable excuse or explanation. In addition to describing degrees of murder and combining types of manslaughter, the Model Penal Code created the new category "negligent homicide" for deaths that resulted from negligence. For a more extensive discussion of voluntary manslaughter, the Model Penal Code's recommendations for homicide laws, derivative homicide laws, and pertinent statute and case citations, see Dix 1988, 121–27.

2. There are other defenses that may be raised by the defendant to absolve him or her from criminal responsibility. These include, for example, in-

fancy, involuntary intoxication, ignorance or mistake of fact, necessity, duress, entrapment, and lack of consent. Self-defense provisions may be written in terms of the justifiable use of deadly force and the justified use of nondeadly force. For a more extensive discussion of these defenses, see Dix 1988.

3. Gillespie 1988.

4. Ewing 1987.

5. Browne 1987, 174.

6. Gillespie 1988.

7. Ewing 1987.

8. Stone 1975, 1978.

9. Heide 1983c; Morris 1986.

10. E.g., Morris 1986.

11. E.g., Pasewark 1981; Heide 1983c; Morris 1986.

12. "Commitment Following an Insanity Acquittal," 1981; Heide 1983c; Morris 1986.

13. Dix 1981; Heide 1983c.

14. Rogers 1986, 223.

15. Rogers 1986.

16. Shapiro 1984; Rogers 1986.

17. Shapiro 1984.

18. Ibid.

19. *Cirack v. State* (1967).

20. The legal elements of a crime consist of legality (no crime without a law), actus reus (forbidden conduct), mens rea (criminal intent or guilty mind), concurrence of actus reus and mens rea, resultant harm, causation (harm would not have occurred were it not for the defendant's conduct), and punishment (no crime without a legally prescribed punishment). For a discussion of these elements, see Vetter and Silverman 1986, 18–21.

21. Intent to kill is one of the several different mental states that if present at the time of the killing are considered to constitute the "malice aforethought" required to convict a defendant who kills another human being unlawfully of (first- or second-degree) murder. In this typology, it is the presence or absence of specific intent to kill that is important because of its clinical significance. Malice aforethought is a broader concept than specific intent to kill and encompasses situations where the intent to kill is implied rather than actual under circumstances that do not otherwise excuse, justify, or mitigate the homicidal conduct to manslaughter. Mental states other than intent to kill that have been considered to constitute the malice aforethought necessary to support a murder conviction when present at the time of the killing include intent to inflict great bodily injury, intent to commit a felony, intent to resist lawful arrest, and awareness of a high risk of death—"depraved mind" or "abandoned and malignant heart" murder. For a more extensive discussion of constructs of malice aforethought, homicide laws, and pertinent statute and case citations, see Dix 1988, 112–14. Empirical verification of the utility of this taxonomy among the population of adult murderers as well as juvenile homicide offenders would also be valuable.

22. Woolf 1977, 601.

23. Ibid., 308.

24. Use of this classification scheme builds upon the work of Buss (1961), who classified aggression as instrumental or expressive. By incorporating intention to kill and desire to hurt the victim into the framework of homicide, it is possible to distinguish between instrumentally and emotionally based killings. Use of the term *nihilistic* was suggested by Fromm (1973).

25. A minor blow would not constitute adequate provocation because it would not be expected to provoke a reasonable person to kill. A violent and painful blow under certain conditions has been deemed to constitute sufficient provocation. Most jurisdictions have held that mere words do not constitute adequate provocation. A few jurisdictions have held, however, that words, particularly if they convey information of a fact that would constitute reasonable provocation if observed (e.g., defendant is told of spouse's adultery), may be sufficient to cause adequate provocation. For a more extensive discussion of voluntary manslaughter and pertinent statute and case citations, see Dix 1988, 121–24.

26. Woolf 1977, 776.

27. *Thompson v. Oklahoma* (1988).

28. In *The Anatomy of Human Destructiveness* (1973), Fromm maintained that it was both theoretically possible and necessary to distinguish between two types of aggression. "Benign" or defensive aggression is similar to the drives of other animals who strive to preserve vital interests. "Malignant" aggression is specifically a human phenomenon. Fromm theorized that some individuals and cultures seem to be driven by a "passion" rooted in their individual or collective characters to destroy members of their own species when no rational gain, either biological or economic, exists.

29. Morgan 1975; "The Youth Crime Plague," 1977; Taft 1983; "Children Who Kill," 1986.

30. Following his arrest for scores of murders, Lucas stated that his mother was not his first homicide victim. While the veracity of Lucas' remarks has been questioned, one fact is certain: If his mother was indeed not his first victim, she was among the first and was far from his last.

31. Darrach and Norris 1984; Egger 1990.

32. Cheney 1976.

CHAPTER 6

1. Those who are designated as mental health professionals vary with state law. People with advanced degrees in medicine or the social and behavioral sciences (psychiatrists, psychologists, mental health counselors, family and marriage counselors, social workers, and the like) are generally recognized as mental health professionals.

2. Preliminary analysis of interviews with 59 adolescent murderers has

suggested that the best source of data in uncovering this destructive pattern was typically not the adolescents' descriptions of their homicidal involvements, because many youths talked about them only guardedly. Unguarded remarks made about seemingly innocuous content areas—activities, pets, girlfriends, sexual partners and fantasies, and so on, proved to be invaluable in suggesting that a few of the sample subjects really seemed to enjoy acting sadistically and destroying other living objects for reasons of which they were usually unaware. Further analysis of these data should provide more insight into the underlying dynamics involved in purely destructive behavior and suggest preventive efforts to eradicate this response pattern. For additional findings from this study, see Heide 1984.

    3. Fla. Stat. § 921.141 (6) (1991).

    4. Rosenhan and Seligman 1989.

    5. Ibid.

    6. Ibid.

    7. Kohlberg 1969.

    8. Harris 1988; Reitsma-Street and Leschied 1988.

    9. Warren 1971; Posey 1988; Van Voorhis 1988.

    10. Sullivan, Grant, and Grant 1957.

    11. Warren 1969, 1971, 1978; Harris 1979, 1988; Heide 1982, 1983a, 1983b. For a summary of I-level's development, classification methods, reliability and validity, current status, and future development, see Harris 1988.

    12. Sullivan, Grant, and Grant 1957.

    13. Warren 1971.

    14. Warren 1966.

    15. Ibid.

    16. The salient characteristics of individuals classified at the two lowest and highest I-levels are given below. For more discussion of all seven integration levels, see Sullivan, Grant, and Grant 1957.

Integration Level 1: Initially, infants do not see themselves as separate from the world. As they try to satisfy basic needs, they learn to discriminate between themselves and the nonself.

Integration Level 2: Most infants who recognize differences between self and nonself will move on to the next integration level, where they come to recognize that there are differences between persons and things.

Integration Level 6: Individuals at this level are able to perceive differences between themselves and the social roles they play. They can recognize and accept role inconsistencies in themselves and others because they are able to see continuity and stability.

Integration Level 7: Individuals at the highest stage of sociperceptual development are able to see the integrating processes in themselves and in others. Sullivan, Grant, and Grant (1957) hypothesize that it is unlikely that anyone completes this stage in our society.

    17. APA 1987, 250.

CHAPTER 8

1. Heide 1983a.
2. Harris 1979; Heide 1982, 1983b.
3. Warren 1966; Heide 1982.
4. Miranda warnings consist of advising suspects who are in custody prior to questioning that they have a right to remain silent, that anything they say can and will be used against them in a court of law, that they have a right to an attorney, and that, if they cannot afford an attorney, one will be provided (*Miranda v. Arizona* [1966]).

CHAPTER 9

1. Warren 1966; Heide 1982.
2. Lowen 1983.
3. I administered the C.A.S.T., an instrument developed by John W. Jones in 1982 to identify children of alcoholics. I read Patty 30 statements to which she was to reply yes or no. If an individual answers affirmatively to six of the 30 statements, she is, according to the test designer, probably a child of an alcoholic. Patty answered yes to 25 of the questions. For this test, see Black 1981, appendix A.
4. Heide 1984.
5. E.g., Bass and Davis 1988; Forward 1989.
6. Giallombardo 1966.

CHAPTER 10

1. Benedek, Cornell, and Staresina 1989.
2. Duncan and Duncan 1971, 78.
3. Duncan and Duncan 1971; Tanay 1973, 1976b; Corder et al. 1976; Post 1982.
4. Benedek, Cornell, and Staresina 1989, 243.
5. References included Kaufman 1945; Reich 1945; Dychtwald 1950; Lowen 1958, 1976, 1983; Berne 1961; Satir 1964; Kübler-Ross 1969; Perls 1969; Janov 1970; Palmer 1975; Kurtz and Prestera 1976; Black 1981; Gil 1983; Gravitz and Bowden 1985; Keleman 1985; Magid and McKelvey 1987; Painter 1987; Whitfield 1987; Bass and Davis 1988; Bradshaw 1988a, 1988b, 1990; Oliver-Diaz and O'Gorman 1988; Forward 1989; Weiss and Weiss 1989.
6. These treatment strategies require specialized training. Readers are advised that engaging in the therapeutic techniques described in this chapter without the requisite training and safe environment described later in the chapter can be dangerous and should not be attempted.

7. Warren 1969, 1971; Palmer 1975; Harris 1988; Reitsma-Street and Leschied 1988; Andrews et al. 1990. The best candidates for treatment are generally those who perceive at I-level 4 or 5. Level 3 clients, whose typical behavioral response is that of the passive conformist—such as Patty Smith in chapter 9—are more amenable to treatment than the other two level 3 subtypes (see Warren 1966, 1971).

8. Benedek, Cornell, and Staresina 1989.

9. See, e.g., Kübler-Ross 1969.

10. Within I-levels 4 and 5, those whose typical behavioral response pattern is "neurotic" (neurotic acting-out or neurotic anxious) would be most likely to hurt themselves (see Warren 1966, 1971).

11. One technique to facilitate the release of explosive anger involves breathing exercises that intensify the feeling. Another has the client exaggerate the way he is holding or using his body to contain the feeling (e.g., having the client clench his jaw until muscles exhaust themselves). A third consists of directly confronting the client with what he is feeling.

Sometimes words or expressions can be used to mobilize and facilitate the direct expression of emotion (e.g., having adolescent shout "Yes!" "No!" "Give it to me. It's mine." "Get off my back!" or "I hate you!" Other techniques include biting or twisting a towel, stamping his feet, and having a temper tantrum.

12. The youth needs to learn to use "I" statements that are indicative of his thoughts, needs, and feelings. In response to unfair treatment, the client might role-play the situation with the therapist and rehearse saying something like, "I feel angry when you tell me how I feel. I would appreciate it if you would let me decide how I feel about things." The therapist might instruct the youth to consider punching a punching bag, screaming in a private place, or engaging in strenuous physical exercise when he feels consumed with anger.

13. One technique to facilitate the release of fear includes breathing exercises that intensify the feeling of fear. Another technique involves having the client exaggerate his body's posture to the point of expressing fear or exhausting the body's ability to contain it (e.g., asking the youth to act out being frozen in fear). A third technique consists of having the APO scream "Help!" "No!" "Go away!" "Leave me alone!" or "Don't hurt me!" The APO can also scream nonsense syllables to get in touch with his fear. Other techniques require that the therapist take a more direct approach (e.g., engaging in prolonged eye contact with the client). Techniques used to facilitate the direct expression of fear include screaming, shaking, panicked running within the room, and panicked crying.

14. Techniques used to facilitate the release of sadness encourage the client to experience his predominant feeling, which may then revert to the underlying feeling of sadness. For example, the youth may initially be expressing anger when he screams. As he becomes exhausted, his body may

collapse, allowing the underlying sadness to surface. Another technique involves having the youth talk about the hurt from his childhood and homicide, express his needs to be nurtured, comforted, or forgiven, physically reach out, and call out "Mother" or "Father." Other techniques include having the client breathe to intensify the feeling, shout nonsense syllables, or exaggerate the body's posture to express the sadness (e.g., by holding breath).

15. Bradshaw 1988a.

16. Gravitz and Bowden (1985, 98–100) present a "Personal Bill of Rights," consisting of 20 rights which they maintain belong to every human being.

CHAPTER 11

1. Moore 1987.
2. Cohn 1983.
3. Donnelly 1991, 105.
4. Some women who were victimized as adults by their husbands were unable to protect their children from harm by these men. See Walker 1979; Browne 1987.
5. Leerhsen and Namuth 1988.
6. Myers 1987.
7. Ibid., 2.
8. Flowers 1986.
9. Davidson and Horowitz 1984.
10. U.S. Department of Justice 1985.
11. J. Wiedenhoft (personal communication [January 9, 1991]).
12. U.S. Department of Justice 1985.
13. Fuller 1988.
14. Donnelly 1991, 101.
15. Ibid., 102.
16. Ibid., 104.
17. See, e.g., Ewing 1987.
18. Donnelly 1991, 102.

APPENDIX

1. Heide 1987.
2. FBI 1978–87.
3. Heide 1987.
4. Ibid.
5. FBI 1978–87.
6. Heide 1987.
7. FBI 1978–87.

■ BIBLIOGRAPHY

A family's nightmare in posh Palos Verdes. (1983, April 4). *Newsweek*, 27.

Ackerman, R. J. (1979). *Children of alcoholics: A guidebook for educators, therapists, and parents* (2d ed.). Holmes Beach: Fla.: Learning Publications.

———. (1986). *Child Abuse and Neglect*. Paper presented at the Second National Conference on Children of Alcoholics, Washington, D.C.

Alexander, S. (1985). *Nutcracker*. New York: Dell.

Alpern, D., and Kasindorf, M. (1982, April 5). Who killed Grandfather? *Newsweek*, 34.

American Psychiatric Association (APA). (1980). *Diagnostic and statistical manual of mental disorders* (3d ed.). Washington: Author.

———. (1987). *Diagnostic and statistical manual of mental disorders* (3d ed., revised). Washington: Author.

Andrews, D. A., Zinger, I., Hoge, R. D., Bonta, J., Gendreau, P., and Cullen, F. T. (1990). Does correctional treatment work? A clinically relevant and psychologically informed meta-analysis. *Criminology 28*(3), 369–404.

Anthony, E. J., and Rizzo, A. (1973). Adolescents who kill or try to kill their fathers. In E. J. Anthony and C. Koupernik (Eds.), *The impact of disease and death* (333–50). New York: Wiley Interscience.

Bad luck for Lizzie Borden. (1982, January 19). *Financial Times*, 14.

Bass, E., and Davis, L. (1988). *The courage to heal*. New York: Harper & Row.

Bender, L. (1959, December). Children and adolescents who have killed. *American Journal of Psychiatry 116*, 510–13.

Bender, L., and Curran, F. J. (1940). Children and adolescents who kill. *Criminal Psychopathology 1*(4), 297–321.

Benedek, E. P., and Cornell, D. G. (1989a). Clinical presentations of homicidal adolescents. In E. P. Benedek and D. G. Cornell (Eds.), *Juvenile homicide* (37–57). Washington: American Psychiatric Press.

———. (1989b). *Juvenile homicide*. Washington: American Psychiatric Press.

Benedek, E. P., Cornell, D. G., and Staresina, L. (1989). Treatment of the homicidal adolescent. In E. P. Benedek and D. G. Cornell (Eds.), *Juvenile Homicide* (221–47). Washington: American Psychiatric Press.

Benefits frozen for kids who kill parents. (1982, October 1). *Juvenile Justice Digest*, 6.

Berne, E. (1961). *TA—Transactional analysis in psychotherapy*. New York: Ballantine.

Black, C. (1981). *It will never happen to me*. Denver: M.A.C.

———. (1985). *Repeat after me*. Denver: M.A.C.

Black, D. (1970). Production of crime rates. *American Sociological Review 35*, 733–48.

Blais, M. (1985, March 10). The twisting of Kenny White. *Tropic (The Miami Herald)*, 10–17.

Bootzin, R. R., and Acocella, J. R. (1984). *Abnormal psychology* (4th ed.). New York: Random House.

Bortner, M. A. (1988). *Delinquency and justice*. New York: McGraw-Hill.

Bowlby, J. (1969). *Attachment and loss: Vol. 1. Attachment*. New York: Basic.

Bradshaw, J. (1988a). *Bradshaw on: Healing the shame that binds you*. Deerfield Beach, Fla.: Health Communications.

———. (1988b). *Bradshaw on: The family*. Pompano Beach, Fla.: Health Communications.

———. (1990). *Homecoming*. New York: Bantam.

Brief of the American Society for Adolescent Psychiatry and the American Orthopsychiatric Association as Amici Curiae in Support of Petitioner, *William Wayne Thompson v. State of Oklahoma* (October 1986).

Browne, A. (1987). *When battered women kill*. New York: Free Press.

Bunker, H. A. (1944). Mother-murder in myth and legend. *Psychoanalytic Quarterly 13*, 198–207.

Burgess, A. W., Groth, A. N., Holmstrom, L. L., and Sgroi, S. M. (1978). *Sexual assault of children and adolescents*. Lexington, Mass.: Lexington Books.

Buss, A. H. (1961). *The psychology of aggression*. New York: John Wiley.

Callaway, J. D. (1989a, March 18). Man given life term in slaying. *Tampa Tribune*, B1, B6.

———. (1989b, March 17). Son's list of things to do included killing mom. *Tampa Tribune*, B1, B13.

Campion, J., Cravens, J. M., Rotholc, A., Weinstein, H. C., Covan, F., and Alpert, M. (1985). A study of matricidal men. *American Journal of Psychiatry 142* (3), 312–17.

Cermak, T. (1988). *A time to heal*. Los Angeles: Jeremy P. Tarcher.

Chambers, M. (1986, October 12). Growing number pleading self-defense in murder of parent. *New York Times*, Y23.

Cheney, M. (1976). *The co-ed killer*. New York: Walker.

Children who kill. (1986, November 24). *Newsweek*, 93–94.

Chiswick, D. (1981). Matricide. *British Medical Journal 283* (14), 1279.

Cirack v. State, 201 So. 2d 706 (Fla. 1967).

Cleckley, H. (1976). *The mask of sanity*. St. Louis: C. V. Mosby.

Cohn, A. H. (1983). *An approach to preventing child abuse*. Chicago: National Committee on the Prevention of Child Abuse.

Coleman, J. (1985). *At Mother's request*. New York: Pocket Books.

Commitment following an insanity acquittal. (1981, January). *Harvard Law Review 94* (3), 605–07.

Corder, B. F., Ball, B. C., Haizlip, T. M., Rollins, R., and Beaumont, R.

(1976). Adolescent parricide: A comparison with other adolescent murder. *American Journal of Psychiatry 133*(8): 957–61.

Cork, R. M. (1969). *The forgotten children.* Toronto: PaperJacks.

Cormier, B. M., Angliker, C. C. J., Gagne, P. W., and Markus, B. (1978). Adolescents who kill a member of the family. In J. M. Eekelaar and S. N. Katz (Eds.), *Family violence: An international and interdisciplinary study* (466–78). Toronto: Butterworth.

Cornell, D. G. (1989). Causes of juvenile homicide: A review of the literature. In E. P. Benedek and D. G. Cornell (Eds.), *Juvenile Homicide* (1–36). Washington: American Psychiatric Press.

Cornell, D. G., Benedek, E. P., and Benedek, D. M. (1987). Juvenile homicide: Prior adjustment and a proposed typology. *American Journal of Orthopsychiatry 57*(3), 383–93.

———. (1989). A typology of juvenile homicide offenders. In E. P. Benedek and D. G. Cornell (Eds.), *Juvenile Homicide* (59–84). Washington: American Psychiatric Press.

Cornell, D. G., Staresina, L., and Benedek, E. P. (1989). Legal outcome of juveniles charged with homicide. In E. P. Benedek and D. G. Cornell (Eds.), *Juvenile Homicide* (163–82). Washington: American Psychiatric Press.

Cravens, J. M., Campion, J., Rotholc, A., Covan, F., and Cravens, R. A. (1985). A study of men charged with patricide. *American Journal of Psychiatry 142*(9), 1089–91.

The daddy's killers? (1979, March 5). *Newsweek,* 54.

Daly, M., and Wilson, M. (1988a, October 28). Evolutionary social psychology and family homicide. *Science 242,* 519–24.

———. (1988b). *Homicide.* New York: Aldine de Gruyter.

Darrach, B., and Norris, J. (1984, August). An American tragedy. *Life.*

Davidson, H. A., and Horowitz, R. M. (1984). Protection of children from family maltreatment. In R. M. Horowitz and H. A. Davidson (Eds.), *Legal rights of children* (262–312). New York: McGraw-Hill.

Deutsch, C. (1982). *Broken bottles, broken dreams.* New York: Teachers College, Columbia University.

Dix, G. E. (1981). *Gilbert law summaries: Criminal law* (12th ed.) Chicago: Harcourt Brace Jovanovich.

———. (1988). *Gilbert law summaries: Criminal law* (14th ed.) Chicago: Harcourt Brace Jovanovich.

Donnelly, A. H. C. (1991). What have we learned about prevention: What should we do about it. *Child Abuse and Neglect 15*(1), 99–106.

Duncan, J. W., and Duncan, G. M. (1971). Murder in the family. *American Journal of Psychiatry 127*(11), 74–78.

Dychtwald, K. (1950). *Bodymind.* Los Angeles: Jeremy P. Tarcher.

Egger, S. A. (1990). *Serial murder: An elusive phenomenon.* New York: Praeger.

Ellerstein, M. S. (1979). The cutaneous manifestations of child abuse and neglect. *American Journal of Diseases of Children 133,* 906–09.

Ewing, C. P. (1987). *Battered women who kill.* Lexington, Mass.: Lexington Books.

———. (1990a). *Kids who kill.* Lexington, Mass.: Lexington Books.

———. (1990b). *When children kill.* Lexington, Mass.: Lexington Books.

Faller, K. C. (1990). *Understanding child sexual maltreatment.* Newbury Park, Calif.: Sage.

Federal Bureau of Investigation (FBI). (1978–87). *Crime in the United States* (1977–1986). Washington: U.S. Government Printing Office.

Florida Statutes §921.141 et seq. (1991).

Flowers, R. B. (1986). *Children and criminality.* New York: Greenwood.

For Janet Reese, death seemed her only way out. (1987, February 15). *St. Petersburg Times,* 1A, 16A.

Forward, S. (1989). *Toxic parents.* New York: Bantam.

Foucault, M. (Ed). (1975). *I, Pierre Rivière, having slaughtered my mother, my sister, and my brother . . . A case of parricide in the nineteenth century.* New York: Pantheon.

Freud, S. (1961). *The interpretation of dreams.* J. Strachey (Ed. and Trans.). New York: John Wiley. (Original work published 1900)

Fromm, E. (1973). *The anatomy of human destructiveness.* Greenwich, Conn.: Fawcett.

Fuller, J. A. (1988, July/August). Guardians ad litem in custody dispute resolutions: Representation of the child's best interests. *Florida Bar Journal,* 27–30.

Garbarino, J., and Garbarino, A. C. (1980). *Emotional maltreatment of children.* Chicago: National Committee for Prevention of Child Abuse.

Gardiner, M. (1985). *The deadly innocents: Portraits of children who kill.* New Haven: Yale University Press.

Gelles, R. J. (1987). *The violent home.* Newbury Park, Calif.: Sage.

Gelles, R. J., and Straus, M. (1987). Is violence toward children increasing? A comparison of 1975 and 1985 national survey rates. In *Family violence* by R. J. Gelles (78–88). Beverly Hills, Calif.: Sage.

Giallombardo, R. (1966). *Society of women: A study of a woman's prison.* New York: John Wiley.

Gil, E. (1983). *Outgrowing the pain.* New York: Dell.

Gillespie, C. K. (1988). *Justifiable homicide: Battered women, self-defense, and the law.* Columbus: Ohio State University Press.

Gillies, H. (1965). Murder in the west of Scotland. *British Journal of Psychiatry 111,* 1087–94.

Girl gets jail term in killing. (1987, October 6). *Tampa Tribune,* 4A.

Goes free. (1988, January 20). *Tampa Tribune,* 6A.

Gravitz, H. L., and Bowden, J. D. (1985). *Guide to recovery: A book for adult children of alcoholics.* Holmes Beach, Fla.: Learning Publications.

Green, C. (1981). Matricide by sons. *Medicine, Science and Law 21,* 207–14.

Greenleaf, J. (1981, April). *Co-alcoholic para-alcoholic.* Paper presented at the Annual Alcoholism Forum of the National Council on Alcoholism, New Orleans.

Groth, A. N. (1981). Chart of sexual offenders against children. (Available from Forensic Mental Health Associates, Inc., Webster, Mass.)

Groth, A. N., and Birnbaum, H. J. (1979). *Men who rape: The psychology of the offender*. New York: Plenum.

Guandolo, V. L. (1985). Munchausen syndrome by proxy: An outpatient challenge. *Pediatrics 75*(3): 526–30.

Harris, P. W. (1979). *The interpersonal maturity of delinquents and nondelinquents*. Unpublished Ph.D. dissertation, State University of New York at Albany.

———. (1988). The interpersonal maturity level classification system: I-level. *Criminal Justice and Behavior 15*, 58–77.

Heide, K. M. (1982). Classification of offenders ordered to make restitution by I-level and by specific personality dimensions. Unpublished Ph.D. dissertation, State University of New York at Albany.

———. (1983a, November). *Classification of adolescent murderers by interpersonal maturity level*. Paper presented at the thirty-fifth annual meeting of the American Society of Criminology, Denver, Colorado.

———. (1983b). An empirical assessment of the value of using personality data in restitution outcome prediction. In W. S. Laufer and J. M. Day (Eds.), *Personality theory, moral development and criminal behavior* (251–77). Lexington, Mass.: D.C. Heath.

———. (1983c, January). *The insanity defense: Abolish it, change it, or leave it alone?* Paper presented at the annual conference of the Florida Criminal Justice Educators, Orlando, Florida.

———. (1984, November). *A preliminary identification of types of adolescent murderers*. Paper presented at the thirty-sixth annual meeting of the American Society of Criminology, Cincinnati, Ohio.

———. (1985, November). *Parricide: An in-depth examination of the prototypical case*. Paper presented at the thirty-seventh annual meeting of the American Society of Criminology, San Diego, California.

———. (1986). A taxonomy of murder: The motivational dynamics behind the homicidal acts of adolescents. *Journal of Justice Issues 1*(1), 3–19.

———. (1987, November). *Parricide: Nationwide incidence and correlates*. Paper presented at the thirty-ninth meeting of the American Society of Criminology, Montreal, Canada.

———. (1988, November). *Parricide committed by adolescents: Retrospective interpretation and identification of high risk subjects*. Paper presented at the fortieth annual meeting of the American Society of Criminology, Chicago, Illinois.

———. (1989). Parricide: Incidence and issues. *The Justice Professional 4*(1), 19–41.

Heide, K. M., and Pardue, B. W. (1986). Juvenile justice in Florida: A legal and empirical analysis. *Law and Policy 8*(4), 437–62.

Hellsten, P., and Katila, O. (1965). Murder and other homicide, by children under 15 in Finland. *Psychiatric Quarterly Supplement 39*(1), 54–74.

Hull, J. D. (1987, October 19). Brutal treatment, vicious deeds. *Time*, 68.

It made terrible sense. (1982, December 13). *Time*, 34.

Janos, L. (1983, March 7). On a windswept Wyoming prairie. *People Weekly*, 34–36.

Janov, A. (1970). *The primal scream*. New York: Dell.

Jones, J. G., Butler, H. L., Hamilton, B., Perdue, J. D., Stern, H. P., and Woody, R. C. (1986). Munchausen syndrome by proxy. *Child Abuse and Neglect 10*, 33–40.

Kaczor, B. (1989, July 1). Precedent-setting defense gets girl cleared in slaying. *Tampa Tribune*, B1, B5.

Kaufman, G. (1945). *Shame: The power of caring* (2nd ed., revised). Cambridge, Mass.: Schneckman.

Keleman, S. (1985). *Emotional anatomy*. Berkeley: Center Press.

Kiremidjian, D. (1976). Crime and punishment: Matricide and the woman question. *American Imago 33*, 403–33.

Kleiman, D. (1986, September 14). Murder on Long Island. *New York Times Magazine*.

———. (1987a, September 14). A case of sexual abuse and silence. *New York Times*, II, 7, col. 3.

———. (1987b, September 22). Boyfriend testifies about his role in having girl's father murdered. *New York Times*, II, 3, col. 2.

———. (1987c, September 15). Girl says hiring father's killer was "like a game." *New York Times*, II, 1, col. 2.

———. (1987d, September 17). Girl tells how she and friend planned killing of her father. *New York Times*, II, 2, col. 5.

———. (1987e, September 2). Murder case on Long Island pierces the silence on incest. *New York Times*.

———. (1987f, September 10). Report urges jail for New York teen-ager in killing of her father. *New York Times*, II, 1, col. 2.

———. (1987g, October 6). Teen-ager who charged sex abuse is jailed for planning father's killing. *New York Times*, II, 1, col. 5.

———. (1987h, September 18). Uncle says he heard of girl's abuse. *New York Times*, II, 1, col. 2.

———. (1988). *A deadly silence*. New York: Atlantic Monthly Press.

Kohlberg, L. (1969). Stage and sequence: The cognitive-developmental approach to socialization. In D. Goslin (Ed.), *Handbook of socialization theory and research* (347–480). Chicago: Rand McNally.

Kritsberg, W. (1988). *The adult children of alcoholics syndrome*. New York: Bantam.

Kübler-Ross, E. (1969). *On death and dying*. New York: Macmillan.

Kurtz, R., and Prestera, H. (1976). *The body reveals*. New York: Harper & Row.

Leerhsen, C., and Namuth, T. (1988, January 18). Alcohol and the family. *Newsweek*, 62–68.

Lewis, D. O., Moy, E., Jackson, L. D., Aaronson, R., Restifo, N., Serra, S., and Simos, A. (1985). Biopsychosocial characteristics of children who later murder: A prospective study. *American Journal of Psychiatry 142*, 1161–67.

Lewis, D. O., Pincus, J. H., Bard, D., Richardson, E., Prichep, L. S., Feldman, M., and Yeager, C. (1988). Neuropsychiatric, psychoeducational and family characteristics of 14 juveniles condemned to death in the United States. *American Journal of Psychiatry 145*, 584–89.

Lewis, D. O., Shanok, S. S., Grant, M., and Ritvo, E. (1983). Homicidally aggressive young children: Neuropsychiatric and experimental correlates. *American Journal of Psychiatry 140*(2), 148–53.

Lewis, D. O., Shanok, S. S., Pincus, J. H., and Glaser, G. H. (1979). Violent juvenile delinquents: Psychiatric, neurological, psychological, and abuse factors. *Journal of the American Academy of Child Psychiatry 18*, 307–19.

Lipson, C. T. (1986). A case report on matricide. *American Journal of Psychiatry 143*, 112–13.

Lowen, A. (1958). *The language of the body.* New York: Collier-Macmillan.

———. (1976). *Bioenergetics.* New York: Penguin.

———. (1983). *Narcissism: Denial of the true self.* New York: Macmillan.

Maas, R. L., Prakash, R., Hollender, M. H., and Regan, W. M. (1984). Double parricide—matricide and patricide: A comparison with other schizophrenic murders. *Psychiatric Quarterly 56*(4), 286–90.

Mack, J. E., Scherl, D. J., and Macht, L. B. (1973). Children who kill their mothers. In E. J. Anthony and C. Koupernik (Eds.), *The child in his family* (319–32). New York: John Wiley.

Magid, K., and McKelvey, C. A. (1987). *High risk: Children without a conscience.* New York: Bantam.

Malmquist, C. P. (1971). Premonitory signs of homicidal aggression in juveniles. *American Journal of Psychiatry 128*(4), 461–65.

Man accused of killing of mother placed in hospital. (1983, May 7). *Los Angeles Times*, II, 1.

Matthews, J. (1983, April 28). Girl molested by father faces prison term for killing him. *Washington Post*, A2.

May, C. D. (1986, March 2). Behind a rise in sexual-abuse reports. *New York Times*, E8.

Mayer, J., and Black, R. (1977). Child abuse and neglect in families with an alcoholic or opiate-addicted parent. *Child Abuse and Neglect 1*, 85–98.

McCarthy, J. B. (1978). Narcissism and the self in homicidal adolescents. *American Journal of Psychoanalysis 38*, 19–29.

McCully, R. S. (1978). The laugh of Satan: A study of a familial murderer. *Journal of Personality Assessment 42*(1), 81–91.

McGraw, C. (1983, April 2). Man held in killing of mother called suicidal. *Los Angeles Times*, II, 6.

McKnight, C. K., Mohr, J. W., Quinsey, R. E., and Erochko, J. (1965). Matricide and mental illness. *Canadian Psychiatric Association Journal 11*(2), 99–106.

Medlicott, R. W. (1955). Paranoia of the exalted type in a setting of *folie à deux.* A study of two adolescent homicides. *British Journal of Medical Psychology 28*, 205–23.

M'Naghten Test. (1843). Daniel M'Naghten's case, 10 C. & F. 200, 210–11,

8 Eng. Rep. 718, 722–23.

Middleton, J. (1984, September–October). Double stigma: Sexual abuse within the alcoholic family. *Focus on Family*, 6–11.

Middleton-Moz, J. (1986, February). *Sexual abuse*. Paper presented at the Second National Conference on Children of Alcoholics, Washington, D.C.

Middleton-Moz, J., and Dwinell, L. (1986). *After the tears: Reclaiming the losses of childhood*. Pompano Beach, Fla.: Health Communications.

Miller, A. (1990). *For your own good* (3rd ed.). New York: Noonday.

Miranda v. Arizona. 384 U.S. 436 (1966).

Mohr, J. W., and McKnight, C. K. (1971). Violence as a function of age and relationship with special reference to matricide. *Canadian Psychiatric Association Journal 16*, 29–32.

Monahan, J. (1981). *Predicting violent behavior*. Beverly Hills, Calif.: Sage.

Mones, P. (1985). The relationship between child abuse and parricide. In E. H. Newberg and R. Bourne (Eds.), *Unhappy families: Clinical and research perspectives on family violence*. Littleton, Mass.: PSG.

———. (1989, November). *A comparison of children who kill family members and children who kill non-related persons*. Paper presented at the forty-first annual meeting of the American Society of Criminology, Reno, Nevada.

Moore, M. H. (1987). *From children to citizens*. New York: Springer-Verlag.

Morgan, T. (1975, January 19). They think I can kill because I'm 14. *New York Times Magazine*.

Morris, G. (1985). *The kids next door: Sons and daughters who kill their parents*. New York: William Morrow.

Morris, N. (1986). Insanity defense. *National Institute of Justice crime file study guide*. U.S. Department of Justice, National Institute of Justice/National Criminal Justice Reference Service, Rockville, Md.

Muffin. (1970, January 26). *Newsweek*, 21, 24.

Myers, G. (1987). National elementary school education project. *The NACoA Network 4*(2), 1–2.

Myers, W. C., and Kemph, J. P. (1988). Characteristics and treatment of four homicidal adolescents. *Journal of the American Academy of Child and Adolescent Psychiatry 27*(5), 595–99.

O'Connell, B. (1963). Matricide. *The Lancet 1*, 1083–84.

Oliver-Diaz, P., and O'Gorman, P. (1988). *12 steps to self-parenting*. Deerfield Beach, Fla.: Health Communications.

Painter, J. (1987). *Deep body work and personal development*. Mill Valley, Calif.: Bodymind.

Palmer, T. (1975). Martinson revisited. *Journal of Research in Crime and Delinquency 12*, 133–52.

Parsons v. State, 2 So. 854, 866–67 (Ala. 1887).

Pasewark, R. A. (1981). Insanity plea: A review of the research literature. *Journal of Psychiatry and Law 9*, 357–401.

Patterson, R. M. (1943). Psychiatric study of juveniles involved in homicide. *American Journal of Orthopsychiatry 13*, 125–30.

Perls, F. (1969). *Gestalt therapy verbatim*. Lafayette, Calif.: Real People.

Poet tried to have father poisoned, police say. (1986, October 11). *Tampa Tribune*, 4B.

Posey, C. D. (1988). Special issue: Correctional classification based upon psychological characteristics. *Criminal Justice and Behavior 15*, 1–136.

Post, S. (1982). Adolescent parricide in abusive families. *Child Welfare 61*(7), 445–55.

Prendergast, A. (1983, May 26). It's you or me, Dad. *Rolling Stone*, 41–44, 66–67.

———. (1986). *The poison tree*. New York: Avon.

Raizen, K. H. (1960). A case of matricide and patricide. *British Journal of Delinquency 10*(4), 277–94.

Reich, W. (1945). *The sexual revolution*. New York: Simon and Schuster.

Reinhardt, J. M. (1970). *Nothing left but murder*. Lincoln, Nebr.: Johnsen Publishing.

Reitsma-Street, M., and Leschied, A. W. (1988). The conceptual level matching model in corrections. *Criminal Justice and Behavior 15*, 92–108.

Roberts, D. (1985). Orestes as fulfillment, *teraskopos*, and *teras* in the *Oresteia*. *American Journal of Philology 106*, 283–97.

Rogers, R. (1986). *Conducting insanity evaluations*. New York: Van Nostrand Reinhold.

Rosen, C. L., Frost, J. D., Bricker, T., Tarnow, J. D., Gilette, P. C., and Duniavy, S. (1983). Two siblings with recurrent cardiorespiratory arrest: Munchausen syndrome by proxy or child abuse? *Pediatrics 71*(5), 715–20.

Rosen, C. L., Frost, J. D., and Glaze, D. G. (1986). Clinical and laboratory observations: Child abuse and recurrent infant apnea. *Journal of Pediatrics 109*(6), 1065–67.

Rosenberg, D. A. (1987). Web of deceit: A literature review of Munchausen syndrome by proxy. *Child Abuse and Neglect 11*, 547–63.

Rosenhan, D. L., and Seligman, M. E. P. (1989). *Abnormal psychology* (2nd ed.). New York: W. W. Norton.

Rosenthal, D. (1985, April 16). When a child kills a parent. *Parade*, 6–9.

Rotter, J. (1966). Generalized expectancies for internal versus external control of reinforcement. *Psychological Monographs 80* (Serial No. 609).

Rubinstein, L. H. (1969). The theme of Electra and Orestes: A contribution to the psychopathology of matricide. *British Journal of Medical Psychology 42*, 99–108.

Russell, D. H. (1965). A study of juvenile murderers. *Journal of Offender Therapy 9*(3), 55–86.

———. (1973). Juvenile murderers. *International Journal of Offender Therapy and Comparative Criminology 17*, 235–39.

———. (1979). Ingredients of juvenile murder. *International Journal of Offender Therapy and Comparative Criminology 23*(3), 65–72.

———. (1984). A study of juvenile murderers of family members. *International Journal of Offender Therapy and Comparative Criminology 28*(3), 177–92.

Russell, F. (1979, June 8). Murder strikes home. *National Review*, 744–45.

Sadoff, R. L. (1971). Clinical observations on parricide. *Psychiatric Quarterly* 45(1), 65–69.

Sargent, D. (1962, January). Children who kill: A family conspiracy? *Social Work 7*, 35–42.

Satir, V. (1964). *Conjoint family therapy: A guide to theory and technique.* Palo Alto, Calif.: Science & Behavior.

Savitz, L. D. (1978). Official police statistics and their limitations. In L. D. Savitz and N. Johnson (Eds.), *Crime in society* (69–81). New York: John Wiley.

Savitz, L. D., and Johnson, N. (Eds.) (1978). *Crime in society.* New York: John Wiley.

Scherl, D. J., and Mack, J. E. (1966). A study of adolescent matricide. *Journal of the American Academy of Child Psychiatry 5*(2), 569–93.

Scwade, E. D., and Geiger, S. G. (1953). Matricide with electroencephalographic evidence of thalamic or hypothalamic disorder. *Diseases of the Central Nervous System 14*, 18–20.

Seixas, J. S., and Youcha, G. (1985). *Children of alcoholism: A survivor's manual.* New York: Harper & Row.

Sendi, I. B., and Blomgren, P. G. (1975). A comparative study of predictive criteria in the predisposition of homicidal adolescents. *American Journal of Psychiatry 132*, 423–27.

Shapiro, D. (1984). *Psychological evaluation and expert testimony.* New York: Van Nostrand Reinhold.

Siegel, B. (1983). Kids and the law: When tortured kids strike back. *Juvenile justice: Getting behind the stereotypes.* American Bar Association.

Simon, R. J. (1967). *The jury and the insanity defense.* Boston: Little, Brown.

Skogan, W. G. (1977, January). Dimensions of the dark figure of unreported crime. *Crime and Delinquency 23*, 41–50.

Solomon, E., Schmidt, R., and Ardragna, P. (1990). *Human anatomy and physiology.* Philadelphia: Saunders.

Solway, I. S., Richardson, L., Hays, J. R., and Elion, V. H. (1981). Adolescent murderers: Literature review and preliminary research findings. In J. R. Hays, T. K. Roberts, and K. Solway (Eds.), *Violence and the violent individual* (193–210). Jamaica, N.Y.: Spectrum.

Sorrells, J. M. (1977, July). Kids who kill. *Crime and Delinquency 23*, 313–20.

———. (1981). What can be done about juvenile homicide? *Crime and Delinquency 16*, 152–61.

Stanford v. Kentucky. 109 S. Ct. 2959 (1989).

State of Florida Guardian ad Litem Program. (n.p., n.d.). Speaking up for children. (pamphlet)

Stone, A. A. (1975). *Mental health and law: A system in transition.* Rockville, Md.: National Institute of Mental Health, Center for Studies of Crime and Delinquency.

———. (1978). The insanity defense. In R. W. Rieber and H. J. Vetter (Eds.), *The psychological foundations of criminal justice: Vol. 2* (162–76). New York: John Jay Press.

Straus, M. (1979). Measuring intrafamily conflict and violence: The conflict tactics (CT) scales. *Journal of Marriage and the Family 41*, 75–88.

Subby, R. (1987). *Lost in the co-dependent shuffle*. Deerfield Beach, Fla.: Health Communications.

Suinn, R. M. (1984). *Fundamentals of abnormal psychology*. Chicago: Nelson-Hall.

Sullivan, C. L., Grant, M. Q., and Grant, J. D. (1957). The development of interpersonal maturity: Application to delinquency. *Psychiatry 20*, 373–85.

Taft, P. B., Jr. (1983, July 11). Juvenile criminals. *Family Circle*, 18–20, 25–28.

Tanay, E. (1973). Adolescents who kill parents—Reactive parricide. *Australia and New Zealand Journal of Psychiatry 7*, 263–77.

———. (1976a). *The murderers*. Indianapolis: Bobbs-Merrill.

———. (1976b). Reactive parricide. *Journal of Forensic Sciences 21*(1), 76–82.

Thompson v. Oklahoma. 43 CrL 4084 (1988).

Townsend, D. (1983, April 30). Miller declared unfit for trial. *Los Angeles Times*, I, 31.

U.S. Department of Justice, National Institute of Justice Reports. (1985, July). OJJDP: Introducing CASA.

Valliant, G. E. (1983). *The natural history of alcoholism—Causes, patterns, and paths to recovery*. Cambridge: Harvard University Press.

Van Voorhis, P. (1988). A cross classification of five offender typologies: Issues of construct and predictive validity. *Criminal Justice and Behavior 15*, 109–24.

Vetter, H. J., and Silverman, I. J. (1986). *Criminology and crime*. New York: Harper & Row.

Wadlington, W., Whitebread, C. H., and Davis, S. M. (1983). *Children in the legal system*. Mineola, N.Y.: Foundation.

Walker, C. E., Bonner, B. L., and Kaufman, K. L. (1988). *The physically and sexually abused child: Evaluation and treatment*. New York: Pergamon.

Walker, L. (1989). *Sudden fury*. New York: St. Martin's.

Walker, L. E. (1979). *The battered woman*. New York: Harper & Row.

———. (1984). *The battered woman syndrome*. New York: Springer-Verlag.

———. (1989). *Terrifying love*. New York: Harper & Row.

Warren, M. Q. (1966). *Interpersonal maturity level classification: Juvenile diagnosis and treatment of low, middle, and high maturity delinquents*. Unpublished manuscript. (Available from California Youth Authority, Sacramento, Calif.)

———. (1969). The case for differential treatment of delinquents. *Annals of the American Academy of Political and Social Science 381*, 47–59.

———. (1971). Classification of offenders as an aid to effective management and effective treatment. *Journal of Criminal Law, Criminology and Police Science 62*, 239–58.

———. (1978). The impossible child, the difficult child, and other assorted delinquents: Etiology, characteristics and incidence. *Canadian Psychiatric Association Journal 23* (Suppl.).

Wegscheider, S. (1981). *Another chance*. Palo Alto, Calif.: Science and Behavior Books.

Wegscheider-Cruse, S. (1985). *Choicemaking*. Pompano Beach, Fla.: Health

Communications.

Weiss, L., and Weiss, J. (1989). *Recovery from codependency.* Deerfield Beach, Fla.: Health Communications.

Wertham, F. (1941). *Dark legend: A study in murder.* New York: Duell, Sloan, and Pearce.

Whitfield, C. (1987). *Healing the child within.* Pompano Beach, Fla.: Health Communications.

Wholey, D. (1988). *Becoming your own parent.* New York: Doubleday.

Wilkins v. Missouri 109 S. Ct. 2959 (1989).

Witness says victim abused family. (1987, April 30). *Tampa Tribune*, 8B.

Woititz, J. G. (1983). *Adult children of alcoholics.* Pompano Beach, Fla.: Health Communications.

———. (1985). *Struggle for . . . intimacy.* Pompano Beach, Fla.: Health Communications.

Woman faces abuse charge after dressing son like a pig. (1988, July 6). *Tampa Tribune*, Section A.

Woman says abuse led to slaying. (1986, September 29). *Tampa Tribune*, 11B.

Writer murdered by adopted son and friend. (1984, October 5). *Publishers Weekly*, 28.

The youth crime plague. (1977, July 11). *Time*, 18–20.

Zenoff, E. H., and Zients, A. B. (1979). Juvenile murderers: Should the punishment fit the crime? *International Journal of Law and Psychiatry 2* (4), 533–53.

■ INDEX

■ ABOUT THE AUTHOR

KATHLEEN M. HEIDE, Ph.D., is Professor of Criminology at the University of South Florida, Tampa. Dr. Heide received her undergraduate degree in psychology from Vassar College and her master's and doctoral degrees in criminal justice from the University at Albany, State University of New York. She is an internationally recognized consultant on homicide and family violence. Dr. Heide is a licensed mental health counselor and serves as Director of Education at the Center for Mental Health Education, Assessment and Therapy in Tampa. She is a court-appointed expert in matters relating to homicide, sexual battery, children, and families. Dr. Heide has been the recipient of several research grants and five teaching awards. She is an internationally acclaimed lecturer and has appeared as an expert on many talk shows, including *Larry King Live* and *Geraldo*. Dr. Heide has been honored by many professional and community agencies for her service to them.